"Dennis McCallum in a clear and concise way provides us with a sure guide through the biblical and experiential evidence about Satan and his role not only in human history but also in church history and in the lives of individual Christians. Not since C.S. Lewis's *The Screwtape Letters* have we had as convincing a presentation that Satan's favorite method of relating to modern people is to convince them he is not real, thereby giving him freedom to operate amongst the unsuspecting. Highly recommended."

— **Dr. Ben Witherington, III,** Asbury Theological Seminary and St. Mary's College, St. Andrews University, Scotland

"Have you ever wondered why the disciples had so much trouble figuring Jesus out? After all, they had all the Old Testament prophecies. Jesus was right there with them. Dennis McCallum's thesis—that all the data is in the Bible but it wasn't until after the resurrection that Jesus connected the dots—is most intriguing. It also explains why the devil so miscalculated the outcome of his plot to kill Jesus. Read with your Bible open and you'll learn how to gain victory in our contemporary war with darkness."

— **Gerry Breshears, PhD,** Western Seminary

"We have long needed a lucid, biblically sound presentation of spiritual warfare and the satanic kingdom. This is it, and it is both readable and deep. Everyone should read it."

— **Grant R. Osborne, PhD,** Trinity Evangelical Divinity School

"Dennis McCallum has written a balanced and thoughtful work on an often overlooked but essential topic: the reality of Satan and his practices as he misrepresents God's goodness and misleads humanity into believing in its own goodness. McCallum writes in a biblical and realistic way, using thorough research to answer vital questions effectively. The chapters on Satan and Your Ministry are especially helpful and ring true to reality. Here is a well-done book full of vital truth."

— **Dr. Bill Lawrence,** Dallas Theological Seminary and Leader Formation International

SATAN
AND HIS
KING
DOM

WHAT *the* BIBLE SAYS *and*
HOW IT MATTERS TO YOU

DENNIS McCALLUM

BETHANY HOUSE
MINNEAPOLIS, MINNESOTA

Published by Bethany House Publishers
11400 Hampshire Avenue South
Bloomington, Minnesota 55438

Bethany House Publishers is a division of
Baker Publishing Group, Grand Rapids, Michigan.

Printed in the United States of America

In keeping with biblical principles of creation stewardship, Baker Publishing Group advocates the responsible use of our natural resources. As a member of the Green Press Initiative, our company uses recycled paper when possible. The text paper of this book is comprised of 30% post-consumer waste.

Library of Congress Cataloging-in-Publication Data

McCallum, Dennis.
    Satan and his kingdom : what the Bible says and how it matters to you / Dennis McCallum.
      p. cm.
    ISBN 978-0-7642-0649-8 (pbk. : alk. paper) 1. Spiritual warfare. 2. Devil—Christianity.
3. Spiritual warfare—Biblical teaching. 4. Devil—Biblical teaching. I. Title.

BV4509.5.M3428   2009
235'.4—dc22

                                       2009012675

Special thanks to Nick Hetrick, Melony Harvey, and my wife, Holly, for their edits. Thanks also to my church community for standing with me in spiritual warfare for all these years.

Dennis McCallum is founder and lead pastor of Xenos Christian Fellowship in Columbus, Ohio, a nontraditional church composed of several hundred house churches. He also leads Xenos's college ministry at The Ohio State University. Dennis holds a BA in history from The Ohio State University and an MA from Ashland Theological Seminary. He is the author of several books, including *Organic Disciplemaking: Mentoring Others Into Spiritual Maturity and Leadership* and *The Death of Truth.*

Dennis married his wife, Holly, in 1973. Their children, Jessica, Joe, and Bret, all lead house churches at Xenos.

CONTENTS

SECTION 3: FOR FURTHER STUDY

Section 1

THE BATTLE THEN *and* NOW

CHAPTER 1

THE SPIRITUAL WAR

After nearly forty years of ministry, I am still surprised that people know so little about Satan. When he brought evil into the world, it changed the course of human history. Arguably, next to God, Satan is the most important being to learn about.

During the past few years, though, when people have asked me questions about Satan and I wanted to recommend a book that dealt with the subject comprehensively, I could think of none that fit the bill. For instance, *The Screwtape Letters* by C. S. Lewis is excellent, but it is fiction and leaves much biblical teaching uncovered. Warren Wiersbe's book *The Strategy of Satan* is also good but relatively limited in what it covers. Many key questions are not addressed.

A number of recent books dealing with Satan reflect an extreme perspective that is not biblically based. Authors who attribute too much to demonic activity do a poor service to believers by assuming matters that are not revealed in the Bible. Hermeneutic restraint—sticking to what is actually written—is in short supply when it comes to books on Satan. Believers need accurate, balanced, biblical information on Satan, not exaggeration. Exaggerated or distorted versions of spiritual warfare have created suspicion on the whole subject in the minds of many Christian leaders.

At the other extreme, there is deafening silence on this subject from many evangelical leaders today. Pursuing my interest in matters of ministry, I have visited many churches in the United States, including most of the well-known mega-churches. Yet for as many services and conferences I have attended, I don't recall ever hearing a teaching on Satan or spiritual warfare—one of the major themes in the New Testament. Personal discussions with leaders from these churches reveal that they do believe in Satan. But for some reason it doesn't seem to get much "airtime" in modern mainstream evangelical churches.

Most liberal and emergent village churches reject the reality of a personal Satan. So too do the majority of Americans who say they believe in God. According to a 2008 Barna Group survey, the majority of both Catholics and Protestants in America reject the reality of a personal Satan.[1] Verbal Kint, the narrator in the 1995 film *Usual Suspects*, says, "The greatest trick the Devil ever pulled was convincing the world he didn't exist."

While most Bible-believing Christians do believe in Satan, confusion often reigns. Our question today should be, "What are the facts?"

WARFARE IS REAL

A spiritual war is raging. The apostle Paul says, "For we are not fighting against flesh-and-blood enemies, but against evil rulers and authorities of the unseen world" (Ephesians 6:12 NLT).[2] You are in the middle of that war. Whether your heart is peace-loving or warlike makes no difference. You can't get out of it. You can only choose whether to fight or to be mowed down as a civilian casualty.

If you are a pastor, a Christian who actively shares your faith, or you lead Bible studies or disciple younger believers, you need to learn about Satan for the sake of your ministry. You need to be able to answer important questions that come up and to anticipate his moves in the lives of your people. This book is for both Christians who need to learn about Satan for their own survival and for workers who need the ability to explain his ways and face him in battle.

WHERE WE STAND

When the allies invaded France on D day, allied leaders knew it was all over for Hitler. With the Russian juggernaut hammering in from the east, and now the powerful allies coming in from the west and the south, Hitler's only possible future was absolute defeat. But the soldiers on the ground didn't feel like anything was over. Bitter battles lay ahead and blood would be shed. Many would die.

This is a partial analogy for our situation today in the church. Jesus won the decisive battle at the cross, as we'll see. But we still have a vicious enemy rampaging all over the world. Satan is just as dangerous as he ever was, even though his ultimate doom is assured.[3]

Battle is a common theme in the New Testament. Our battle today is part of a dramatic struggle that has gone on for thousands of years. As God's plan rolls up to our own day, we take our place as combatants in the struggle.

Many Christians prefer to see the church as the family of God or the loving community, and both are valid pictures. But we are also at war—a war we could easily lose in our locality, in spite of the fact that Satan was defeated in the final sense at the cross. And in war, people must either be willing to fight or face death or captivity. Satan's ultimate defeat will be small comfort, here and now, if we allow our lives and churches to be shattered in the meantime.

Whether Christians see their lives in the context of spiritual war becomes quickly evident. Before considering how this war works, and how to fight, consider how our outlook should change just from knowing that we are engaged in a spiritual war.

WARTIME VS. PEACETIME MENTALITY

The last time America fought an all-out war was World War II. During that struggle, the country had to devote its whole energy to win. The need for sacrifice and effort profoundly affected every person in the country. Although America has fought wars since then, none of them has been large enough to drive the whole country into a wartime mentality. Life went on as usual for most people during the smaller wars since. Most of us have grown up without ever knowing the need for a true wartime mentality.

The Bible tells us the church is locked in the grip of all-out spiritual warfare. But many of us in the church have never seen a spiritual wartime mentality either. Too often, today's church functions in a mentality suitable to peacetime, but utterly inappropriate during war.

Waste

During times of peace, someone might ask, "What's wrong with enjoying myself by accumulating some goods and possessions?" But in times of war, people need to mobilize everything they can for the struggle. We can enjoy ourselves after the war—if we win. But if we lose, our survival is at stake. During World War II, the government rationed daily goods carefully; rubber, copper, gasoline, and food were all grudgingly given out because the country needed those things to fight the war. Civilians all over the country gathered up extra silverware, pots, pans, and other pieces of metal and turned them over to the military. They put their money into war bonds. People with a wartime mentality realize this is no time to indulge self and accumulate goods.

Sacrifice

During times of peace, it's reasonable to avoid suffering and hardship as much as possible. But war always involves extreme suffering and hardship. Whether fighting on the front line or behind the lines, people know they can't win a war without painful sacrifice and suffering.

Autonomy

A person enjoying peace could well say, "If I don't feel like showing up or putting out sometimes, that's my business." Yes, we live in a free society, but in war, failure to show up and do your part may be the difference between victory and defeat. Soldiers aren't free to show up only when they want to. War requires discipline. In war, failure to do your part could cost others' lives. During war the stakes couldn't be higher. Any force that accepts autonomous wartime attitudes is headed for defeat.

Individualism

During peacetime you could say, "I decide what goals to pursue and how to pursue them." But this won't do for war. Warriors come under a unified strategy and must comply with orders. Any force where people decide what to do on their own is a rabble, not an army. Yes, individual initiative is also important, but soldiers must exert initiative within the scope of the overall strategic goals.

Danger

People enjoying peace are glad that no particular danger faces them, and see no reason why people should perish before their time. But people in war face mortal danger every day, and many die violently. War is supremely dangerous.

Time-out

In peacetime, people may play sports; they tire, and then call time-out. But in war, there are no time-outs. Imagine yourself in one of the battles portrayed in the motion picture *Braveheart*. As the screaming line of Scots races forward, you step out in front of your troops and hold your hands up in a T. "Time-out!" you cry. Well, you can take a time-out if you want to, but they aren't going to give one. Actually, this would probably only make them charge even harder. In war, exertion may often be to the point of utter exhaustion.

IS THIS EXAGGERATION?

Is it fair to draw conclusions about the church based on analogies with all-out human warfare? Yes it is, and in fact the stakes are even higher in our war. People aren't just dying physically. Some lose their souls forever. Make no mistake: Satan destroys lives, both of Christians and non-Christians. We can expect spiritual warfare to be every bit as vicious and harsh as human war. Jesus promised his followers peace, but he referred to inner peace, not peace with God's enemy; as he warns, "Here on earth you will have many trials and sorrows" (John 16:33).

When the church ignores the reality of spiritual warfare, we suffer from slack, individualistic attitudes that weaken us and guarantee defeat. Evidence on all sides shows that many Christians and even entire churches live in a peacetime rather than a wartime mentality.

People with a peacetime mentality simply cannot understand what all the fuss is about. They feel happy to be Christians, but see their spirituality as mainly something to bring them comfort. The things of God deserve some attention when one has the time, but it's hard because "I have a lot of things to do." When peacetime Christians see others getting hard-core about God, they feel perplexed. Why get so extreme? In contrast, when believers accept what God tells us about our war, we see a sharpness and commitment that God can use to bring victory to the church.

THE IMPERATIVES OF WAR

All wars have certain things in common, and spiritual warfare is no different. Consider some of the elements that go into winning a war.

Intelligence

One of the first rules of war is to know your enemy well enough to anticipate his moves. Combat intelligence has won many battles in the history of human warfare. At Midway, the Japanese had poor intelligence, while the Americans knew how to read Japanese code. The result was a decisive defeat inflicted on Japan. America has recently seen the problems caused by its poor intelligence regarding weapons of mass destruction (WMDs) in Iraq.

One advantage we should have in our struggle with Satan is good combat intelligence. In 2 Corinthians 2:11, Paul says "We are not ignorant of his [Satan's] schemes" (NASB). Or are we? Unfortunately, many Christians cannot say with Paul that they know the schemes of Satan, and the result is extreme vulnerability.

Morale

While it may seem too obvious to say, those in war must be willing to fight. But this is not always the case. History is loaded with examples of smaller forces defeating larger ones mainly because the larger force had lost the will to fight. In World War II, a single British jeep herded in several thousand Italian prisoners during the North African campaign. These men would no longer fight.

Are we ready to face the savagery of an enemy who has destroyed human lives for thousands of years? We must not underestimate the fury of spiritual war. Any time the church moves ahead, the people of God pay a price. Many of our fellow believers have already become so bewildered and dismayed by the battering in this war that they will no longer "stand fire."

Satan actively undermines Christians' fighting spirit by sowing defeatism in their minds. He also tries to divert attention from important issues by baiting believers into taking undue interest in unimportant things. Christians caught up in fixation with entertainment, materialism, sex, or obscure theology cannot be effective combatants. Satan doesn't need to persuade us to bow down to him; all he needs is for us to back off a bit and relinquish our fighting spirit. Once believers stop taking the offensive, the initiative goes over to Satan.

Equipping

Christians need to be equipped to fight just like any force in war, and Scripture says church leaders are supposed to prepare God's people for works of service (Ephesians 4:12). God has provided Christians with an arsenal of powerful weapons (2 Corinthians 10:3–4), yet unless we learn how to wield them, our plight is pitiful. A country that sent its soldiers into battle armed with spit wads would be a farce. But we sometimes see churches sending their people into battle virtually unarmed—they are ignorant and inexperienced. This is a failure of leadership.

Warring forces also need reliable direction and reasonable plans. The plans need to be suitable for the situation and for the enemy in question. When a group unites around a good plan, it is in good position to win victories.

Defense

Successful offensives win wars, but defense is also important. There's nothing wrong with building a base of operations where people can rest and be refitted, where supplies can be gathered and stockpiled, and where plans can be considered and established. We are finite creatures, and we can't withstand the constant tension of slugging it out with crafty spirit beings unless we get refreshed. We also have to train people and nurture the young. Having a place where people can enjoy the safety of support and nurture is part of a winning strategy in all wars.

WHAT WE NEED

This book will give you the necessary basics for becoming an effective player in spiritual war. Toward that end, we need to think through a number of things:

1. Who is Satan? Where did he come from? Why is he still on the loose? How do we even know he's real?

2. What has already happened in the cosmic collision between God, God's people, and Satan during the generations before us? Where do we stand? (Understanding God's plan of the ages is crucial.)

3. What's the plan today? What are we supposed to be doing? And what is Satan's plan?

4. What practical steps can we take? Where does this play out in daily living?

Let's get started.

CHAPTER 2

WHO IS SATAN?

Many, including some Christians, wonder whether Satan is a real being. How do we know he is a being and not just, for example, a personification of evil? For those interested in this question, later in this book (appendix 1) I speak of my own struggles and how I came to find answers.

Aside from Satan's existence, other important questions emerge: Where did this being come from? Why does he exist? How could God let this happen?

Even if the Bible said nothing about the origin of Satan, we could deduce primary facts based on what we know about God and about Satan as he now is. He must be a created being, because God alone is infinite and has created all things, including principalities and powers in the heavenly places. It follows that Satan must have been created as a good being, because his creator is good. We could then deduce that he must have experienced a fall from God. And since we do have the Bible record, we know that this fall occurred sometime before the fall of humankind, because he shows up already fallen in the account of creation.

PASSAGES CLAIMED TO BE ABOUT SATAN'S FALL

Commentators identify two or three passages as referring to the fall, or origin, of Satan, but not all of them agree. Let's look at these.

ISAIAH 14

> How you have fallen from heaven,
>   O star of the morning, son of the dawn!
> You have been cut down to the earth,
>   You who have weakened the nations!
> But you said in your heart,
>   "I will ascend to heaven;
>   I will raise my throne above the stars of God,
>   And I will sit on the mount of assembly
>   In the recesses of the north.
> I will ascend above the heights of the clouds;
>   I will make myself like the Most High."
> Nevertheless you will be thrust down to Sheol,
>   To the recesses of the pit" (vv. 12–15 NASB).

Although this passage purports to be about the king of Babylon, some interpreters think it points to the fall of Satan and his eventual judgment. One key reason is that verses 13 and 14 say, "But you said in your heart, 'I will ascend to heaven; I will raise my throne above the stars of God.' " Who, these interpreters ask, would be able to say such things but Satan? They also argue that in verse 12, God calls the being "star of the morning," or "shining one." The King James Version translates this term "Lucifer": "How art thou fallen from heaven, O Lucifer, son of the morning!"

I (along with most interpreters) think that this passage is *not* about Satan. For one thing, although *Lucifer* is a traditional name for Satan, people base that tradition *solely* on this passage. Nowhere else does the Bible call Satan *Lucifer.* Using the name *Lucifer* here as proof that this passage is about Satan would be a circular argument. More modern translations have abandoned the translation as "Lucifer" because the Hebrew here is not a proper name but an expression meaning "shining one."

The other argument for this passage being about Satan (i.e., that only he could make such claims) also carries no weight. The form of literature here is a "taunt" (see v. 14), which usually refers to a sarcastic or mocking form of address that may exaggerate for effect. We can see how this taunt

(vv. 13–14) would mock a human king's claim to deity. And strange as it may sound to contemporary ears, not only did ancient rulers claim to be gods, but their people also often believed them. (Consider, for example, the Roman Caesars.) Finally, and most important, the one addressed in this passage is a human being, not an angel. Verse 11 says,

[You] have been brought down to Sheol;
Maggots are spread out as your bed beneath you
And worms are your covering.

This description only fits a physical body; it would be nonsense if addressed to a purely spiritual being. Also, verse 16 says, "Is this the man who made the earth tremble?" Later, it describes his "trampled corpse" (v. 19). We have no good reason to attribute this to anyone other than the king of Babylon, as the text says (v. 4). Some authors argue that it refers to the king of Babylon primarily, but to Satan in a secondary sense. However, we need some kind of authorization or clue from the text to see "secondary senses." People who respect biblical authority should be very reluctant to read meanings into passages unless the text clearly warrants them.

As mentioned earlier, hermeneutical (interpretive) restraint is a sore spot in studies about Satan. The Bible says plenty about the Evil One without needing any exaggeration or insertions from us. Much of the related literature available today exhibits carelessness by failing to limit conclusions to those warranted by the Bible.

EZEKIEL 28

Many believe Ezekiel 28 contains a section about Satan. Here again, a human king was claiming deity for himself, and God mocked his pretensions through the prophet in verses 1 through 10. For instance,

Son of man, give the prince of Tyre this message from the Sovereign Lord:

21

> "In your great pride you claim, 'I am a god!
> I sit on a divine throne in the heart of the sea.'
> But you are only a man and not a god" (vv. 1–2).

However, this passage has a subsequent section that seems to redirect the address. Beginning in verse 11 we read,

> Again the word of Lord came to me saying, "Son of man, take up a lamentation over the king of Tyre and say to him, 'Thus says the Lord God, "You had the seal of perfection, full of wisdom and perfect in beauty. You were in Eden, the garden of God ..." (vv. 11–13 NASB).

This passage differs from the one in Isaiah in that its second section is clearly marked off from the one preceding it: "Then this further message came to me from the Lord" (v. 11). Instead of addressing the "prince of Tyre" or "ruler," or "leader" (e.g., NIV, NASB) like at the chapter's beginning, God now calls him "the king of Tyre." This might seem like an insignificant use of poetic variation except for the interesting fact that the people of Tyre worshiped a Baal they called *Melquart*, which means "King of the City." The prophecy may address the human ruler of Tyre as a prince, or underling, while the actual ruler (as the Tyrians believed) was this false god, Melquart. Both the Old and New Testaments teach that idols are really demons in disguise, as Paul says: "The things which the Gentiles sacrifice, they sacrifice to demons" (1 Corinthians 10:20; see also Deuteronomy 32:17; Psalm 106:36–37 NASB). This suggests a demonic connection with Melquart, king of the city of Tyre. While not conclusive, the background supports the idea that this prophecy could address an evil spirit.

Ezekiel's continued description—"You were the model of perfection, full of wisdom and exquisite in beauty. You were in Eden, the garden of God" (v. 13)—hardly would fit any human ruler. Satan *was* in Eden and could have been described this way before his fall.

Next, we see a description of this being's magnificent adornment: He'd been covered in gemstones that range in color through the whole rainbow. God says this had been "given to you on the day you were created" (v. 13). Clearly, the one in question was not born, like humans, but created, like an angel.

Most important, God says, "I ordained and anointed you as the mighty angelic guardian" (v. 14). The NASB more literally translates this as the "anointed cherub who covers" (or "who guards"—see NASB margin). Cherubs are angels, *nothing* like the flying babies pictured in popular mythology, but rather lofty, mysterious creatures of the highest rank.[1]

If Ezekiel 28 is describing Satan, then he must have been created as a cherub, and a special one. God calls him "the anointed cherub," which is a way of saying "chosen." This probably means he had a role as a guardian, in the sense of being a steward or manager over others.

When interpreting this passage, we should again notice the genre (type) of literature. Unlike the passage in Isaiah, a sarcastic "taunt," this poem is a "lamentation" (see v. 12 NASB). A lamentation is a song of mourning, not normally characterized by sarcasm or satire. This is a song of genuine sorrow about actual events. Note that God doesn't say this being *claimed* these things for himself; he simply states that these things happened.

All these factors lead me, along with most conservative scholars, to conclude that this passage *is* in fact a description of Satan and his fall from God.

Elements in the Fall of Satan

Accepting this interpretation, we learn some important facts about Satan. First, consider God's statement "You were the model of perfection, full of wisdom and exquisite in beauty" (Ezekiel 28:12). For the God of the universe to declare that another is perfect in wisdom is remarkable. Satan must have incredible intellectual powers; repeatedly the Bible stresses his brilliance. His beauty and majesty also must be unimaginable.

We likewise learn the reason for Satan's fall:

Your heart was proud because of your beauty;
    you corrupted your wisdom

23

for the sake of your splendor. (v. 17 NLT)

Both statements suggest that pride was the original sin. Satan apparently concluded that he was so magnificent he didn't need God. Like the first humans, he probably felt he could be his own god. Satan moved self to the center.

Once Satan enthroned himself and rejected God's moral guidance, a whole series of negative character traits automatically developed. Any moral being who rejects God's leadership finds it psychologically necessary to justify that decision. We will see later that Satan justified his rebellion by finding fault in God. Why rebel against a loving, all-wise leader who only does what is best for those who serve him? Well, what if that leader *portrays* himself as such, but in reality is self-serving? Such a leader could not be trusted. Furthermore, any leader harsh enough to judge an old friend just because he sees things a little differently could hardly be loving, right?

When Satan rebelled, he became the supreme accuser of God's character. From that day forward, Satan has been raising suspicions about God in the minds of others. Scripture reveals that the logic of rebellion quickly becomes an interlocking system of thought that drives the rebel to discredit his creator.

But the Lord's position with Satan was firm:

I cast you as a profane thing from the mountain of God. . . .
I cast you to the ground. (vv. 16–17 NRSV)

God's just character required him to pass judgment on Satan's sin. And yet his judgment could have been much more severe. Why did he leave Satan alive and free? Why not destroy or imprison him? These are among the most intriguing theological questions; later our study will reveal fascinating answers.

The Fire From Within

We should consider one more enigmatic statement in Ezekiel's prophecy. In verse 18 (NRSV), God says, "I brought out fire from within you;

24

it consumed you." The NASB translates similarly, "I have brought fire from the midst of you; it has consumed you." Apparently, this destroying fire comes from *within Satan himself*—something within him guaranteed his own destruction. Rebelling against God is always ultimately self-destructive, and this is one key reason God cannot accept it. In Satan's case, we will learn how his twisted character eventually caused him to sign his own death warrant.

REVELATION 12

In Revelation 12, we read, "A great red dragon, with seven heads and ten horns, and seven diadems on his heads. His tail swept down a third of the stars of heaven and threw them to the earth" (vv. 3–4 NRSV). This is soon explained:

> And there was war in heaven, Michael and his angels waging war with the dragon. The dragon and his angels waged war, and they were not strong enough, and there was no longer a place found for them in heaven. And the great dragon was thrown down, the serpent of old who is called the devil and Satan, who deceives the whole world; he was thrown down to the earth, and his angels were thrown down with him. (vv. 7–9 NASB)

People debate why this vision appears in the context of Revelation 12. Is it a future event, where Satan will be barred from heaven in a new way? Or did these events happen long ago? Deciding this question goes beyond our scope; for our study, the significant part of this passage is "his tail swept down a third of the stars of heaven." These stars refer to other angels, according to verse 9. So a third of the angelic host has joined Satan's side. We know from other passages that Satan is not the only angel that rebelled against God (see Jude 6; 2 Peter 2:4). Many others joined him, and these became the evil spirits, or demons.

These heavenly beings had seen and known God, yet a third of them decided to follow Satan! How could this happen? We don't know the exact answer, but it should make us at least acknowledge how awesome Satan's persuasive power must be. Angels are exalted creatures, but even they succumbed to Satan's arguments. They weren't overpowered, they were deceived. Like humans later, they believed what Satan was saying and voluntarily joined him.

Because of this tragedy, our world is afflicted not by only one dangerous evil being but by many. In fact, passages referring to numbers of angels indicate there are probably millions or even billions of angels, and a third of them now serve evil.[2] This means that even though Satan is not omnipresent like God, through his numerous followers he can act in many places at once.

CHAPTER 3

THE REBELLION SPREADS TO HUMANITY

We have seen that after Satan launched a rebellion against God, he persuaded untold millions of angels to follow him. Then he turned his attention to us. We should pay careful attention to how Satan (as the serpent) advanced the logic of rebellion, because this pattern is so typical of how he works.[1]

A STRANGE BEGINNING POINT

Satan wanted humans to defy God's order not to eat the fruit from the Tree of Knowledge of Good and Evil. When moving in to tempt Eve, he started with "Did God really say you must not eat the fruit from any of the trees in the garden?" (Genesis 3:1). It may seem odd that Satan would open his attack with this question. However, the more we learn about him, the more predictable his approach becomes.

"Did God really say?" *Satan begins by questioning God's Word.* If we were trying to persuade, we might start differently: "Nice-looking fruit, eh?" But not Satan. He knows that in the spiritual realm, the players gain or lose power based on issues of truth and faith in what is true. He knows all about the power of the Word of God. He knew that if Eve began to question or doubt what God said, she would be helpless to resist Satan's proposals. As we saw in Revelation 12:9, Satan is "the one deceiving the whole world." The first step in satanic deception is sowing seeds of doubt in a person's mind about God's Word. As long as he or she has faith rooted in what God says is true, Satan's suggestions will have little effect.

Satan's deliberate misquotation "you must not eat the fruit from any of the trees" (God actually forbade only one tree, not all of them) was a spin-job that took careful aim at Eve's mind. By wildly exaggerating God's restrictiveness, he was planting ideas. "What's wrong with God that he would so limit what you can do out here?" He portrays God's moral will as restrictive, oppressive, and suffocating.

What was Satan's spin? Casting a vision of God as too tyrannical and controlling to be trusted. *Breaking down trust is the key to disrupting relationship.* The more he could make Eve wonder if something might be wrong with God's character, the more open she would become to his other suggestions. He probably knew she wouldn't accept his misquotation, but he must have felt that it would have lingering effect. He was already lining up for a direct shot at God's character. Surely this most brilliant of creatures had carefully thought this through. Perhaps when Eve saw through what Satan said so easily (in that she knew his claim was inaccurate), she had actually accepted more than she thought. She denied one aspect of what he said but may have accepted the other part. Already, doubts about God must have crept into her mind, because by verse six it becomes clear she "was convinced."

EVE'S WEAK DEFENSE

At first Eve defended what God said:

> "Of course we may eat fruit from the trees in the garden," the woman replied. "It's only the fruit from the tree in the middle of the garden that we are not allowed to eat. God said, 'You must not eat it or even touch it; if you do, you will die'" (Genesis 3:2).

Eve seems to have it right, although she too misquotes God. We see his actual statement a few verses earlier: "You may freely eat the fruit of every tree in the garden—except the tree of the knowledge of good and evil. If you eat its fruit, you are sure to die" (2:16–17). How much should we make of Eve's addition to God's Word—that even touching the fruit would cause death? Some commentators think this is significant, and I tend to agree. Remember, Eve wasn't around when God spoke his directive to Adam—that happened before she was created. Therefore, Adam probably had to convey what God had said. Perhaps he decided to play it safe and, just in case, add a restriction that God never mentioned. If so, his addition is similar to what believers have historically done with God's Word. Instead of sticking with what God has said, we tend to add extra restrictions, as layers of protection or control. If God forbids worldly sin, then wouldn't it be even safer for us to stay away from places where worldly sin happens? Maybe we should stay away from "sinful people" altogether—that way they won't influence us with their sinful views.

Here is another pattern: When people add to the Word of God, they tend to add more boundaries and guidelines than he gave in the original. Such additions can become openings for Satan because they represent God as being needlessly restrictive and portray the Christian life as stuffy and unlivable. Satan then uses this to call God's character into question.

We don't want to make too much of Eve's (or Adam's) misquotation, but we do notice that during a later confrontation between Satan and Jesus, we see no similar inaccuracies coming from the Lord.

CLOSING THE DEAL

Satan moved in: "You won't die!" (Genesis 3:4). Now, instead of questioning, he boldly denies the Word of God. Ironically, Satan, the Father of Lies, constantly accuses God of lying. How can anyone trust a liar? But he doesn't leave it there. For a punch line, the Evil One quickly adds an ingenious rationale: "God knows that your eyes will be opened as soon as you eat it, and you will be like God, knowing both good and evil" (v. 5).

This statement has little to do with the fruit, and everything to do with God. The implications are clear. First, Satan alleges that the real motive for God's command is that he's self-serving, so intent on holding exclusive power that he can't risk giving freedom to others. A God who would deliberately try to hold others down so he can be number one cannot be trusted. This kind of God is not interested in the well-being of his creatures, only in protecting his own status.

Second, Satan influentially suggests the awesome joy and fulfillment one can get by sinning, thus presenting sin in the most glorified light possible. What an incredible power—to be like God, knowing good and evil! And Satan's claim is partially true. They did become like God in one respect: They no longer had to refer to any standard outside themselves (i.e., God) when determining what was evil. Instead, from then on, they could decide what was evil or good according to their own view.[2]

Of course, Satan didn't mention that assuming God's role for oneself, without his infinite, omniscient, all-good nature, would be utterly self-destructive. Satan's presentation of Eve's choice has no moral content; he only mentioned what she could gain for herself. No thought of Adam. No thought of God. Self-gratification and self-aggrandizement were at the heart of this temptation. He also said nothing about how humans would come under the ruthless power of a new ruler—Satan himself.

Satan's enticement would never have made such a claim on Eve's heart unless Satan had first undermined her confidence in God and his Word. Once he had questioned and denied God's Word, he replaced it with his own accusing word. But his word had devastating power because he had carefully laid the groundwork.

A NEW PERSPECTIVE

Eve looked back to the fruit with new eyes: "She saw that the tree was beautiful and its fruit looked delicious" (Genesis 3:6). She had seen it before. Why did its beauty and succulence have such power over her now? It wasn't the fruit. Her problem was that she had believed Satan, "and she wanted the wisdom it would give her" (v. 6). If she thought the fruit would make her wise, she must also have believed Satan's implied charge against God. Once she began to suspect on some level that the essence of this rule about not eating the fruit was God holding out on her, the power of sensual lust became overpowering. She had already believed God wasn't going to take care of her, so she had to take care of herself. Once she accepted the self-first thesis, she was defenseless.

From Satan's first appearance, we see a frightening picture of how he works. We recognize these moves, and we see how influential they still are today. Satan didn't cast a spell on Eve. He didn't fling her bodily across the garden or belch fire at her. Instead, he attacked the truth in her mind: the truth about what God had said, the truth about God himself, and the truth about Eve and her situation. In each case he had a dishonest but highly plausible alternative explanation.

Included toward the end of this book is section 3: For Further Study. There you can survey the rest of the Old Testament's teaching on Satan, and you will notice the same pattern—in Job, in Daniel, and elsewhere. We always see Satan repeating himself: hurling accusations, arguing his point of view, suggesting different interpretations, and thoroughly opposing God. Satan has never changed his tactics in all of the millennia since human beings first fell. He has no need to change, because these tactics are just as effective today as they ever were.

CHAPTER 4

GOD'S PLAN

Our collision with Satan is part of a larger picture—a picture of the cosmic collision between God and Satan we refer to as spiritual warfare. Before we can properly appreciate our involvement in spiritual warfare, we have to understand the flow of God's plan and Satan's reactions. We already noted that God, in his response to Satan's fall, seems to have been somewhat passive, and in chapter 19, surveying Satan's Old Testament appearances, you will see further evidence of this. God seems to let Satan rampage with more impunity than we might expect. We're now ready to learn the answers to some of the baffling questions raised by the interactions between God and Satan, including why God has allowed him to continue his evil work.

EARLY HINTS

Although God *apparently* has been passive in the face of Satan's evil actions, he hasn't really been. We can rest assured that he saw the whole thing coming. Before he ever created Satan or humans, God knew about their future rebellion, and he formed a colossal, startling plan that suddenly and shockingly burst onto the world when Jesus did the unthinkable. Paul makes it clear that God had this plan long ago, "even before he made the world" (Ephesians 1:4).

To the casual reader, it may seem like the biblical story meanders; that God was reacting to events that came up, trying this, trying that, being let down by people, blessing, judging, and eventually, after exhausting other options, sending Jesus. But this is not the case. Right from the beginning, God hinted that his plan was afoot. In Genesis 3, in the shadow of humanity's fall from grace, he said to the serpent,

> I will cause hostility between you and the woman, and between your offspring and her offspring. He will strike your head, and you will strike his heel. (v. 15)

Adam and Eve almost certainly couldn't tell exactly what this foretelling meant, but it indicates a definite plan resulting in a negative fate for the serpent. The agent of the serpent's destruction would be the "seed of woman."

ISRAEL'S MISSION

God proceeded with his plan when he called Abraham and his descendants for a mission, one that included the all-important recording and transmission of the Scriptures. Dozens of authors contributed books or sections to the Old Testament over many centuries. This text records not only the history of Israel and other ancient peoples but also contains crucial information about the one true God. His nature, his will, and his ways are all represented in a variety of modes—direct teaching, legal passages, symbols, types (e.g., the tabernacle, sacrifices, and the festival system), and narrative accounts of the relationship between God and his people. God had them lay down a body of revelation that would eventually become the tool used to foil Satan forever.

For example, how are we to know what is good or evil? People in the world generally agree that good and evil exist, but they cannot agree on what constitutes good or evil; different cultures have differing views on the matter. The Old Testament reveals that *we are to base our views of good and evil on the character of the creator God.* "You must be holy because I, the Lord your God, am holy" (Leviticus 19:2). God gave laws and confronted evil through his prophets.

In the Old Testament he also reveals that he is a God of justice. He is outraged at sin and is compelled by his own nature to judge it rightly. The Bible recounts many situations requiring divine justice. He called on his people to offer guilt offerings—sacrifices to remind them constantly that his justice must and will be served.

At the same time, Scripture reveals God as abundant in love and graciousness:

> I am slow to anger and filled with unfailing love and faithfulness. I lavish unfailing love to a thousand generations. I forgive iniquity, rebellion, and sin. But I do not excuse the guilty. (Exodus 34:6–7)

How can God forgive rebellion but not excuse the guilty?

Non-believing observers frequently insist that the Bible's portrayal of God's justice and love is self-contradictory. Most of us have read articles or heard arguments that if God would do something as cruel as casting down judgment, then he can't be loving. But the Old Testament faithfully holds these attributes of God in tension. God reveals that he doesn't enjoy judging people:

> "As surely as I live," says the Sovereign Lord, "I take no pleasure in the death of wicked people. I only want them to turn from their wicked ways so they can live" (Ezekiel 33:11).

Nevertheless, in concert with his perfect righteousness, he firmly maintains that judgment remains inevitable for those committed to sin: "When righteous people turn to evil, they will die" (v. 18).

GOD'S DILEMMA

God's love and his justice are not contradictory, but they do create a dilemma. What is God to do? Will he maintain his love for people at the expense of his justice? Liberal theologians long have suggested this solution, called "universalism" (where everyone ultimately goes to heaven). But God never compromises one of his attributes in favor of another.

On the other hand, if God remains just, how can he avoid judging the very ones he loves? This dilemma becomes Satan's favorite opportunity to incriminate God. He claims God is unloving because he insists others follow him and judges those who refuse to do so; all, allegedly, for self-serving reasons. These pernicious accusations have convinced millions to rebel against God, and they still appeal to many people today.

Each part of Satan's carefully crafted lie contains self-validating aspects that could prevent God from opposing it effectively. What if God struck Satan down the first time he voiced this view? Wouldn't that suggest the accusation was true? Imagine God destroying Satan, then turning to the rest of his creatures and saying, "Any other questions?" Clearly, such "solutions" wouldn't resolve the matter. God needed to resolve the dilemma once and for all.

KING MESSIAH

The Old Testament records God's promises about the future. One of these is that Messiah, the chosen one, would come and restore the world to its intended state. He would come as ruler of a kingdom founded on the throne of David. King Messiah is foretold in one passage after another. One of the best-known is Isaiah 9:6–7:

> For a child is born to us, a son is given to us. The government will rest on his shoulders. And he will be called: Wonderful Counselor, Mighty God, Everlasting Father, Prince of Peace. His government and its peace will never end. He will rule with fairness and justice from the throne of his ancestor David for all eternity. The passionate commitment of the Lord of Heaven's Armies will make this happen!

From this, you can see that King Messiah is a human being, born like other people but also divine. The titles "Mighty God" and "Everlasting Father" would never be used for any mere human. He will reign over the whole world forever, sitting on the throne of his ancestor David. Micah 5:2–5 adds that he will be born in the little village of Bethlehem:

But you, O Bethlehem Ephrathah, are only a small village among all the people of Judah. Yet a ruler of Israel will come from you, one whose origins are from the distant past. The people of Israel will be abandoned to their enemies until the woman in labor gives birth. Then at last his fellow countrymen will return from exile to their own land. And he will stand to lead his flock with the Lord's strength, in the majesty of the name of the Lord his God. Then his people will live there undisturbed, for he will be highly honored around the world. And he will be the source of peace.

Micah also affirms that Messiah existed before his incarnation as a human. His rule will begin after the Jewish people have been exiled from their land and have returned.

Numerous other passages predict that human history is moving toward the reign of this chosen one. Put together, predictions about the Messiah and his kingdom fill hundreds of pages in the Old Testament.

THE SUFFERING SERVANT

Alongside the prophecies about King Messiah are numerous predictions of a "servant of the Lord" who seemingly is of a different kind. Humble, obscure, despised, and persecuted, the servant offers himself as a sacrifice for human sin. Instead of ruling forever, he dies horrifically.

Today, believers know that the suffering servant and King Messiah are the same person—Jesus Christ. But there are issues. For some reason, the predictions of the suffering servant are ambiguous in one way or another. For interested readers, we examine these passages in more detail in appendix 2. For now, we can summarize the difficulties as follows:

1. None of the passages about the suffering servant identify him as Messiah.

2. The servant's career appears to contradict that of Messiah; he is not an eternal king but a rejected and obscure person who dies badly.

3. The context for many passages creates confusion, easily leading the reader to miss the point.

4. No Old Testament passage indicates that Messiah will come twice. This startling omission makes it virtually impossible to interpret the passages correctly unless you already know the story of Jesus.

5. In some cases, predictions about the suffering servant are immediately next to prophecies about King Messiah, without any mention of a more-than-two-thousand-year gap between them (e.g., cross-reference Isaiah 61:1ff and Jesus' commentary in Luke 4:21).

This pattern is so consistent, so lacking in any exception, that it *demands* an explanation. Jewish interpreters (as well as others skeptical about Jesus) have a ready answer. They argue that Christians wanted to believe the Old Testament predicts Jesus but that it never does. In their desperation, supposedly, the early Christians "read in" their interpretation, forcing their desired meaning into passages that don't say what believers claimed. The results, then, are predictable: broken contexts, bizarre leaps in chronology, and assumed material that simply is not in the text.

But the predictions of Messiah's first coming are *not* mistaken readings. They are amazing confirmations of Christ's authenticity. Passages like the servant songs in Isaiah do refer to Jesus and to no one else (as we explain in appendix 2). And while we might read some of the prophecies in more than one way, we certainly can see them in the Christian light without distortion.

SURPRISING CONFUSION

Still, questions remain. Why did God often present predictions in confusing contexts? Why did he omit any mention of Messiah in the servant passages? Why would he not include *even one Old Testament reference* to two comings of Messiah?

Only one answer satisfies these questions: God must have created this situation *deliberately*. The pattern in the predictions of Messiah's first coming crystallize into a single picture: God intentionally had these predictions written in such a way that readers couldn't understand them until *after* the life of Jesus. God was purposeful in omitting the key information that would have made them easy to grasp in advance. Everything the passages say is true; it's what they *don't* say that makes them ambiguous.

For some reason, God was keeping Messiah's mission during his first coming a secret. God didn't want to reveal what Jesus was going to do. At the same time, he wanted to show that he had predicted it all in advance—*but only after Jesus' life.*

Jesus followed the same pattern. He purposely presented himself and his teachings in a way that people would understand them one way before his death and a different way afterward. (We discuss his teaching on Messiah's two comings in appendix 3.)

If God wanted people to recognize Jesus' advent and mission, there's no way he would have left out the part about two comings from the Old Testament. This omission alone makes one passage after another seem incomprehensible. However, if he had mentioned that Messiah would come twice, *even in one verse*, the same passages would become as clear as day. In fact, the conflation of the two comings into a single passage (the so-called "prophetic gap") seems calculated to create the impression that Messiah will come only once. Interestingly, it's always the first coming that is obscure, never the second.

Liberal theologians and Jewish readers say this is because these passages don't predict the first coming. They claim these "prophecies" are an invention of early Christians' wishful thinking. In the New Testament, though, we see an explanation that astoundingly and convincingly fits the text. In fact, the answer opens the door not only to understanding Old Testament prophecy but also to a new and marvelous comprehension of New Testament teaching and the nature of God himself. The resolution to this problem takes us directly into the heart of God's plan, including the defeat of Satan.

CHAPTER 5

SATAN'S ODD BEHAVIOR

During Jesus' ministry, people were confused about what he was here to do. At one point they wanted to force him to become a king (John 6:15). Clearly, nobody, including his followers, had any category for a Messiah who was not a king (see appendix 2). All of them, even his closest disciples, had missed the predictions of the suffering servant.

But nobody behaved more strangely during this time than Satan. At the Last Supper, the devil had already put into the heart of Judas Iscariot, the son of Simon, to betray Jesus (John 13:2). Why? If Jesus had come to die for humanity's sin, why would Satan actively cooperate in his death? Hadn't Jesus just warned that the cross would be Satan's undoing? (12:31–32). Wasn't it because of the cross that Paul could later say, "[God] disarmed the spiritual rulers and authorities. He shamed them publicly by his victory over them on the cross"? (Colossians 2:15).

On first take, this part of the story seems like a poorly written novel where the characters' motivations don't line up with the action. Why would a creature as brilliant as Satan actively assist in doing the very thing that would be most destructive to himself?

POSSIBLE REASONS

Some suggest that Satan was *compelled*—that God sovereignly made him do what he did. Since the cross was God's plan, he made Satan play his part in that plan. This suggestion is certainly possible, although it is speculative. The Bible never claims Satan was acting under compulsion;

only that the cross was part of the "predetermined plan and foreknowledge of God" (Acts 2:23 NASB). Certainly God knew what Satan would do; he also knew the other players, Pilate and Herod, would do what they did. But unlike the human players, Satan had everything to lose and nothing to gain from the cross.

Others have argued that Satan was so arrogant he thought he could hold Jesus in death after the cross. Again, it's possible, though speculative. We have no direct evidence to back this theory. Certainly Satan is arrogant, and he is said to wield "the power of death" (Hebrews 2:14). But would he be so foolish? He definitely knew who Jesus was. We see him backing down from God's power in cases like the story of Job. He knew Jesus could command demons to depart. How could he think he would be able to hold the Son of God in death?[1]

Others maintain that Satan knew the cross would destroy him, but he couldn't resist the pleasure of watching Jesus suffer. Again, we can imagine this—it makes sense to envision Satan as being capable of irrational hatred. Yet it seems like quite a stretch to see the once-anointed cherub behaving so self-destructively for nothing more than a sadistic thrill.

Maybe Paul offers us a better explanation:

> We do speak wisdom among those who are mature; a wisdom, however, not of this age, nor of the rulers of this age, who are passing away; but we speak God's wisdom in a mystery, the hidden wisdom, which God predestined before the ages to our glory; the wisdom which none of the rulers of this age has understood; for if they had understood it, they would not have crucified the Lord of glory. (1 Corinthians 2:6–8 NASB)

Could it be that Satan, the great adversary, *didn't know* that Jesus actually intended to die? If so this would explain why he helped orchestrate Christ's death.[2]

Paul seems to be saying that the brilliant, bitter enemy of God acted freely, thinking he was disrupting the divine plan to take over and rule the world through Jesus as King Messiah. Instead, he played directly into Jesus' hands, demonstrating in the process God's character as true, self-giving love. Therein he also clearly demonstrated his own self-centered hatred.

Imagine Satan looking on when Jesus quoted Psalm 22:1 from the cross: "My God, my God, why have you forsaken me?" (NASB). Perhaps only at that moment did he realize that this psalm (which he would have known by heart) fully predicted the crucifixion. He may have suddenly realized, too late, that he had done exactly what Jesus wanted him to do. *At the cross, Satan disproved his own accusations against God.*

DID SATAN KNOW?

Some find it difficult to believe that Satan would have made such a colossal blunder when all the information was right there in front of him for hundreds of years. But let's think about it. How would he have known what Jesus was doing? He would have had the same information everyone else had—the predictive Scriptures. But we have seen that God crafted those in such a way that a reader before the time of Christ could not have discovered the plan for two comings; the missing information made it impossible to reach this conclusion. In this arena, why would Satan be different from anyone else? (We discuss the challenges to this idea more fully in appendix 4.)

Again, if we accept the premise that God intentionally veiled his intentions in the first coming, the hanging question remains: Why would he do so? Here, we may have an answer. Perhaps in God's eternal plan of salvation, he was also putting the permanent smack-down on Satan and his accusations.

Suppose for the sake of argument, when Jesus came, Satan, like everyone else, concluded that he had come not as a suffering servant but as reigning king. The Bible says King Messiah will destroy his enemies and rule the world with an "iron rod" (Psalm 2:9). Satan could have interpreted this picture of dominance in line with his concept of God as self-serving. Aside from anything in prophecy, Satan would be inclined to see Messiah this way because of his prejudice against God.

Satan probably made this exact mistake. He thought Jesus had come to rule immediately. Indeed, he tried to kill Jesus when he was a baby. Jesus' self-effacing behavior must have been confusing, but most people thought he would unveil his power any day (Luke 17:20; 19:11; Acts 1:6), and Satan may have thought this as well. In one instance, when demons cried out to Jesus—"Why are you bothering us, Son of God? You have no right to torture us before God's appointed time!" (Matthew 8:29)—apparently they were surprised to see him there earlier than expected, but they saw his mission only as one of bringing torment. How typical this is of demonic thinking.

THE COSMIC OUTCOME

If Satan were mistaken about Jesus' intentions, he naturally would have concluded that arranging to kill him could short-circuit the planned kingdom. Suddenly, his actions with Judas make sense. But what was the outcome? Again, too late, he realized that he had facilitated not the destruction of God's everlasting reign but the salvation of the human race! He never imagined God would come in person, not to punish, but to take his punishment upon himself! At the same time, the most reliable war-tools in his arsenal, his accusations, were now useless. The cross undeniably demonstrated God's loving and sacrificial nature. Satan proved *himself*, not God, to be utterly vindictive and cruel.

As Paul says in Colossians 2:15, the cross forever disarmed Satan by crushing his main weapon: his accusation that God is self-serving and unjust. What Christ did at the cross was the antithesis of the picture Satan paints. No wonder Jesus said, "Now judgment is upon this world; now the ruler of this world will be cast out" (John 12:31 NASB).

OPENING EYES

Once Jesus died, and especially after he rose from the dead, the message encoded within the prophecies was suddenly clear. After the resurrection he rejoined his disciples:

Then he opened their minds to understand the Scriptures, and He said to them, "Thus it is written, that the Christ would suffer and rise again from the dead the third day; and that repentance for forgiveness of sins would be proclaimed in His name to all the nations, beginning from Jerusalem" (Luke 24:45–47 NASB).

Imagine how excited they must have been to realize God had been in control the whole time!

Just before "opening their minds" Jesus said, "When I was with you before, I told you that everything written about me in the law of Moses and the prophets and in the Psalms must be fulfilled" (v. 44). We saw earlier how the prophets and the psalmist spoke of the suffering servant, but when did Moses (the Pentateuch—Genesis through Deuteronomy) predict him? The answer is that the whole sacrificial system, the ark of the testimony, and the festival calendar also predicted, in amazing detail, Christ's work in his first coming. The disciples knew Jesus had been crucified on the day of Passover. But they probably didn't grasp the whole picture until this meeting. The language here suggests this was the first time they understood both the prophecies of the suffering servant and the significance of their own ceremonial law.

We must see that initially nobody realized these Old Testament sacrifices and festivals were "only shadows of the reality yet to come. And Christ himself is that reality" (Colossians 2:17). Only when he had already atoned for sin was the curtain pulled back. Then God revealed that the elaborate system of ceremonial law was like an immense jigsaw puzzle—now assembled—showing Jesus on the cross! Here again, God had encoded his message in a way that was unmistakable, *but only after the work was complete*. Hebrews 5–10 explains this message and how it foreshadows Christ's work.

THE "MYSTERY"

The aggressive anti-Christian rabbi Saul of Tarsus also failed to grasp that the Old Testament completely laid out the work of Jesus, even though he was an expert on Scripture. Only when Jesus opened his eyes did he realize how this picture had been laying right in front of him the whole time.

In several places, Paul tells us that God had recently revealed a secret "mystery" after hiding it for thousands of years.

My gospel and the preaching of Jesus Christ, according to the revelation of the mystery which has been kept secret for long ages past, but now is manifested, and by the Scriptures of the prophets, according to the commandment of the eternal God, has been made known to all the nations. (Romans 16:25–26 NASB)

Notice God was indeed keeping something secret for ages (Greek: *aeons,* or eons)   something that then had recently been revealed. Paul says this "mystery" or secret is his gospel, "the preaching of Jesus Christ." Paul is referring to the cross and God's whole redemptive plan in Messiah's first coming. It was secret because, although God predicted it, he did so in a way that was undecipherable until after Satan had made his violent move against Christ, and then the whole truth emerged.

In another passage Paul says,

As I briefly wrote earlier, God himself revealed his mysterious plan to me. As you read what I have written, you will understand my insight into this plan regarding Christ. God did not reveal it to previous generations, but now by his Spirit he has revealed it to his holy apostles and prophets. (Ephesians 3:3–5)

Paul says God gave him a special revelation about the plan. He clearly states that this mystery was not revealed to people before his time. The particular aspect of the mystery addressed here has to do with how God has united Jews and Greeks (non-Jews) in Christ. But other passages reveal that Paul's idea of the mystery extends well beyond this aspect, and he goes on to draw out the cosmic significance of God's secret plan:

To me, the very least of all saints, this grace was given, to preach to the Gentiles the unfathomable riches of Christ, and to bring to light what is the administration of the mystery which for ages has been hidden in God who created all things; so that the manifold wisdom of God might now be made known through the church to the rulers and the authorities in the heavenly places. This was in accordance with the eternal purpose which He carried out in Christ Jesus our Lord. (Ephesians 3:8–11 NASB)

Several points are interesting here. For one thing, he says the mystery was for ages "hidden in God." Apparently, *God alone* knew what he was intending to do. Here is clear confirmation that God was actively concealing his intentions in Christ from the whole world and even from the angelic hosts.

This passage also mentions one result of the mystery: that the "rulers and authorities in the heavenly places" (angels and probably demons) will learn something about God. Probably they now see his character of love and self-sacrifice for what it is. Certainly, they saw his "manifold wisdom" unfolded in his vast, eternal plan, now exposed in all its brilliance. The cross, a unique event in the history of the universe, has laid to rest—for anyone who understands it—any suspicion about God's character.

Notice also that the church plays a key role in this revelation to the heavenly hosts: to them these secrets are "made known through the church." As recipients of grace, we forgiven humans are in a unique position. We know what it's like to live apart from God, to harbor suspicions of God, even to hate God. But we also know what it's like to experience his grace and love—an incredible gift that cost him everything and us nothing. Even unfallen angels have never experienced such love, and we alone can explain what it's like to experience grace, "so that in the ages to come He might show the surpassing riches of His grace in kindness toward us in Christ Jesus" (Ephesians 2:7 NASB). Someday you may be invited on a speaking tour to recount what life was like in a fallen world!

THE DEMONSTRATION

This mystery is central to what Paul calls God's "eternal purpose." He planned all this out from eternity and for eternity. Never again will there be a revolution against God, even though free-will creatures populate the universe. That's because all will recall what happened last time. We will remember how God demonstrated his nature as all-good, all-loving, and all-just, while his accusers revealed their character as evil, bitter, and deceptive.

The idea of God demonstrating his character appears also in Romans 3.

> God displayed [Jesus] publicly as a propitiation in His blood through faith. This was to demonstrate His righteousness, because in the forbearance of God He passed over the sins previously committed; for the demonstration, I say, of His righteousness at the present time, so that He would be just and the justifier of the one who has faith in Jesus. (vv. 25–26 NASB)

The cross was a public demonstration of God's goodness. What does the phrase "just and the justifier" mean? At the cross, God demonstrated his justice, because he fully punished the sins of humans rather than ignoring them. At the same time, he is the justifier, because he paid that penalty himself at incredible cost. How perfectly this resolves the dilemma regarding God's justice and love that we discussed earlier.

Paul brings the mystery up again in Colossians 1:

> Of this church I was made a minister according to the stewardship from God bestowed on me for your benefit, so that I might fully carry out the preaching of the Word of God, that is, the mystery which has been hidden from the past ages and generations; but has now been manifested to His saints, to whom God willed to make known what is the riches of the glory of this mystery among the Gentiles, which is Christ in you, the hope of glory. (vv. 25–27 NASB)

In this very similar passage we again see that the mystery "has been hidden from the past ages and generations." Yes, it was there, right in front of them through the prophets and in ceremonies, but because of the key omissions no one could see it. Paul then says God has recently manifested it, or brought it to light. The content of the mystery, it says here, is "Christ in you, the hope of glory." Only the cross could open the door to the new intimacy between God and us; an intimacy so deep that he actually indwells us through the Holy Spirit.

Again Paul makes it very clear that God was keeping a secret, a mystery he has only recently revealed. Once more we not only see that God was keeping Jesus' mission secret, but we also see why.[3]

THE BIG PICTURE

As we ponder the mystery hidden for eons past, the mass of information begins to congeal into a spectacular panorama.

God wanted to create personal beings, and personal beings, by definition, must be un-programmed, free-choosing moral agents. Anything less is a machine, not a person; love is impossible for creatures lacking free will. Imagine programming a recorder to say "I love you" every time you come home from work. Is this love? No. It's only saying what you programmed it to say. No wonder the God of love puts high value on free-choosing creatures. Without freedom, outside God the creation would also be without love. Yet the creation of freedom inherently entails the possibility and indeed the likelihood that eventually someone would use his or her freedom the wrong way.

We know this happened when Satan rebelled against God, and that rebellion then spread to our world, nearly ruining it. Of course, God saw all this coming, and he had a plan. He laid down a well-attested scriptural record that promised he would one day intervene to return the world to its proper state with him as its leader. Inserted into this same predictive material, though, was another message—a message that was clear in one way but hidden in another, almost as though written in code.

Then, at the right time, Christ came, and as Satan pitted his limited wisdom against God's infinite wisdom, he was completely outclassed and ended up only proving how good is God and how bankrupt was his own revolution. We saw earlier that when Satan fell, God said, "So I brought fire out from within you, and it consumed you" (Ezekiel 28:18). The destroying fire came from within Satan himself: At the cross, Satan was ruined by his own bloodthirsty hate.

The outcome is clear. To anyone who understands it, the cross forever refuted the ravings of Satan and his followers. In light of what happened, the citizens of the universe can feel inexpressible confidence in God and his character, a confidence so complete that revolution will never again taint the course of eternity future. Jesus defeated Satan in the first place, not by power and force, but by something Satan cannot comprehend: sacrificial love.

CHAPTER 6

SPIRITUAL WARFARE TODAY

From God's eternal viewpoint, Jesus utterly won the war at the cross. Yet like Nazi Germany even after D day, Satan still has plenty of fight left. Since the ascension of Jesus, the church, his body, has taken the front line in this conflict. This is where we get involved. Before studying how to battle Satan, we need to reflect on the overall strategies: What is he planning to do and what should we be trying to accomplish?

WHAT IS SATAN THINKING?

One might envision Satan as being very depressed these days. He's up against the infinite God of the universe; he blew it badly at the cross; his own doom is assured; and the hated human race now has open access to eternal life. What keeps him going? We get a clue from Revelation 12:12:

> Terror will come on the earth and the sea. For the Devil has come down to you in great anger, and he knows that he has little time.

Knowing he has been defeated doesn't bring melancholy to Satan; it makes him furious. Seeing his end draw near makes Satan even more frantic to destroy. In the psychology of hatred, rage becomes irrational, and Satan apparently has become angrier than ever. But his strategy is far from irrational. He continues, in calculated and effective ways, to pursue his course of opposition to God's plans.

Satan's strategy is essentially defensive. He already has his stake in the world, but as the kingdom of God grows, his stake shrinks. Therefore, he guards his turf by trying to keep people from coming under God's leadership and forgiveness. To steer people away from God, he can draw on a number of measures aimed at all people, both believers and nonbelievers.

MEASURES DIRECTED AGAINST NON-CHRISTIANS

Counterfeit

Satan works to convince people that God is someone he actually isn't. Religion is one of his most powerful tools for keeping people away from the true God. Far from the postmodern idea that all religions are valid and more or less the same, the Bible says the false gods people worship really are demons (1 Corinthians 10:19–20). Sometimes Satan fosters religion that allows people to view themselves as gods, and by so guiding, he causes them to believe they're close to God when in fact they are not.

Slander

Satan constantly strives to convince non-Christians (and even Christians) that the God of the Bible is a dangerous jerk. Following God, he claims, is the worst possible experience—it will result in losing everything that makes life enjoyable. The message is clear: God wants something from you—a lot, in fact—and if you listen to him, your life could be impoverished.

According to Satan, God cannot be trusted. At most, it might be smart to do a few things to keep God pacified, but he's not the kind of being you'd ever want to get close to. Satan wants to convince people that God is menacing and demanding, that he's essentially a cosmic police officer.

Stereotyping

Most non-Christians have never seen Jesus, and many have never read the Bible. But they have met Christians. To them, Christians *are* Christianity. That's why Satan is eager to make Christians seem odious and offensive. When others are disgusted and offended by believers, they avoid the gospel like the plague. They never want to see themselves as "one of those people."

While Satan is often unable to gain control of true believers, he can still create this portrayal by infiltrating his own operatives into "Christianity." Once there, they usually become the loudest and most aggressive "Christians" and are used to propagate the negative stereotype Satan seeks.

At the university in my city, a vicious, shouting man stands on the campus green and insults passersby. Often with a cross behind him, the Bible in front of him, and Jesus on his lips, this guy is so notorious that every person on this fifty-thousand-student campus is aware of him. We have never heard him preach the gospel of forgiveness. If he is a Christian, he is a terribly misguided one, and we have good reason to think he's not a Christian at all. Believers on campus shudder in embarrassment whenever he starts to bellow.

Throughout history Satan has succeeded in getting so-called Christians to outrage the rest of the world. Even real Christians can be deceived and taken over to help in this work. Jesus warned this was coming and put people on their guard to "beware of false prophets who come disguised as harmless sheep, but are really wolves that will tear you apart" (Matthew 7:15).

Mark Mittelberg and Bill Hybels record a measure of Satan's success in our world today:

> *The Day America Told the Truth*, a book by James Patterson and Peter Kim, reports that when a national survey asked respondents to rank various professions for their honesty and integrity, TV evangelists came out almost at the very bottom, below lawyers, politicians, car salesmen, and even prostitutes. Out of the seventy-three occupations compared in this integrity rating, only two ended up lower on the scale: organized crime bosses and drug dealers![1]

Satan doesn't have to make all Christians behave in offensive ways. Assigning guilt by association is a powerful psychological tendency in most people. Just a few negative examples can be effective in marring all of Christianity in the minds of many.

Slavery

Satan knows that, as Jesus said (John 8:34), sin has the power to enslave humans. He's an expert in the dynamics of addiction, and he knows that the more heavily people's minds become enslaved to sin, the less likely they'll be to turn to God. Because people know God is a moral being and opposed to sin, they fear him, intuitively sensing that coming to him would be a threat to the sin that controls their lives. Highly destructive addictions may backfire, resulting in conversion to Christ. While cultural approval may make more subtle addictions (like materialistic greed) highly effective.

Distraction

People in our church recently interviewed local students on their views of the afterlife. After asking what they believed, we asked a follow-up question: Why do you believe that? One of the most common answers was something like, "I don't know. I've never really thought much about it."

How could people reach adulthood without thinking much about a matter as crucial as the afterlife? This illustrates the power of distraction. Many people have spent their lives so preoccupied with temporal pursuits that they have never seriously considered life's larger questions. "Satan, who is the god of this world, has blinded the minds of those who don't believe. They are unable to see the glorious light of the Good News" (2 Corinthians 4:4).

Through his impressive *kosmos* system (which we'll study in chapter 11), Satan can so engross people in ultimately meaningless aims that they won't consider anything else. Even when some desire to know more about God, they often can't find time to learn much because of the demands of their pursuits in the *kosmos* (world-system).

Death

Death is the seal of finality on people's lives when they fail to come to God. Satan is eager to see us die, but the story of Job makes it clear that Satan cannot just kill anyone he wishes. God restricts his ability—based on unrevealed rules, probably involving human free will—but Satan has proven effective at getting people to kill each other or even themselves. Jesus says he was "a murderer from the beginning" (John 8:44) and that "the thief's purpose is to steal and kill and destroy" (10:10).

In addition to working for the early death of humans, Satan uses the fear of death to manipulate them.

> Only by dying could [Jesus] break the power of the devil, who had the power of death. Only in this way could he set free all those who have lived their lives as slaves to the fear of dying. (Hebrews 2:14–15)

Satan uses fear of death to drive people into living frenzied lives, striving to gain as much self-advantage as possible during their short time. Their fear of death makes them so uncomfortable they don't want to think about it, or anything connected to it, especially the possibility that they may be accountable to God.

Taken together, these measures constitute an enormously effective network of deception and manipulation leading people away from God and his saving gospel.

MEASURES DIRECTED AGAINST CHRISTIANS

Satan attacks believers, which can seem to us like an offensive strategy, but these actually are "spoiling attacks." Sometimes offense is the best defense: Military leaders who realize an enemy is about to launch an offensive often attack first, seeking to upset the attackers' plans and throw them into confusion. Not all our problems come from Satan—we are more than capable of making trouble for ourselves without any help from him. But when he does strike, he can be very effective.

Destroying Christians' Spiritual Lives

Every healthy, growing Christian poses a potential threat to Satan's kingdom. That's why he seeks opportunities to destroy or retard our spiritual growth. Peter says, "Stay alert! Watch out for your great enemy, the devil. He prowls around like a roaring lion, looking for someone to devour" (1 Peter 5:8). We will examine how he does this in the coming chapters.

Rendering Christians Ineffective

Satan is unable to destroy Christians, so his ultimate goal is to make us ineffective in our mission. Whether he can destroy faith or stalemate us in other ways, his point is to block Christians' efforts to rescue those currently under his control. While personal hatred plays a role (so he may feel pleasure just from harming God's people), we have every reason to believe Satan's main motivation is pragmatic: he wants to guard his captives from the power of the gospel. Satan can convince most Christians never even to try to advance God's cause on earth. Others do try, but he can frustrate their plans or redirect them into fruitless projects.

He attacks both individuals and groups, sometimes inciting them to do his work for him. He can divide believers or get them to pursue foolish, doomed-to-failure tactics. And he has been remarkably successful getting believers to preach a message so alien to the gospel that no one could meet Christ through their message.

CHAPTER 7

OUR STRATEGY

How you understand Satan's strategy and ours will shape your entire vision for Christian living and church life. One of the main reasons Christian groups are so different from one another is their understanding of grand strategy.

TAKING THE OFFENSIVE

As Christians, our strategy is supposed to be offensive (i.e., attacking), not toward people but toward the kingdom of darkness. Jesus said, "How can anyone enter the strong man's house and carry off his property, unless he first binds the strong man? And then he will plunder his house" (Matthew 12:29 NASB). The strong man in this context is Satan; Jesus, who had just released a man from a demon's power, illustrates himself and his followers plundering Satan's house. This fits his revelation that Satan is the "god of this world," holding people in bondage apart from God, who sends us to liberate captives, if we can get past the strong man.[1]

Rescue

Paul explained that our ministry is the same as Jesus' own.

Now all these things are from God, who reconciled us to Himself through Christ and gave us the ministry of reconciliation, namely, that God was in Christ reconciling the world to Himself, not counting their trespasses against them, and He has committed to us the word of reconciliation. (2 Corinthians 5:18–19 NASB)

Just as God sent Jesus to reconcile people to himself, so we, Christ's body, are to continue and expand on this work. The "goods" plundered from Satan's household are *people* we release from his prison, build up and make whole, and release to play their part in the battle. Of course the ministry of reconciliation involves evangelism, but also much more than that. Reconciliation begins when people meet Christ, and it continues as they are nourished, discipled, healed, and melded together into a healthy local body (church).

So many different gifts and ministries are involved in this complex task of reconciling the world to God, and Paul clearly teaches that this is our purpose, encouraging the Philippians to be "standing together with one spirit and one purpose, fighting together for the faith, which is the Good News [gospel]" (Philippians 1:27).

Jesus agrees: "As the Father has sent me, so I send you" (John 20:21; cf. 17:18, where he prays to the Father about his followers: "As you sent me into the world, I am sending them into the world"). Jesus sent his followers into the *kosmos*, just as he had earlier been sent, and for the same reason. Why was Jesus sent into the world?

The Son of Man has come to seek and to save that which was lost. (Luke 19:10 NASB)

God did not send the Son into the world to judge the world, but that the world might be saved through Him. (John 3:17 NASB)

Even the Son of Man did not come to be served, but to serve, and to give His life a ransom for many. (Mark 10:45 NASB)

Theologians point out that the purpose of the church is to glorify God, because all that he has done for us is "to the praise of His glory" (Ephesians 1:12 NASB). What glorifies God? Jesus said, "I brought glory to you here on earth by completing the work you gave me to do" (John

17:4), and the grand purpose for God's people is no different. In Jesus, God invaded the world-system to liberate the vast slave population held in bondage by Satan. *We are on a rescue mission for the human race.*

John describes Jesus' (and our) mission in these words: "The Son of God came to destroy the works of the devil" (1 John 3:8). God calls believers to infiltrate and subvert Satan's kingdom. As Jesus put it when he called Paul,

> I am sending you to the Gentiles to open their eyes, so they may turn from darkness to light and from the power of Satan to God. Then they will receive forgiveness for their sins and be given a place among God's people, who are set apart by faith in me. (Acts 26:17–18)

Infiltration

God's strategy for taking ground back from Satan's kingdom is to infiltrate it with his own people. We are to build a new kingdom of God, coexisting within Satan's domain. This infiltrating version of the kingdom is the church, or the body of Christ. By building up the body, we progressively erode Satan's kingdom. Any real growth of the true church is an act of aggression—an attack on Satan's *kosmos*.[2]

THE PRICE OF A DEFENSIVE VIEW

Many Christians fail to understand that our strategy is offensive. Consider our common misunderstanding of Matthew 16:18, where Jesus says, "Upon this rock I will build my church; and the gates of Hades will not overpower it" (NASB). The NLT says, "all the powers of hell will not conquer it." But wait: How do the gates of a city "overpower" or "conquer" an army? Don't armies attack gates when they are storming a city? Gates are *defensive* structures! This verse should read, "The gates of Hades will not *withstand* [the church]."[3] How could gates ever "overcome" the church? Many interpreters and translators have completely missed the point here.

This traditional translation and the outlook that goes with it sees the universal church in danger of being destroyed, but God preserves it faithfully. But Jesus is saying that *Satan's* fortress is in danger and that God will back the church's assault to victory. *We* are the invaders. *We* seek to knock down the walls and release the prisoners inside.

Paul confirms this reading when he says, "The weapons we fight with are not the weapons of the world. On the contrary, they have divine power to demolish strongholds" (2 Corinthians 10:4 NIV). Satan owns the strongholds we must batter down.

This is a crucial point. When the church sees its strategy as defensive, or as one of self-preservation, we depart from the vision God gives us in the New Testament. One could argue that Israel's Old Testament strategy was more defensive, but at any rate Jesus is clear that we are to attack.[4] Churches on the defensive not only are unable to effectively release Satan's captives, but they also develop spiritual illnesses because they are not doing what God wants.

Remember, we never attack *people*; rather, we attack Satan's fortresses that imprison people. The whole reason the disciples were to wait in Jerusalem is that Jesus promised, "You will receive power when the Holy Spirit comes on you; and you will be my witnesses in Jerusalem, and in all Judea and Samaria, and to the ends of the earth" (Acts 1:8 NIV). God didn't give them power to survive (as a defensive theology would argue); he gave them, and us, power to move out into the world and win people back to God. The Great Commission makes this clear as well:

> All authority in heaven and on earth has been given to me. Therefore go and make disciples of all nations, baptizing them in the name of the Father and of the Son and of the Holy Spirit, and teaching them to obey everything I have commanded you. And surely I am with you always, to the very end of the age. (Matthew 28:18–20 NIV)

The commission's central imperatives are *go*, and *make disciples*. That is our mission. But when Christians fail to see the mission's offensive nature, the result is what some have called *fortress theology*,[5] which accounts for much of the Western church's current ineffectiveness in reaching significant numbers of non-Christians.[6] While many believers today maintain that the evangelical church is growing and reaching large numbers, studies show that over 90 percent of so-called church growth in America is nothing but people transferring from other evangelical churches.[7] Meanwhile, the public's view of Christians has reached new lows.[8]

SUBVERSION

Paul describes spiritual war in 2 Corinthians 10:3–5:

For though we walk in the flesh, we do not war according to the flesh, for the weapons of our warfare are not of the flesh, but divinely powerful for the destruction of fortresses. We are destroying *speculations* and every lofty thing raised up against the *knowledge* of God, and we are taking every *thought* captive to the obedience of Christ. (NASB, italics added)

Notice the italicized words. *Speculations, knowledge,* and *thoughts* apparently make up the fortresses we are to destroy. These words are the language of thought processes and ideas. The spiritual war described here is mainly an *ideological struggle.* To advance the kingdom of God and rescue captives from the world-system, we are to subvert their current belief systems with the truth. The powerful weapons mentioned here are truth, prayer, and spiritual conviction that enable believers to win over the minds and hearts of people laboring under Satan's deception.

We read in Revelation 12:9 that Satan is "the one deceiving the whole world." To release people from the spell he has put on them, Christians are to answer with truth each lie hurled at them by the enemy. Somehow, we must show people the deceptions. Every choice to follow God has to be a free-will decision—not made under compulsion. Thus, with God's power, we need to convince people how the doctrine of the world is wrongheaded and show them how God's way is the better choice. "It is because we know this solemn fear of the Lord that we work so hard to persuade others" (2 Corinthians 5:11).

We've seen the warning that "Satan, who is the god of this world, has blinded the minds of those who don't believe. They are unable to see the glorious light of the Good News" (2 Corinthians 4:4). Every Christian who has had a hand in the task of reconciling people to God knows how difficult it can be to break through this inflicted blindness. While we wonder how anyone could turn down an offer as awesome as the free gift of eternal life, it happens all the time. Witnessing believers must be well aware of the cloud of confusion and preconception that seems to block people from seeing what is right in front of their eyes.

To overcome such deception, we need powerful weapons indeed. This means the church also has a large task to accomplish in training and building up its people. Paul calls for leaders to equip members for ministry:

> Their responsibility is to equip God's people to do his work and build up the church, the body of Christ. This will continue until we all come to such unity in our faith and knowledge of God's Son that we will be mature in the Lord, measuring up to the full and complete standard of Christ. Then we will no longer be immature like children. We won't be tossed and blown about by every wind of new teaching. We will not be influenced when people try to trick us with lies so clever they sound like the truth. (Ephesians 4:12–14)

So building maturity into our members is biblical, and not only so we can enjoy each other more. A big part of the reason we need mature members is that maturity is crucial to winning our war with Satan. Immature believers lack the understanding and fiber to match up consistently with the Evil One. They don't know how to wield the weapons of righteousness.

Conviction

The persuasive presentation of truth from God's Word accounts for much of spiritual warfare, but we can also impact people in other ways. Through prayer and example, we can appeal directly to their hearts and consciences even before speaking to them. Jesus said that when the Holy Spirit comes, "he will convict the world of its sin, and of God's righteousness, and of the coming judgment" (John 16:8). When working in cooperation with God, we can anticipate cases in which people may become unexpectedly receptive. They seem to have already sensed their need for God in their hearts. Often this happens after they hear God's Word declared. It may happen after they visit a loving Christian community and sense its people have something real. The forces of the Bible, the example lived out by believers, and prayer, combine to generate great power. No wonder Paul calls the weapons of our warfare "divinely powerful" (2 Corinthians 10:3 NASB).

WHY STRATEGY MATTERS

Knowing and agreeing on our grand strategy is crucial to the church's success in spiritual war. Our vision of the church's mission shapes our attitudes and actions. If most of God's people on earth today adopt self-protective or inward-looking goals, we can expect little progress toward our true goal of reconciling the world to God. Do some Christians today see the church as little more than a family entertainment center or country club—a place to be with similar people and enjoy uplifting performances? Think what a view like this does to our battle worthiness and readiness.

How different it is when we realize we're in the midst of a desperate struggle with eternal life and death at stake! Under this vision, things become reasonable that would never make sense under softer outlooks. When believers realize that discipline, self-denial, and suffering might be more typical of church life than personal gratification or mere self-improvement, they can identify with the militant language found in one New Testament passage after another.[9] Enjoying times of worship or improving oneself become lesser goals, intended to contribute to the larger spectrum.

Understanding grand strategy enables Christians to appreciate the smaller pieces, shift competing values, and put it all together in readiness for battle.

CHAPTER 8

HOW THE SIDES MATCH UP

Before going into battle, it makes sense to size up your enemy. Jesus recommended this when he asked, "What king would ever dream of going to war without first sitting down with his counselors and discussing whether his army of ten thousand is strong enough to defeat the twenty thousand soldiers who are marching against him?" (Luke 14:31). How strong are Satan and his forces? How strong are we?

SATAN'S ADVANTAGES

Satan has a number of advantages in spiritual warfare. In fact, when considered together, his advantages can be downright frightening.

Experience

In the first place, he's been doing this for thousands of years. As a result, he and his demon followers are supremely experienced. Satan has seen it all many times. He's studied human nature for ages and knows exactly how we work. In the tension of battle, it's easy to lose your nerve and run away, especially if you aren't used to war. But Satan doesn't have to worry about that with his battle-hardened fighters. While our green troops are still trying to figure out what battle is, Satan's followers have each fought thousands of battles.

Intellect

Satan and his followers are superior to the body of Christ in intellect. None of us has any hope of matching up with his brilliance or education. The Bible presents Satan as extraordinarily smart; again, God said he was perfect in wisdom (Ezekiel 28:12). Satan's intellect includes both book knowledge and field experience.

Many of our people aren't too smart even as humans go, and others won't take any time to study. Some don't even believe that thinking, learning, and study are worthwhile spiritual activities. The contrast between our confusion and Satan's sharp, well-informed forces is pitiful. Intellectually, Christians are hopelessly outclassed.

Numbers

Satan's side can also be superior in numbers. Although the Bible never gives us the number of demons in existence, we can infer that they exist in vast numbers—at least hundreds of millions and perhaps billions.[1] Also, with their unlimited mobility as spirit beings, Satan can arrange to outnumber God's followers in any particular locality. If a group of Christians begins to influence spiritual battle, we have every reason to believe Satan can quickly send in reinforcements and outnumber them. Satan is not omnipresent, but he gets excellent coverage with his numerous and mobile underlings.

Stealth

A key advantage for evil spirits is their stealth. To humans, spirits are invisible unless they want to be seen, and this is a terrible handicap for us. In 2 Kings 6, we read that Elisha's servant was alarmed one morning to find the town where they were staying surrounded by a hostile army. But Elisha told him:

> "Don't be afraid!" . . . "For there are more on our side than on theirs!" Then Elisha prayed, "O Lord, open his eyes and let him see!" The Lord opened the young man's eyes, and when he looked up, he saw

that the hillside around Elisha was filled with horses and chariots of fire. (vv. 16–17)

How different things would look if we could see the spirit world. Believers would probably walk much more carefully if they could see actual demons following them around. Instead, we too often find that Satan has already done his work among us and departed by the time we begin to wonder if he might be involved. Sometimes the idea of his involvement never even occurs to apathetic Christians who stand gaping at spiritual tragedy, confused, and with no idea why or how it happened. We spend most of our time doing damage control because of Satan's stealth.

Discipline

Satan apparently commands a well-disciplined army. While we have no evidence that their discipline is perfect, Jesus discounted the idea that they might fight against each other (Matthew 12:26). Well-coordinated work is typical of satanic attacks; his followers know what to do, and they do it with extreme reliability. Our people, on the other hand, frequently are more like a loose rabble. We feel happy if our people even show up, let alone take a hand in the struggle. And too often our people do Satan's work for him—arguing his case or even attacking and destroying fellow Christians.

Fearless, Relentless, and Heedless of Loss

All firsthand accounts of battle emphasize how terrifying it is. Seeing friends cut down on every side is unnerving. But Satan's forces are fearless. They come, and they keep coming, no matter what happens. Any local victory we score will be answered quickly by another attack. Casualties are common in the church. How jolting it is to see believers you thought would never falter fall apart completely.

Relentless pressure like this becomes demoralizing to fearful people like us. Humans tend to keep score and to lose heart when they're behind. But the demons don't seem to care how often they lose—they remain just as determined during times of loss as during times of victory. Satan capitalizes on fear, often convincing Christians that their struggle is hopeless, and this is particularly true in groups that are aggressively doing God's work. While do-nothing groups may live in comparative serenity, active, forward-moving groups can expect a relentless battering.

Staying Alert

Staying alert is important in war, whereas an unexpected move (such as Pearl Harbor) often brings defeat. Many passages on fighting with Satan stress the need for alertness (e.g., Acts 20:31; 1 Corinthians 16:13; Ephesians 6:18; Colossians 4:2; 1 Thessalonians 5:6; 1 Peter 5:8), but this is a sore spot for most Christians. We might be alert at certain times, but usually we're preoccupied by other interests. Some are so preoccupied they "forget" for months at a time that a war is going on! Satan's forces have no problem with lack of alertness; they have no other interests. While they may be surprised at times, this appears infrequent, and they seem to adjust quickly.

One time someone in our home group reached a student who lived in a small nearby suburb. The new believer turned out to be very influential, and within a few weeks a dozen others had come to Christ or were close to faith in a group we started in their town. But Satan rapidly enticed one leader to fall into an affair and another to fall into drugs. Then he set them against each other, and within another two weeks the group disintegrated and disappeared.

Freedom to Cheat

The fact that Satan is not constrained by ethics can be a significant advantage. Total pragmatism—winning at any cost and by any means—is hard to combat. We, on the other hand, have to wage war according to God's rules. In human combat, always telling the truth would be unthinkable; deceiving your enemy is a crucial wartime operation. Satan does this all the time, but we don't have the freedom to lie. While we wouldn't have much chance of deceiving him anyway, we could deceive his human servants if we were permitted. He uses manipulation and intimidation to good effect, but these are out of bounds for us as well.

We are not to play into the culture's popular desires but instead generally confront people with a message they find offensive. Satan is free to tell them exactly what they want to hear. He promises them the very thing they desire even though he has no intention of delivering.

God won't overrule human free will in most cases; he waits for a choice from feeble humans at multiple points. But Satan won't hesitate to enslave people and overtake them to various extents, even without their knowledge. In a word, God often forbids us to do the pragmatically useful thing and instead calls us to forfeit results for the sake of faithfulness to him.

Leadership

Good leadership is crucial to winning battles. Our leader is Jesus, the head of the body (Colossians 1:18); we have the superior leadership. But our lines of communication with Jesus are often poor. Many Christians rarely read or study the Bible, where God clearly teaches his battle plan. And following the subtle, inner leading of the Holy Spirit isn't easy for carnally minded Christians who don't even remember to pray.

In practice, God usually leads through human delegates, and this becomes a major difficulty. Human leaders frequently are corrupt and self-serving. Lying, instability, hypocrisy, and misdirected ego-trips characterize far too many.

Satan also is an excellent leader, consistently guiding his forces to victory. He also has direct communication with his fellow-spirit beings, and they understand what he says.

Unbelief

Finally, Satan's forces never have any problem with unbelief. They all know exactly what's going on and who God is. They waste no time wondering what's real. Conversely, our people sometimes don't even believe spiritual war exists. We doubt our leader, we doubt his Word, and we doubt one another, often with devastating results. Even when we're only briefly immobilized by unbelief, this may allow sufficient time for Satan to make his move. When Christians live in perpetual doubt, they offer no resistance at all. Unbelief cuts off the supply of God's power.

PROBLEMS WITH OUR GROUP

We've already seen a number of problems on our side of this struggle, and there are more. Aside from being incompetent, fearful, ignorant, distracted, and unbelieving, we sometimes suffer from even more serious handicaps. For one thing, *many Christians are secretly in love with the other side.* These may follow Christ outwardly, but in their hearts they are intent on currying favor with Satan's world-system. And this despite the warning that "friendship with this world [*kosmos*] makes you an enemy of God" (James 4:4).

Spiritual beings are completely uninterested in temporal goals like pleasure and making money. Humans, on the other hand, often are obsessed with temporal goals but unable to articulate any specific spiritual goals in their own lives. Some of our fellow travelers couldn't care less about God's goals and haven't lifted a finger in years to move his purposes forward in the world.

Our forces frequently suffer internal division, with members too bitter toward their comrades to contribute anything but discord and distress. We have members right in our midst that Satan can energize and use any time he wants. A significant proportion of Christians are simply too lazy and too selfish to wage spiritual war. Others are so gullible they're just as likely to believe what Satan and his people say as what God says. At this time, very few of our people are adequately equipped for real battle.

Considering this list of advantages for Satan, it may seem surprising that Christians ever win any victories at all. Clearly, we have our work cut out for us! Nevertheless, we have some advantages of our own.

OUR ADVANTAGES

Looking at the big picture, we realize that any victory scored by God's people is nothing short of a miracle. But we must have something going for us or we never would have grown to the size we are today. And we have several key advantages.

Power

Christians possess one advantage so great it's impossible to exaggerate: We have God on our side. This means that in any situation, even a single Christian has infinitely more power available than any demonic combination. Psalm 89 says,

> Who in all of heaven can compare with the Lord? What mightiest angel is anything like the Lord? The highest angelic powers stand in awe of God. He is far more awesome than all who surround his throne. (vv. 6–7)

If we know how to access God's power, and if we work in cooperation with what he wants to do, we can expect victory in one battle after another, in spite of our weaknesses. God has given us "divinely powerful" weapons with which to fight (2 Corinthians 10:4). But he doesn't automatically exert his power. He expects us to learn how to fight the war using these weapons, and he often withholds his power until we use them appropriately.

This must be the case, or God would have no reason to give us instructions about spiritual armor and resisting Satan. If everything were up to him, he wouldn't imply that we have an active role to play. Prayer, for example, would be pointless. We must assume that even though God has more than enough power to control Satan completely or even to eliminate him at any time, he restrains his own intervention based on unrevealed rules that govern spiritual warfare.

Grace

Another advantage for us grows out of God's grace. Because he deals with us under grace, our errors and foolishness are often overlooked. Though God often covers blunders and sin that should spell certain defeat, and while he may discipline us as we go, he frequently grants success well beyond what our performance merits.

I've always been confused about why God uses me like he has, but during one period of my life it was particularly baffling. I became so disappointed and angry at how poorly my marriage was going that my walk with God deteriorated. I almost completely stopped praying. I felt like a stranger to him. I was teaching a weekly Bible study at the time, and I always felt awkward urging others to follow the God I was hardly following myself. My ministry did suffer. But the biggest shock was seeing God continue to work in that group, though at a reduced level. I was amazed every time people came to Christ; it seemed like a contradiction. I realized that God was more gracious than I had known, and that his love for lost people is such that he was prepared to bear fruit even through the ministry of one who should have been discredited.

Truth

We have God's words in the Bible. When dealing with the Father of Lies, what could be more important than knowing truth directly from God himself? This treasury perfectly answers every argument Satan brings and every tactic he employs. The Word of God has the power to turn back the attacks of Satan and to win people away from his power. People who grow deep in the Word are well-positioned to wage spiritual warfare.

Predictability

Even though Satan outclasses us in intellect, we have an advantage in that he tends to act in relatively predictable ways, probably because his long-established tactics are so successful he feels no need to change them. When Paul says that "we are familiar with his [Satan's] evil schemes" (2 Corinthians 2:11), he's referring to an important strength for our side: the ability to anticipate what Satan will try next. If we are successful in anticipating Satan's next move, we should be able to appropriate God's superior power through the Holy Spirit to defeat the Evil One's intentions. This advantage underscores the importance of learning Satan's tactics.

We are ready to consider how to battle Satan, first in the church, then in our personal lives, and finally in our sphere of ministry.

CHAPTER 9

BATTLING SATAN INSIDE
THE CHURCH

Hatred animates Satan's actions. He hates God and anything or anyone God loves, and that puts you and me in the crosshairs of his bitterness. As we've already seen, undermining the spirituality, balance, and effectiveness of Christ's body are essential to Satan's plan to guard his kingdom against the "plundering" work God sent us to do.

INDIVIDUALS VS. COMMUNITIES

For thousands of years Satan has perfected his tactics for neutralizing God's people. In this chapter we'll discuss Satan's attacks against local churches. Unlike many Christians, Satan agrees with God on the church's importance; they both know that a highly relational and motivated local church is the most potent force possible for invading the world-system. Jesus didn't leave behind various free-lance ministry organizations or wandering individuals; he left the church. The rest of the New Testament advances his body as God's main plan for reconciling the world to him. Nobody understands the church's centrality for God's purposes better than Satan.

Because of this knowledge, Satan directs immense efforts at subverting Christian communities. He knows that lone individuals pose little threat to his kingdom. They are also easy prey he can dispatch at his leisure. Only the body of Christ worries Satan enough to draw his best efforts, and when Satan gives his best, that's bad news for the people of God! He attacks with deception, division, persecution, and infiltration.

CORPORATE DECEPTION

Satan is the great deceiver. We saw how he undermines truth as a necessary precursor for other moves he wants to make. Jesus says Satan "always hated the truth, because there is no truth in him. When he lies, it is consistent with his character; for he is a liar and the father of lies" (John 8:44). He deceives leaders and uses them to carry entire groups of people into falsehood, away from God and their mission. Satan doesn't come into the church to cover people with open sores or explode their skulls like in the movies. He comes to deceive them.

Extreme Corporate Deception

Sometimes Satan is so successful at extreme deception that it's hard to fathom. Satan has convinced the church to believe incredible lies. Today, people who reject all biblical authority lead whole denominations with millions of members. By infiltrating nonbelievers into places of Christian higher learning, the Father of Lies has successfully churned out thousands of pastors and priests who have lost their faith in Scripture and now take their lead from the variable thought patterns of Satan's own world-system. Churches led by these people cannot and will not point people to Christ because their leaders don't believe the gospel themselves and never preach it.

Other formerly Christian groups have been deceived into placing additional sources of authority alongside the Bible. Any time we reckon a second authority as equal to Scripture, it ends up eventually *replacing* Scripture as the true source of revelation. These cult groups and churches drift further and further from biblical teaching with essentially no constraint, and once the church authorizes humans to generate rulings and visions that have equal authority with the Word of God, anything can happen. Satan can literally take over such groups, leading them to commit atrocities in the name of Christ: slaughtering, stealing, lying; you name it. They may present an image so grotesque and bizarre that they drive the watching world away in horror.

Cases of extreme deception in church history make for fascinating study. How could a church become so misguided that they would believe God called them to torture people to death? Why would millions of people give their hard-earned money to leaders who deny every aspect of the Christian gospel and even God's existence? How could "Christian" cult members ever come to believe that stealing, killing, assault, and even suicide are the will of Jesus Christ? These are baffling questions with one central answer: the awesomeness of Satan's power to deceive. He has proven ability to convince millions of normal people that they are following Jesus even while they directly or indirectly support evil.

Since this book is for mainstream believers, we will not dwell long on egregious examples of Satan's deceiving work. But these cases are important to examine for two reasons.

First, these masterpieces of deception have shaped the non-Christian world's view of Christianity to a saddening degree. Believers will have difficulty understanding why some nonbelievers feel such hostility and scorn for the church if we fail to learn what they know about the sad record of "Christian" misbehavior and foolishness. Most churches are reluctant to discuss such events in any detail, perhaps because they worry that it would be "divisive" or because they don't want to be too negative. A surprising percentage of Christians go so far as to defend, minimize, or excuse past wicked actions, thus further implicating themselves and Jesus in the evildoing. Neither Jesus, Paul, nor the other New Testament authors had any such reluctance when sternly denouncing false teaching and wrongdoing in the church.[1] Christians should learn about church atrocities and denounce them firmly.[2]

Second, these extreme cases should give all of us a healthy respect for Satan's lying power, and even a measure of fear, because that same power is headed our way and is already among us. What makes us think we are any different or better than the millions of other Christians (including well-trained leaders) who have succumbed to his lies to such devastating effect? Apathy or sloth in the face of such power is amazingly foolish.

Defense

It may seem simplistic, but the best defense against outlandish deception is the public reading of the Scriptures. Paul tells Timothy, "Until I get there, focus on reading the Scriptures to the church, encouraging the believers, and teaching them" (1 Timothy 4:13). When we exposit entire books of the Bible in context for people in the church, they become more resistant to deception.[3]

The church also should heed Paul's instruction to "learn not to exceed what is written" (1 Corinthians 4:6 NASB). Any time we view church leaders or tradition as having authority on the level of Scripture, we are wide open to deception. Most of the worst episodes in church history have been based on extra-biblical authority: visions, discovered texts, special translations, or bodies of tradition considered fully binding. The church must listen to Proverbs 30:5–6:

> Every word of God proves true. He is a shield to all who come to him for protection. Do not add to his words, or he may rebuke you and expose you as a liar.

Church leaders need to be accountable to their congregations, and that means their people should be able to read and interpret the Bible for themselves. In some extreme cases Satan has been able to remove the Bible completely from the hands of most Christians and thereby has removed their ability to hold leaders accountable to the truth. For a thousand years it was illegal to translate the Bible into languages laypeople could read. Today, thousands of churches still have their members convinced that the Bible is indecipherable and useless unless one has professional training. In this environment, the church is rendered defenseless against false teaching.

Subtle Corporate Deception

Satan's subtle forms of deception are far more germane to mainstream evangelicals, and these can be just as effective in blocking God's purposes in the church. Satan doesn't need to convince us that evil is good to achieve victory; all he has to do is move the church somewhat off the center of God's revealed counsel. This arguably can be even more effective than outlandish deception; it's harder to recognize and therefore has great staying power.

In subtle deception, Satan also doesn't need to persuade believers to deny central teachings, such as Christ's atoning death, his resurrection, or even biblical authority. Instead, he seeks to shift the *emphasis* from the important to the unimportant and misleads people on more peripheral issues. The resulting group may bear little resemblance to the church described in the New Testament.

We've already seen one clear example of this. Churches in the grip of fortress theology become incapable of being "all things to all men" (1 Corinthians 9:22 NASB), like Paul did, and the result is predictable: Ingrown churches don't reach meaningful numbers of people for Christ and instead merely compete to attract one another's members. These groups usually agree with all the major scriptural doctrines but have put a spin on more peripheral biblical teaching in a way that stalemates their witness.

Extremist groups abound today, and they often unintentionally heap disgrace and contempt on Jesus. Many TV preachers, snake-handlers, and legalistic groups are in this category. All of us know local groups that are exceedingly strange not because they deny central Christian teaching but because they dwell on minor or even questionable issues to such an extreme that it overshadows any truth they may teach. The overall picture presented to the world is bizarre and creates aversion to Christ.

Defense

To counter subtle deception, Christians must learn not only to teach what Scripture teaches but also to *emphasize what Scripture emphasizes.* Emphasis matters when we seek to reflect the full counsel of God. Thinking Christians in any church should constantly be asking themselves, "Does this take on Scripture accurately reflect the emphases found there, or are we camping out on issues the Bible hardly mentions? Are the issues we talk about out of date because the Bible itself says they've been superseded by later developments? Are we ignoring important teachings in the Word?" Scripture repeats emphasized truths often or teaches them with emphatic language, and we should do likewise.

Members also should examine the effect a group's teaching has on their progress toward achieving God's mission for the church. Careful discernment is important. Huge churches may only be filled with people lured away from other churches, and we've noted that mere numbers say little about whether churches are impacting Satan's kingdom. Popularity contests between churches have nothing to do with our mission, and they don't win people to Christ. On the other hand, a group reaching large numbers for Christ and seeing those new believers discipled, trained, and released into ministry must have something right. Speaking about how to discern false teachers, Jesus said, "A good tree produces good fruit, and a bad tree produces bad fruit (Matthew 7:17).

DIVISION

Jesus said, "Any kingdom divided by civil war is doomed. A town or family splintered by feuding will fall apart" (12:25). Contextually, he was pointing out that Satan is too smart to allow his household to be divided. Unfortunately, the church can't make the same claim.

After warring for millennia, Satan knows military doctrine like nobody else, and one of war's basics is "divide and conquer." Anytime a general can divide enemy forces, he's in a position to defeat them in detail; the smaller segments are no match for the power he can concentrate against them.

To divide Christian groups, Satan uses his preferred weapon, the one for which he's named: accusation (*diabolos*, the devil, means accuser). We often think of his accusation as being against God, or accusing a believer in the sense of making him feel too guilty to draw close to God. But he also launches accusation against fellow Christians. Satan plants hostile interpretations of others' actions and words in the minds of his victims.

By planting accusations in minds on both sides of a divide, he makes communication and reconciliation difficult. (E.g., "These people can't be trusted, they can't be dealt with; they must be fought or avoided.") Sowing suspicion is the name of Satan's game. He can usually ground suspicions in facts, at least partially, subtly adding assumptions about people's motives. But even when people are in the wrong, we are called to help fellow believers overcome their problems, not fight with them or hold them in contempt.

Some people are remarkably susceptible to suspicious thoughts about fellow Christians. They never consider that the accusing voice in their heads might be Satan. The Evil One knows which individuals in any fellowship have immature conflict-management skills. These self-centered believers rarely go to people they harbor suspicions against with a humble spirit and open mind. Instead, they become bitter and spread their suspicions to others, often exaggerating for effect. Believers tell tales heedless of the effect they may have on local church unity, and they do so without fairness, context, or key information that would ruin their intended spin-job.

Satan watches churches, identifies negative players with unresolved bitterness, and moves in to fan the flames. Paul says that in the context of bitterness and enmity, "anger gives a foothold to the devil" (Ephesians 4:27). Again, discussing lack of forgiveness, he says we should forgive "so that no advantage would be taken of us by Satan" (2 Corinthians 2:11 NASB).

Some biblical evidence suggests that Satan can virtually take over the minds of certain people in the church. In 2 Timothy 2, Paul tells Timothy to gently reprove those in opposition in the hope they "will come to their senses and escape from the devil's trap. For they have been held captive by him to do whatever he wants" (v. 26). In the context of this pastoral advice, these prisoners of Satan could well be believers. They aren't demon possessed; they're just so deceived and guilty that they can no longer tell the difference between right and wrong or between the voice of God and the voice of Satan.

This process of taking people under bondage for use in the church is usually associated with unresolved sin. In another passage, Paul tells Titus, "Reject a factious man after a first and second warning, knowing that such a man is perverted and is sinning, being self-condemned" (Titus 3:10–11 NASB). As we will study later, Satan knows how to use sin in a believer's life to alienate him from God, confuse him, and create a host of destructive measures for self-justification. High on the list of these strategies are blame-shifting and bitterness (especially for those untaught in God's grace). If he wants to, Satan can progressively take control of the thinking of those who fail to repent.

Lying dormant until the right moment, these people are secret weapons that Satan can unleash when he's ready. Experience suggests he may have several people substantially under his control in the same church. The sudden nexus of several bitter people with the same agenda is a sure mark of Satan's handiwork. Bitterness and suspicion then spread with incredible speed from person to person. The danger such coordinated attacks pose is so severe that it justifies the most serious form of church discipline: removal from fellowship.

Division can destroy entire local churches. I still remember the shock of seeing the power of division for the first time. A dynamic group of over two hundred (mostly recent converts), seeming poised to sweep the entire city, was rent asunder by internal division. Within a period of months they were completely wiped out. I tried to take a hand in reconciling the warring factions, and I was amazed at the irrationality and distorted perceptions that held people in their grip. They were being manipulated by a force greater than themselves. The satanic flavor of church division is unmistakable, and so are the outcomes—most in this group lost their walk with God altogether.

In division, Satan is able to orchestrate the best of all worlds for his side. Christians not only stop pursuing their mission of building the kingdom of God, they actually begin destroying each other. The lingering effects of division can go on for years, and those left in the church usually feel a spiritual depression that inhibits ministry efforts. Distrust and cynicism afflict leaders and workers, making it more difficult to love from the heart.

Not all division involves active conflict; passive division is also dangerous. God calls us to a unity that is tangible and characterized by love (Ephesians 4:3ff; 1 Corinthians 12:25). A disengaged group where people don't bother to relate deeply to one another is also divided, for Satan knows that fostering apathy and distraction can produce a disunited church just as easily as hostility.

Many Christians worry about mega-divisions like those that have created the many denominations today. As problematic as such large-scale conflicts may be, though, I believe Satan is most interested in division within particular local churches. After all, when the church was all one denomination he was effective at working his ways. This was no golden age. I believe God is less interested in all churches working together as a single denomination than he is in unity between brothers and sisters looking at one another in the same room. Personal love relationships are the basis of true unity in the church, and we find these in healthy local churches, not in international organizations. Whenever imperatives come up in the New Testament about preserving unity, these have to do with relational unity in a given locality (e.g., Ephesians 4:3; 1 Corinthians 1–3).

Defense

Churches are never safe from division—a sudden onslaught of which can surprise even the best churches. But we can minimize the risk in five ways:

1. The church must teach its members that Satan fosters division using human beings. People in the grip of division find it hard to realize Satan is manipulating them. They think it's all about those who are offending or hurting them, and they fail to see the invisible foe orchestrating the division. Christians who stop to think that they may be used to fuel a church division often stop long enough to get the mature counsel and help they need to resolve conflicts in a godly way.

2. A well-equipped church may have enough members who know

about basic relational ethics to prevent a budding division. Mature members can confront bitter members with their wrongdoing and send them back to their adversaries after they gain insight into their own contribution to the conflict. Teaching principles of godly conflict-resolution is effective in preventing many potential divisions.[4]

3. Churches hoping to avoid division must teach the primacy of forgiveness over avoiding offense in the first place. The Bible is crystal clear on this point: "Make allowance for each other's faults, and forgive anyone who offends you. Remember, the Lord forgave you, so you must forgive others" (Colossians 3:13). *Anyone* means "everybody minus nobody." This is explicit language ruling out all excuses. Paul qualifies it even further, saying that our forgiveness should be "just as the Lord forgave you" (NASB). And we know the forgiveness we receive in the finished work of Christ is absolute and all-encompassing. Even when our attitude is poor, Jesus' death provides for our complete forgiveness. During divisions, the hardest commodity to find is forgiveness, whether for real or imagined slights and offenses. We will never be able to arrange for a church where people don't offend and wrong one another. Our only hope is forgiveness, grace, and reconciliation.

4. God and members usually tip off leaders early on that division threatens their church. But overworked church leaders often just hope it will go away. This isn't as foolish as it may sound—many threatening divisions do go away. Still, just one successful division can decimate a church. Leaders have to learn to act quickly when rumblings come to their attention. This is a good argument for having many leaders; if a large church has only a few leaders, they usually don't have time to intervene in emerging divisions. But when many well-trained and mature members are given leadership roles, they are more likely to discover local fights and help heal the damage before it spreads. When we counsel the alienated or angry parties early, division becomes far less likely. Of course, we need to make sure our leaders don't fight with each other.

5. When counseling and admonition fail, the church must be willing to take a strong stand. The Bible is clear that dividing the church is so dangerous that it cannot be allowed. Leaders should warn divisive people, and if they persist, their peers in the church should confront them. If the divisive are leaders, they should be removed from leadership. If they will not repent, the church should remove them from fellowship rather than risk division. When leaders value their people and their mission for God, they will be strong enough to refuse to tolerate divisive activity.[5] Any weakness on this issue means we lack love and faithfulness to our stewardship from God. All too often churches put discipline off too long. By the time they finally act, a larger faction has formed and the division goes on, now made worse as people sympathize with disciplined ringleaders.

PERSECUTION

Satan has employed persecution against the church from its first days. He can mobilize non-Christians against God's people at any time, and with devastating effect. Death, imprisonment, and community shunning can retard the church's progress.

Authors throughout church history have argued that persecution only makes the church grow more. This is sometimes true but not always. History also reveals cases where persecution has exterminated entire Christian groups, even on a national scale. For example, the surprise nationwide attack on the sixteenth-century Huguenots succeeded in permanently eliminating their voice in France. The medieval underground group known as the Waldensians was virtually exterminated and finally silenced.[6] Other countries have remained almost "God-proof" to this day because of persecution.

If persecution were completely ineffective, Satan wouldn't use it. While he may enjoy seeing Christians suffer, this lofty being is too smart and disciplined to purposely enjoy himself at the expense of his own kingdom.

Satan also attacks through more subtle forms of persecution. In these, he doesn't physically attack Christians but causes them to be slandered and held in contempt by others, sometimes by entire cultures. In some areas, reaching people for Christ has become so difficult that most believers have given up. In such environments, only those who fight with all their hearts to rescue people can succeed.

Defense

Scripture teaches us how to respond to persecution. First Peter and 1 and 2 Timothy are key texts, as are Acts and Philippians. We should study and teach these texts when persecution threatens.

Some key strategies when persecution arises:

1. Not retaliating. By returning a blessing for a curse we "heap burning coals" on the heads of those who persecute us (Romans 12:19–21 NASB).

2. Living lives that cannot be accused. The apostles repeatedly stress the importance of living careful, inoffensive, and loving lives under persecution. "If people speak against you, they will be ashamed when they see what a good life you live because you belong to Christ" (1 Peter 3:16). Christians should not carry a chip on their shoulders but rather be humble and submissive to the government (2:13–25).

3. At the same time, we can defend ourselves, mainly by arguing our case. "If someone asks about your Christian hope, always be ready to explain it. But do this in a gentle and respectful way" (3:15–16). God does not require pure passivity under persecution. Our tone and demeanor need to be gentle and respectful, but we can plead our case persuasively.

INFILTRATION

As mentioned earlier, Satan can take control of people in the church, and he can also send in people who work for him. "Even Satan disguises himself as an angel of light. So it is no wonder that his servants also disguise themselves as servants of righteousness" (2 Corinthians 11:14–15). As this passage implies, Satan benefits most when infiltrators attain to leadership. Once we so entrust a servant of Satan, all bets are off. He has repeatedly demonstrated the ability to take over whole congregations, leading them away from the truth and from their mission. Other infiltrators may start divisions or create so much distraction that they divert believers from their mission.

Defense

This tactic is very difficult to defend against, because we usually can't tell infiltrators from authentic servants until they begin their work. Even then, leaders will naturally be reluctant to identify anyone in their church as a satanic infiltrator. We can tell people work for the other side if they begin to foist obvious false teaching onto the church and won't relent. Successful leaders of divisions also are easy to see, but only after they have done far too much work.

Since God has given us no means for detecting infiltrators in advance, we apparently have to withstand them until it becomes apparent they work for the other side. Then we can move in to refute, confront, and possibly remove them from the church. God must feel we can handle this since he has not provided us with insight about how to recognize an infiltrator, unless the spiritual gift of discernment of spirits would be helpful here (1 Corinthians 12:10). However, allowing such people into leadership is far worse than their mere presence in the church. We should follow the biblical guidelines for discerning qualified leaders, including careful study of their character and a significant time of testing wherein they demonstrate for all to see that they are self-sacrificial servants (1 Timothy 3:1–13; Titus 1:5–9). If our examination process fails, we must have the courage to remove without delay leaders who come out as wolves in sheep's clothing, no matter how popular they are.

CONCLUSION

Considering how powerful and effective Satan can be at derailing and even destroying local churches, leaders need to be constantly on guard. The alert, roving eyes of well-trained leaders as they pray over their groups is the best defense we have. That's why Peter brings up alertness and *sobriety* (a term meaning level headedness or sound judgment) in connection with leaders protecting their people from Satan (1 Peter 5:8).

Every time I see some powerful movement of the Spirit in our church I have to wonder, "What's going to be Satan's rejoinder to this?" Will he let major outbreaks of evangelism and discipleship go unchallenged for long? Not likely. We have effective countermeasures for each type of attack he may launch, but our biggest problems are our own apathy and blindness. We recognize Satan's hand too late to try opposing him. How many times do Christian leaders square off against Satan with prayer, the Word of God, and the Holy Spirit and meet defeat anyway? Not often. Usually leaders are scrambling to do damage control well after the fact.

Section 2

SATAN *and* YOU

CHAPTER 10

YOUR PERSONAL BATTLE WITH SATAN

If you are a believer, you have entered into a lifelong battle with the anointed cherub. A popular saying goes, "If you haven't run head-on into Satan, it's probably because you're both going the same direction." The closer you grow to God and the more effective you become in serving him, the more frequently you will meet Satan. Success in your Christian life depends in large part on your ability to win these battles. To overthrow his schemes, you have to learn to recognize Satan's works and his voice. You will need to understand his plans for you, and you will need to learn how to draw on God's power.

SATAN'S LIMITATIONS

Satan's power is great, but he also has limitations. Some are inherent in his own nature because he is a created being and therefore finite. He also has powers God doesn't allow him to use. We get glimpses of the afore-mentioned rules governing spiritual war but never a full picture. Christians should learn as much as possible about Satan's limitations; doing so keeps us from overestimating his powers and suffering intimidation as a result.

Power

We aren't sure how much power Satan actually has, but it must be great:

You used to live in sin, just like the rest of the world, obeying the devil—the commander of the powers in the unseen world. He is the spirit at work in the hearts of those who refuse to obey God. (Ephesians 2:2)

Even so, we can be sure much of his power never comes into play. We know, for instance, that Satan can kill people, because he killed Job's children. But God also forbade him to kill Job, so this power doesn't go unchecked. If Satan could kill people anytime he wanted, why wouldn't he immediately kill someone like the apostle Paul? To the contrary, Paul indicated he was invulnerable to death until he finished his course (Philippians 1:23–25; 2 Timothy 4:6–8).

We know Satan can make people sick. He gave Job boils and held a woman in a disabled state for eighteen years (Luke 13:11). Yet the Bible does not attribute most disease to Satan, contrary to the teaching of other ancient religions, most of which explain virtually all disease as caused by demons. The biblical worldview is compatible with modern science, because when living in a fallen world we can expect things like disease and disaster apart from the action of spirits.

Another example of limits placed on Satan is God's promise that he "will keep the temptation from becoming so strong that you can't stand up against it" (1 Corinthians 10:13). God protects believers from the full force of temptation Satan could bring. We can safely conclude that he does not have a free hand to exercise his power on earth but is strictly limited in what he can do, especially to believers.

In all likelihood, people regularly overestimate the danger that comes from Satan's power. Animistic and tribal peoples are terrified of evil spirits, convinced that demons often kill people or make them sick. Yet when we study the sick and the dead, we find they were not killed by Satan but by malaria, AIDS, encephalitis, or other natural causes. Strangely, at about the same time we introduce Western medicine to a village, Satan stops killing so many people.

This is not to say Satan is never involved. He convinces people that he can and does kill, and then he persuades them to turn to occult religion for protection. While Satan may not have made these people sick or killed them, he has deceived them. We will see later that most powers claimed by occultists are phony or exaggerated. Satan uses these claims to deceive people, not to curse them.

Reading Our Minds

Interestingly, we have no evidence that Satan can directly read our minds. In fact, the Bible implies that he cannot. Jesus said he had to finish speaking about confidential matters soon because Satan was coming (John 14:30). This would have been pointless if Satan could have read his mind or those of his disciples. The secrecy we saw earlier about Jesus' intentions at the cross would have been impossible if Satan could have read his mind. So one of Satan's limitations is his apparent inability to know exactly what you are thinking or planning. But this isn't as limiting as we might think. As one who has studied human nature for millennia and has seen all your history, he can predict with a high level of accuracy what you are thinking and how you feel. Even though he can't read our minds, it seems wise to assume that Satan probably knows what you've been thinking or planning most of the time.

Controlling Our Minds

We have no evidence that Satan can *take* control of our minds in a direct way. This is particularly true of Christians who have the indwelling Spirit of God. *If he does gain control of our thinking, it's because we have given him control.* The control he exerts is not forceful in the sense that he compels us to think in a certain way. Instead, he persuades. When we end up thinking Satan's thoughts, it's because we have believed so many of his lies that we lose track of reality. The slippery slope of his persuasion leaves our minds tumbling downward into ever darkening understanding. Even in cases of demon possession, people usually (or maybe always) have given themselves up to it.

Predicting the Future

Unlike God, Satan cannot see the future. He can make predictions based only on two things: (1) high probability short-term predictions based on his knowledge of cause and effect, and (2) short-term predictions that he fulfills himself, possibly by having one or more humans under his control to do the thing he predicts. These are sufficient to explain the occasional, irregular, accurate predictions made by occultists.

Such predictions are different from God's ability to predict even long-term future events that go beyond the current cause-and-effect sequence. In Isaiah, God makes it clear that he alone can foretell long-term events with specificity and accuracy:

I am the Lord; that is my name! I will not give my glory to anyone else, nor share my praise with carved idols. Everything I prophesied has come true, and now I will prophesy again. I will tell you the future before it happens. (42:8–9)

He challenges the idols Israel was worshiping:

Let them tell us what the future holds, so we can know what's going to happen. Yes, tell us what will occur in the days ahead. Then we will know you are gods. (41:22–23)

Only omniscience would allow someone to make the kind of predictions God does. Satan can only guess, and God often makes sure his guesses fail:

I am the Lord, who made all things. I alone stretched out the heavens. . . . I expose the false prophets as liars and make fools of fortune-tellers. I cause the wise to give bad advice, thus proving them to be fools. But I carry out the predictions of my prophets! (44:24–26)

Still, with his limited ability to predict the future, Satan tries to convince people that he does know the future and that they can know it through accessing his power. People become involved with fortune-tellers, psychics, and phony premonitions that lead them to wrong conclusions. They even come to believe that people are prophets of God when they are actually false prophets.

SATAN'S CAPABILITIES

While Satan is not free to exercise supernatural power as he wishes, and while he inherently lacks certain capabilities, he still has plenty of tools with which to accomplish his goals.

Intellect

We have less to fear from Satan's power than from his intellect, for the balance of power ultimately is on our side: "The Spirit who lives in you is greater than the spirit who lives in the world" (1 John 4:4). We should remember that Satan also knows this verse and believes it, so we can expect him to avoid direct tests of power with growing Christians. That doesn't mean he won't attack, but he will choose ground for the fight where he will have an advantage.

In Satan we face an opponent far smarter than we are. Even the most brilliant Christian pales when compared with this being and his many centuries of education. We have seen that countless ages ago, before his fall, God already described him as "perfect in wisdom." Think of how easily adults can fool a child. Without much effort you could make a child believe things that are obviously false. Their underdeveloped minds make them vulnerable to manipulation, and that's why we try to protect them from crafty adult liars.

Christians who make the mistake of arguing with Satan on his own ground find their minds tied up like a pretzel. Have you ever debated someone far smarter than you are? You feel you're in the right but sense yourself losing the argument anyway. Skilled debaters are trained to argue either side of an issue and win regardless. Getting into it with someone like this is usually a bad idea. How much worse it would be if this brilliant debater had intimate knowledge of your own inner prejudices, life experiences, emotional makeup, and thought tendencies!

Satan's goal is to cause Christians to believe that which is false. Think about these typical examples of things he wants believers to buy in to. What kind of person would he speak these things to, and what would he be trying to accomplish in each case?

1. God is continually looking down at you in disappointment or even disgust. He is incredulous that you could be so unfaithful, selfish, and sinful. It's a small wonder he hasn't turned his back on you. He's probably lining you up for a crushing punishment of some kind.

2. Christians are dangerous and cannot be trusted. Opening up to them would be extremely foolish. They're just waiting for a chance to judge you ferociously. You have to tell them what they want to hear and never let them know how badly you're messing up.

3. The Bible may have some good points, but obviously you can't believe it completely. Internal contradictions, questionable miracle stories, and faulty historical and scientific claims show this book to be fallible like any other book written by humans. In fact, you can't really know which parts to take literally.

4. Your efforts to serve God by sharing your faith are doomed to failure. First, nobody wants to hear this, and they will feel offended when you bring it up. Besides, your incompetence makes it even less likely that anyone would listen; the person will probably come up with advanced questions you can't answer, and not only will you look stupid, but you'll also make Jesus look stupid. You'd be better off waiting until you're more prepared.

5. When you feel depressed and far from God, the only solution is to get alone by yourself for a good while. You don't need to go hang out with Christians as much as you need to relax and maybe surf the Net.

6. You don't have to go crazy with this area of sin. Just a sample, just a reminder, just a taste, could hardly do any harm. You're not

going to give yourself over; you're just going to get close enough to remember what it's like.

7. In your fleshly state of mind, it would be pointless to go to a fellowship meeting or other place where you'll need to give out spiritually. If you go, you're just going to be bringing others down. You'd better get your head together before going back.

8. It looks like this moral problem you have is never going to change. You might as well decide how you're going to manage your existence as a lifelong screw-up in this area. God has already shown he isn't going to help, so give it up.

9. Prayer isn't working. It's probably because of your lack of faith, or maybe God refuses to answer because you're so irregular in prayer. Maybe he just doesn't care. Whatever the case, it feels more and more ridiculous to go on pretending you believe in this.

10. There was that time when God was blessing your life, but that was a long time ago. Something has gone terribly wrong; you can't feel his presence like you could then. He doesn't bless you like he did then. It could well be that you've been dealt out of the game. God has moved on to others who are more deserving.

11. If you keep listening to this talk about surrendering all for God, you're going to miss incredible opportunities that may never come again. Your career is going to suffer irreversibly. You're going to miss the love of your life. You're going to become a fanatic and a weirdo. You're on the verge of robbing yourself of real happiness. You've got to take a more moderate position in spiritual matters. We're not talking about denying God here, just more sense of balance in life.

12. So what if you hate that sister in Christ? She's got it coming, and no sane person could possibly react any other way. Besides, you're not saying you would *never* forgive her. You can think about it when she comes to grovel and finally acknowledge what she's done.

13. If you keep serving so regularly, you're going to be all used up! Start looking out for yourself—you don't want to burn out.

14. It's one thing to talk about trusting God, but you're facing real dangers here. Don't be stupid! Of course God wants you to take measures to secure your future. You're not in some fantasy world—this is real life! You've got to start taking life into your own hands.

15. Your plan to go and admonish your friend about an area of sin is unwise. First, who do you think you are? Is your life so pure that you should go around trying to set others straight? Isn't that a little arrogant? Who's casting the first stone here? Besides, if you think about it, you'll see abundant evidence that he'll never listen anyway—he'll probably retaliate, maybe even dangerously. Look, people have to move at their own pace, and if God wanted him to see this he would make it clear himself. If someone should go and say something, aren't there plenty of others who would be way more capable than you? Maybe you should just mind your own business.

16. If only you had done what you really wanted to do in that situation a year ago, you'd probably be having the time of your life right now. You're listening to all this legalism and you're not being true to yourself. If you keep this up, you're going to ruin your life.

17. God probably has decided already what's going to happen in this ministry situation, so it doesn't matter what you do. Who do you think you are, anyway, arrogantly thinking you could make a difference?

18. This kind of person probably won't respond to words. You should just witness with your life, and meanwhile you can pray. Only God can bring someone to faith. If you go shooting your mouth off, it almost certainly will make matters worse.

19. It sure is annoying to see how these Christians just do what everybody expects. There's terrific groupthink going on here. I can't see someone as authentic as you conforming that way to the expectations of others.

20. If you keep pushing your boyfriend away during your make-

outs, he's going to think you don't really like him. He'd have no problem finding a girl who would never push him away.

When Satan lies, his arguments are very persuasive. He bases each one on your actual life experience and states it in terms you will find most appealing. All of them usually contain some truth or at least possible truth. He can manipulate certain circumstances or people in your life in ways that seem to confirm his arguments. But the net effect of each lie is to move you away from God, away from the people of God, away from total commitment to God, and away from serving God. *Each satanic lie argues that it is both reasonable and balanced to live your life for yourself.*

Christians who begin believing even one of Satan's lies find themselves on a slippery slope. For each of the examples above, he has ready follow-up suggestions that will be hard to resist once we concede the original point, even if we only partially agree. The mental battle with him is rarely a single encounter but rather a day-in, day-out, wearying dialogue that tends to break us down. He piles evidence onto evidence as he builds his case. No sooner do you begin to wonder if Christians can be trusted than you find out one of them has been talking behind your back. No sooner do you begin to worry that you're not putting enough energy and time into your financial standing than your car breaks down and a big unexpected bill hits. You begin wondering if witnessing might be too risky because people could be offended, only to hear a neighbor angrily describing how offended he was by a recent encounter with a Christian.

Many believers don't see how dangerous these mental arguments are. We tend to think that even if we mess up and draw the wrong conclusion here or there, we'll get through, and any damage will be minor and temporary. But this radically underestimates Satan, who doesn't stop after he wins one small argument. He will relentlessly pursue any opening and seek to expand it into a major breach; complete destruction is his goal. If we find it difficult to avoid deception before losing an argument with Satan, it becomes much more difficult once we believe any one of his cases, partially or fully.

Look around and ask yourself, "Why do I see so many Christians with mediocre, unfruitful lives? How could those who looked so awesome walk away from God? Why are so many churches around here dead, barren, and weird? Where is the Christian community that looks like the one presented in the New Testament?" These problems are not accidents. They don't signal that God is unreal or that his promises are false. Rather, all these and many other factors around us point to the same thing: the deadly effectiveness of Satan's powers of persuasion.

Instead of arguing with Satan, Christians must learn to declare the Word of God to him, like Jesus did. To match up with someone this smart, we need the help of someone even smarter, and God is infinitely smarter than Satan. We already saw how outclassed Satan was when he matched his intellect up against God's wisdom. Shallow knowledge of Scripture is one reason young Christians are particularly vulnerable. Without a deep knowledge of God's Word we are truly "sheep among wolves" (Matthew 10:16). Later we'll examine how to use his Word in these battles.

Speaking to Our Minds

We know Satan can speak directly to our minds. Jesus talked about his snatching the gospel from people's hearts before they can understand it, which implies that he can work on the inside of people. In 1 Chronicles 21:1, he put into David's mind the idea of numbering the people of Israel. He is called the tempter, and few of us have heard audible voices tempting us; if Satan is tempting and accusing Christians, he must be doing it through mental communication. Therefore, thoughts coming into our heads could be from Satan.

This is bad news for subjective Christians who assume that every thought springing into their heads is the voice of God. For a liar and a fake like Satan, who can disguise himself as an angel of light (2 Corinthians 11:14), we have no reason to doubt that he would present himself to our minds as God's voice. Discerning one voice from the other is an important ability we must develop if we plan to successfully avoid deception.

Too many Christians are too lazy to learn God's Word, instead opting for the easier—but treacherous—view that God is talking to them when they hear thoughts in their minds. Yes, God does speak to us this way, but so can Satan. When I once confronted a Christian woman and expressed my dismay that she had abandoned her husband and kids for another man, she reassured me that God had told her he didn't want her to be unhappy. Most Christians involved in ministry have heard more of these kinds of stories than we care to think about. Ignorant Christians with no external basis for judging inner thoughts are at constant risk for deception.

How do you recognize the voice of Satan? Not by how it makes you feel. You recognize Satan's voice by the things he says—things God would never say. Only Christians who know God's Word can accurately judge this.

Casting Moods

We see slender biblical evidence that Satan may be able to cast negative moods onto people temporarily. We read about when King Saul turned away from God: "Now the Spirit of the Lord had left Saul, and the Lord sent a tormenting spirit that filled him with depression and fear" (1 Samuel 16:14). The language is indefinite, since the spirit came from God. We can't even be sure this was a demon; it may be referring to Saul's own state of mind in response to conviction from God. Certainly what Saul experienced is not normative for Christians. Most interpreters think this was a demon, and experience suggests as well that demons can make us feel terrible for short periods. They may not directly cast emotional states onto people but rather get people to think in ways that are depressing or cause anxiety.

Agents

One of Satan's most pernicious powers stems from the fact that he controls some humans, at least part of the time. Such people need not be possessed by a demon; they may just be particularly susceptible to satanic suggestion. Through these agents he can directly impact Christians.

Paul reminds us that "we are not fighting against flesh-and-blood enemies, but against . . . evil spirits in the heavenly places" (Ephesians 6:12). He knew that when human attackers came against him, they were just pawns being used by the real Enemy. Jesus said to the church at Smyrna, "The devil will throw some of you into prison to test you"

(Revelation 2:10). No doubt humans would actually do the throwing, but Jesus attributes the action to Satan's control over them.

How many of us involved in evangelism have seen a new Christian who hasn't been able to get a date for a year suddenly find that the hottest girl in school wants him soon after—or even just before—he meets Christ? Another convert no sooner meets Christ than her company wants to promote her and move her to another city. Satan often foments persecution because he controls those doing the persecuting.

Watching

Satan is not omnipresent. Even through his many demonic followers he cannot be in every place at once. We may be able to operate at times without his influence, although if we become effective for God, we can anticipate that he will assign more demons to interfere with our ministry. Therefore, even though he is not omnipresent and does not know all things, we should assume Satan usually knows what we have done, what we are doing, and what we plan to do. While this is not always true, it's a safe assumption.

The Physical World

Satan can sometimes affect physical events. With Job, we see his ability to create a deadly whirlwind and to inflict sickness. In all likelihood he can do things like make machines break down or move objects. He can perform counterfeit miracles (2 Thessalonians 2:9). These capabilities could come into play when you need equipment to work correctly for a meeting; your car might break down on the way to meet a person to whom you're witnessing; an apparent miracle could lead people to believe God is at work when it's actually Satan.

The Kosmos

In addition to these tactics and capabilities, Satan has one great pitch to throw. His world-system is so powerful that it deserves its own chapter.

CHAPTER 11

SATAN'S TRUMP CARD

Satan has a trump card in the world-system that both keeps people away from God and mangles Christians' spiritual lives. The world-system is Satan's masterpiece, and although the doctrine of the *kosmos* is well taught in the New Testament, most Christians seem to have only a modest understanding of what it is or what to do about it.

WHAT IS THE *KOSMOS*?

The word *kosmos* is usually translated "world" in English Bibles, but it suggests more than our word *world* implies. The Greeks used *kosmos* to refer to a "unifying harmony," connecting all things. The term means a "harmonious order," or a "system," and this aspect is absent from *world*. To retain more of its original meaning, the term should often be translated *world-system*.

We get the words *cosmetics* and *cosmopolitan* from *kosmos*, and both contain the implications of a beautiful ordered system. Another Greek expression used far less often but usually referring to the same thing is *aeon houtos*, which means literally "this present age" and is usually translated *the world*, just like *kosmos*. *Aeon houtos* contemplates the world-system from the aspect of time, while *kosmos* refers to its essence.

The following chart summarizes some of the main New Testament teachings about the *kosmos*.

What Is the Kosmos (World-System)?

The Bible sometimes uses *kosmos* to refer to the physical globe of the earth or to the universe in general (Matthew 4:8). These uses are not in view here. Satan does not own the world itself; Psalm 24:1 makes it clear that the earth is the Lord's.

At other times, *kosmos* can refer to the whole human race as alienated from God (e.g., John 3:16, "For God so loved the world . . .").

We begin to sense the idea of a system of values when Scripture refers to the underlying abstract qualities that animate the world:

1 Corinthians 2:12	The spirit of the world.
1 Corinthians 3:19	The wisdom of this world.
1 Corinthians 7:31	The way of the world.
Titus 2:12	The lusts of the world.
2 Peter 1:4	The corruption that is in the world.
2 Peter 2:20	The defilement of the world.
1 John 2:15	The things that are in the world.

The New Testament often refers to the world-system's hostility toward God and Christ.

1 Corinthians 1:21	The world knew not God.
John 7:7	The world's works are evil.
John 14:17	The world cannot receive the Spirit.
John 15:18	The world hated Christ.

Jesus made illuminating comments about his own relationship to the world-system.

John 18:36	"My kingdom is not of this world."
John 16:33	"I have overcome the world."
John 12:31	"Now judgment is upon this world."

Christians should recognize what the world-system is and should take a stand against it.

James 4:4	Friendship with the world is enmity with God.
1 John 2:15	If anyone loves the world, the love of the Father is not in him.
John 17:14	The world hates followers of Jesus.
1 John 5:4	Our faith overcomes the world.
The hostility between God, Christians, and the *kosmos* results because this entire system is owned and run by Satan.	
John 12:31	"The time for judging this world has come, when Satan, the ruler of this world, will be cast out."
John 14:30	"The ruler of this world approaches."
John 16:11	"Judgment will come because the ruler of this world has already been judged."
1 John 5:19	"We know that we are children of God and that the world [*kosmos*] around us is under the control of the evil one."
2 Corinthians 4:4	Satan, who is the god of this world [*aeon houtos*], has blinded the minds of those who don't believe.
Ephesians 6:12	In Greek, the "world rulers" are *kosmokrators*.

Perhaps the definitive passage on the *kosmos* is 1 John 2:15–17:

> Do not love the world nor the things in the world. If anyone loves the world, the love of the Father is not in him. For all that is in the world, the lust of the flesh and the lust of the eyes and the boastful pride of life, is not from the Father, but is from the world. The world is passing away, and also its lusts; but the one who does the will of God lives forever. (NASB)

Accordingly, the *kosmos* is primarily a system of values. The lust of the flesh refers to living for ungodly pleasure. The lust of the eyes refers to owning beautiful things or gaining control over beautiful people. The boastful pride of life refers to the way humans try to establish identity and importance by competing with each other for attention, power, and admiration. Satan has been able to orchestrate a situation in which people are motivated primarily by these goals. This is his substitute for a life lived for God. Satan doesn't remove God; he simply substitutes a new values-system in place of the one God advances, and he backs up the rewards of temporary pleasure with a system of punishment for anyone who resists. Friends, co-workers, and family members will be quick to point out how foolish anyone is who passes up opportunities to advance in the world-system.

THE CHURCH AND THE KOSMOS TODAY

Many Christians think of "worldly" things as gross sins like wanton sex, for example. They are likely to imagine the world's pathetic victims lying in a gutter with a paper sack and saliva running down their unshaven chins. And yes, this *is* worldly.

Many of the same Christians, however, would never recognize the world-system when looking at the Harvard University green or the Sears Tower. A glossy magazine advertisement showing a family luxuriating in a hot tub in Tahiti or a shiny new SUV would not ring the *kosmos* bell in their minds. Nor would they think of the world-system while watching a sports team celebrating a world championship. The problem is, these Christians have taken a slice out of the pie and identified *that* as the world while accepting the rest of the pie as legitimate. Imagine cutting a slice of pie and as you lift it out of the pan noticing it's full of worms. Would you cast that piece aside but unhesitatingly gobble down the rest of the pie?

In particular, the Western church has consistently failed to see greed and the quest for personal prestige as worldly—at least as long as they aren't taken "too far." Notice how many Christian parents are worried and angry about how the violence and sex in today's TV shows might affect their children. Isn't it interesting, though, that many of those same parents have never spent a moment worrying about the influence that advertising and programs exhibiting flagrant greed and glorifying wealth and fame might have on their kids?

The result of exempting some aspects of the *kosmos* from our definition is an uneasy accommodation or compromise with the world-system. Some values are embraced while others are rejected, but the result is not 50 percent or even 30 percent spirituality—it is a *completely broken* spirituality. Jesus warned, "No one can serve two masters" (Matthew 6:24). Those who fall into this trap lose the love of the Father (1 John 2:15), for friendship with the world is enmity with God (James 4:4). How could it be otherwise when we are compromising with the kingdom of Satan? He knows that to the same extent he can get Christians to compromise with the world, they will become ineffective for God.

Many observers, me included, think the number-one illness afflicting the church in the West is its unspoken peace treaty with the *kosmos*. Of course, the church continues to deplore "worldliness" and "worldly people." But here we see the problem. Is it even correct to speak of such a thing as "worldly people"? That designation suggests that some people, even non-Christians, are *not* worldly. The Bible presents the whole human race, apart from Christ, as captive to this system. Only by surgically removing key aspects of the world from our definition do we conclude that some people are more "worldly" than others. Why can't we see that clean-living, success-oriented people are just as caught in the world's vise as the helpless addict?

THE ACCOMMODATED CHRISTIAN

When Christians compromise with the *kosmos*, they may continue to attend church and even pray and read their Bibles. The problem is that the things of God occupy a section of their lives, while the main thrust of their affections is devoted to the world-system. Jesus' warning that "no one can serve two masters" is illustrated on every side by Christians in the West today.[1] Ironically, however, those caught up in this mentality usually have no idea that their minds have been captured by Satan's system.

Jesus said this would happen:

Your eye is a lamp that provides light for your body. When your eye is good, your whole body is filled with light. But when your eye is bad, your whole body is filled with darkness. And if the light you think you have is actually darkness, how deep that darkness is! (Matthew 6:22–23)

Given in the context of living for money, these words say that *love of the world-system actually affects our perception of reality until we can no longer tell we're in the wrong.* Our eyes, the lamp of our bodies, no longer work. Christians compromised in this way cannot understand the problem. They go to church; they follow God and stay out of trouble; they even give their tithe. So what's the issue?

As stated earlier, it's that their primary affection and energy are devoted to the *kosmos.* The amount of time, thought, effort, and emotion devoted to the goals of the world can outdistance what's devoted to God many times over. But accommodated Christians may never stop to consider how pitiful is their spiritual intensity compared with what they show toward their careers or their homes. Their words broadcast the importance of God, but their lives say that other things are actually more important.

Sometimes the truth about our values comes out in strange ways. How often those of us doing campus ministry have seen Christian parents more worried about Junior's GPA than whether he has a heart for God! They drive their kids toward worldly accomplishments and accolades—athletics, academics, etc.[2]—and anything suggesting the kids are falling behind in the race throws them into a frenzy of anxiety. Yet as their kids' hearts grow cold toward God and they lose all interest in serving him, there is no corresponding concern. When their kids get excited about following the Lord and living all-out for him, some Christian parents even worry that they're getting carried away or becoming fanatical. At times like these, value systems become painfully evident.

Christians compromised with the world-system can't find time for God. They're too busy to get equipped for ministry, too stressed to devote themselves to leading others, too self-interested to invest in younger Christians through personal discipleship. They feel that showing up at a weekly service should be enough—anything more is extraordinary devotion. If time demands from their careers conflict with times needed for God or his people, they announce that they "can't be there" because of a work engagement. But the truth is that servants of the world-system have just as many hours in their week as anyone else. It's not that they don't have the time; they've just decided to allocate their time to the world-system, and little is left over.

Christians at peace with the world have agreed with the world-system on key values. They may see nothing wrong with laying up treasure on earth, and they become angry or cold when someone suggests otherwise. But Jesus said, "*Don't* store up treasures here on earth." What does this mean? We all have to make a living, and such is the will of God (2 Thessalonians 3:12). However, people can interpret "making a living" in a wide variety of ways, and Satan is smart enough to win Christians over to a definition that perfectly matches their secular neighbors' definition. We often find little or no difference between Christians and non-Christians on this point. They have the same expensive possessions, enjoy the same affluent lifestyle, love receiving worldly prestige and honor, and seem to see nothing wrong with this picture.

WHAT IS WRONG WITH THE KOSMOS?

Jesus isn't trying to cramp our style when he calls on Christians to turn away from materialism and worldly prestige. He gives a key reason for his admonition against laying up treasure: "Wherever your treasure is, there the desires of your heart will also be" (Matthew 6:21). This is why we dare not dabble with investment in the world-system any more than we would risk taking "just a little puff" from a crack pipe: Satan has set up this system to lure people in. Our own affluence, success, and glorification *will* affect our hearts, and we *will* want more. Those who think this isn't dangerous are probably already so compromised that spiritually they no longer know up from down.

Christians who have inwardly made peace with the values of the world-system often show amazing competence at work, but as Christians they remain relatively incompetent. People cannot lead others into completely following Christ when they aren't radical followers themselves. God will not honor ministries secretly in love with Satan's world-system. Their fruitfulness in accomplishing the mission becomes weak or nonexistent. Most have given up trying; Satan has won.

Even in poor countries people feverishly serve the world-system. In this global marketplace, religion and tribalism are steadily losing place to greed as life's prime motivation. Those planting churches around the world face the challenge of members working sixty to eighty hours a week in an effort to get their children into private colleges or to keep upgrading their cell phones. Serving the world-system is a state of mind that can afflict the poor as well as the rich.

HOW THE WORLD-SYSTEM WORKS

Because of the human consensus that materialism, sensuality, and egotism are legitimate and worth living for, people find it very difficult to avoid buying into these values for themselves. Advertising and media constantly reinforce the message. Anyone who refuses to conform to the *kosmos* will be treated with contempt; only a fool would fail to see the worth of these values. Those who obediently devote themselves to their pursuit, on the other hand, have the opportunity to be welcomed and admired.

People get so wrapped up in this *kosmos* pursuit that they become obsessed. This happens because the pleasure they receive from attaining the world's goals doesn't really satisfy; in fact, it only produces more desire. No matter how much money people make, no matter how famous they become, a gnawing emptiness remains, causing them to strive and grasp even harder. Envy and bitterness become common.

THE BIBLE'S CRITIQUE OF THE KOSMOS

People overlook one important negative in all the world's goals, and John explains it simply: "The world is passing away, and also its lusts" (1 John 2:17 NASB). This is a fatal critique of the *kosmos*. What if your job paid you with checks that melt into goop after you leave the office? Nobody would work for that company. What good is money if we can't keep it and use it in an ongoing way?

All the rewards of the *kosmos* are exactly like that melting money. We only get to have them for a while, and then we're left with nothing. On the other hand, "the one who does the will of God lives forever" (2:17b). Here is real treasure! We may not get the world's immediate gratification, and we may have to pass up some opportunities for pleasure or pride, but the things God gives us never go away.

When you think about it, comparing the rewards of the *kosmos* and those of following God is not a value of, let's say, 1 compared to 10. The actual difference is 0 compared to infinity. At least, that's what these rewards will be worth just a short time from now *if we believe the Word of God.* This should make the choice easy.

No wonder Satan tries to keep us from anticipating the ultimate value of following the way of the *kosmos* versus the way of God! He exerts phenomenal effort to keep people looking only at the near future, not at the more distant future.

THE PRICE OF COMPROMISE

Christians can only peacefully coexist with the *kosmos* if they agree to live for the values of the world. That's why John says, "If anyone loves the *kosmos,* the love of the Father is not in him" (1 John 2:15 NASB). Does he mean that only those who don't love God would fall in love with the *kosmos* in the first place? Or does he mean that falling in love with the *kosmos* kills your love of the Father? Is being without the Father's love the *cause* or the *result* of loving the world? It's hard to say, and probably both are true. But losing our love for God is definitely one of the results of loving the world.

Remember, Jesus says, "Where your treasure is, there your heart will be also" (Matthew 6:21 NASB), and he also says those who try to serve God and the *kosmos* will hate the one and love the other (v. 24). If we begin to pursue the goals of the world-system, it will put a real chill on our love for God. We will resent the constraints and "nuisances" he places on us. What used to seem fun will seem burdensome.

God calls loving the kosmos adultery (James 4:4) because it neutralizes our spirituality just as unfaithfulness would spoil your marriage. Christians who fall in love with the world can remember a time when the love of God filled their hearts with joy. But now it seems ho-hum. Though they may feel confused and guilty, they fail to connect the dots between their love of the *kosmos* and their loss of love for God.

Likewise, those who fully follow the Lord come to hate the world-system and what it does to its victims. The idea of playing to the world becomes repulsive on one level, at the same time it continues to beckon on a different level. Christians never fully escape the temptation of the *kosmos*, but their attitude toward the world's values changes dramatically as they give their lives and their priorities over to God.

KEEPING PEOPLE AWAY FROM GOD

For many non-Christians, the feverish pursuit of lust and pride is so intense that they resist anything that might interfere with it. Most people sense that getting involved with God could interfere massively with their affinity for the world. Satan is able to frighten them by threatening that coming to God is all about giving up the awesome things they have or could have in the *kosmos*. Of course, he never mentions that eventually they're going to lose everything they get from the *kosmos* anyway.

So the struggle between the *kosmos* and God's kingdom really is a struggle between the temporal (time-bound, temporary) and the eternal. It's also a struggle between the notion that happiness comes from what I can get for me and the fact that it comes from what I can give for God and others. For both these reasons, there is no middle ground between the kingdom of Satan and the kingdom of God. Any effort to pursue both will result in bondage to the world-system. We must renounce the *kosmos* and all its values if we want to pursue God.

GOD'S VERSION

As we studied earlier when considering fortress theology, God doesn't want us to leave the *kosmos* or try to avoid it. We are to live in its midst, partaking in its activities. We work for money. We enjoy sensual experiences ranging from good food to great sex to enjoyable music. We derive pleasure from a solid sense of identity and from knowing why we matter. In fact, we believe we enjoy all these things *more* than those who serve the world. So what's the difference?

Design

For one thing, Christians enjoy the things in the world because we partake of them according to God's design, which gratifies without destroying us. Satan didn't create things like enjoying our senses or enjoying accomplishment; God did, and he gave them to us for our delight. But he also gave us the design for each, and ignoring this design turns beautiful things into things that enslave.

God, for instance, created sex *before* the fall of humans, and we are to use it in the context of a relationship where "the man and wife become one" (Genesis 2:24). Sex is a way to give and receive love in such a relationship. But if we put self at the center, sex becomes a hunting ground where we hope to take as many pleasurable experiences as possible, usually at the expense of others. This doesn't result in more sexual gratification but in more sexual hunger. As we rip others off, consuming sex but refusing to be committed, we fail to experience the true joy of sex and instead feel emptiness that drives us to seek more sex and more far-out sex. Sex becomes a classic case study in diminishing returns.

For another example, consider accomplishment. Before the fall, God put Adam in the garden to cultivate it and keep it (v. 15). Adam was to enjoy his work and the things he accomplished. But when self is at the center, work becomes a competition for ego-enhancement and acquisitive greed. We can't stop thinking about what we might buy or comparing our success with others. But because this was not the design for creative accomplishment, it never satisfies. Again, the deficiency we feel makes us strive ever harder to derive pleasure from something never intended to bear that load.

God tells us how to have a sense of identity and importance: Our identity is that we are in Christ, and our importance derives from God's valuation of us. When we try to establish identity apart from him, the only basis for our value and importance is how we compare to others. The resulting competition turns into an ego trip, where insecure beings try to reassure themselves that they matter. This is what John calls the "boastful pride of life."

Eternal Perspective

We have already discussed how foolish it is to strive for rewards that quickly pass away, especially when we have the option right in front of us to "lay up treasure in heaven." Once we see and believe this, the temporary rewards of the *kosmos* lose much of their allure. Christians with a clear vision of their future with God simply cannot get very excited about minor temporalities. The psalmist says,

> Those who are wise must finally die,
> just like the foolish and senseless,
> leaving all their wealth behind. (49:10)

But vision for our future has to be continually nourished and rekindled. Our personal times with God and his Word can nurture vision and remind us how foolish it would be to turn aside to the things of the world. Unless we draw close to God regularly, our vision will dim, and the luster of the world will rise.

114

Others-Centeredness

Paul says one of the main reasons for having a paying career is "so that [we] will have something to share with one who has need" (Ephesians 4:28 NASB). Christians become excited about the good they can do for others with their money instead of using it to keep score or to fill their lives with unnecessary luxuries. A simple life without extravagance becomes more attractive. Artistic creativity, sex, food, and all other things also can become opportunities to give instead of opportunities to take.

Someone like me who enjoys the culinary arts can create good dishes to show hospitality or draw others to join in dinner parties where we discuss the things of God. An investor earning big bucks could become a power-giver, relieving suffering and advancing God's work worldwide. Those possessing physical beauty could use their attractiveness to convey the gospel to those who enjoy talking to attractive people (as opposed to using physical beauty as an exercise in self-glorification).

Insight

God wants to renovate our thinking completely:

> Don't copy the behavior and customs of this world [*aeon houtos*], but let God transform you into a new person by changing the way you think. Then you will learn to know God's will for you, which is good and pleasing and perfect. (Romans 12:2)

Growing Christians experience a mental transformation that utterly contradicts the world's outlook.

In thousands of ways, Christians can partake of the same activities as others but with completely different motives and outcomes. This doesn't always happen, however; we have to be aware that whenever we touch the world-system we are touching Satan's kingdom, and this places us in possible danger with each activity or enjoyment. Since Satan uses such things to capture people, only a foolish Christian would fail to realize the perils. Careful reflection before God and his Word will show us if we are sliding into the love of the world.

This is not an easy matter but a daily struggle that lasts a lifetime. Holding on to God's perspective on the *kosmos* requires constant reminding and honest inward examination. We have to refute lying thoughts, planted by Satan, with God's Word, point for point. We may have to struggle in prayer to believe what God says in contrast to the attractive but deceptive picture painted by Satan.

Rarely do we meet a Christian who remembers consciously deciding to live for the world's values; in fact, most worldly Christians don't even know how worldly they are. This transition from a God-centered to a self-centered life is gradual and deceptive. Most world-defeated Christians continue to maintain that they think eternal values are the most important, even though their lives cry out that the *kosmos* is what matters most to them. Jesus described the process of spiritual decay: "The worry of the world and the deceitfulness of wealth choke the word, and it becomes unfruitful" (Matthew 13:22 NASB). Insight and revelation granted by God can show us when worldliness is growing in our hearts.

Peter says, "Be of sober spirit, be on the alert. Your adversary, the devil, prowls around like a roaring lion, seeking someone to devour" (1 Peter 5:8 NASB). We need to realize that the *kosmos* is Satan's premier tool for devouring believers. Being alert means watching for deception in this area; being of sober spirit means being wise and understanding about how Satan pitches the *kosmos* to us. When believers keep a guard up, they become conscious of Satan's efforts to lure and deceive and can bring the power of God to bear upon a situation.

Many Christians are doomed to be captured by the world-system, in part because their churches encourage them to serve it rather than be critical of it. Churches all across the West are preaching versions of Christianity that amount to an endorsement and even sanctification of the world's way. Such groups don't view the things of the world as Satan's snare for people but as God's reward. Rather than selecting a church and teachers who will pat you on the back for loving money, glory, and sensuality, find other believers who will join you in being faithful to God's Word.

Replacement

Instead of helping to build the kingdom of Satan, Christians are called to take delight in building the kingdom of God. We mentioned eternal rewards as part of this; what are these? Paul mentions one of the best:

> After all, what gives us hope and joy, and what will be our proud reward and crown as we stand before our Lord Jesus when he returns? It is you! Yes, you are our pride and joy. (1 Thessalonians 2:19–20)

Paul is pondering how wonderful it will be to spend eternity in heaven with people he led to Christ. Those who occupy themselves with the gospel have current joy as well as eternal joy awaiting them.

Believers who discover the thrill of being used by God in others' lives are often able to resist the allure of the *kosmos*, while those who never develop a personal ministry cannot resist it.[3] Since humanity's creation, God intended that we accomplish something for him with our lives. If we don't, we will be lured to seek accomplishment in the world-system. This is why a version of Christianity that merely focuses on praising God and enjoying church meetings is inadequate. People need a sense of purpose, and goals toward which they can strive. Failure to develop and pursue spiritual goals produces apathy and spiritual depression that makes the world's playthings irresistible. On the other hand, when our eyes are fully opened to the reality and power of the world-system, we're in a good position to evade Satan's ultimate trap for our lives.

CHAPTER 12

COUNTERING SATAN'S MOVES

We are ready to study two key New Testament passages on how to conduct spiritual warfare from our side.

DESTROYING FORTRESSES

We saw Paul's description of spiritual war in 2 Corinthians 10:3–6: "destroying speculations and every lofty thing raised up against the knowledge of God, and . . . taking every thought captive to the obedience of Christ," which makes up the main field for spiritual battle.[1] The fortresses Satan builds are usually belief systems in the minds of his captives, and our weapons are divinely powerful to tear these fortresses down. Entire groups and subcultures typically share similar assumptions about the world, and such false beliefs, fostered by Satan, stand in the way of a true understanding of the gospel.

False belief can invade the church as well. In fact, Paul wrote this passage in the context of a group of false leaders in the church at Corinth. That's why he says he is ready to discipline these teachers after he wins over the rest of the church to the truth (v. 5). The important thing to see is that Satan deceives both Christians and non-Christians. But believers, and not just leaders, are empowered to counter Satan's lies with truth backed by the power of the Holy Spirit.

THE ARMOR OF GOD

What are the powerful weapons we can use to destroy these fortresses? Elsewhere in his letters Paul is more explicit, comparing our weapons to those of a Roman soldier of the time. Because Ephesians 6:10–18 is in one of the Prison Epistles, Paul was probably chained to a Roman soldier as he wrote it.

Let's look at several insights he offers into our own struggle with Satan.

In God's Power

Paul first admonishes us to "be strong in the Lord and in his mighty power" (v. 10). We are powerless against Satan in ourselves. How could we ever oppose such a being when we can't even see spirits? We have no idea how to oppose them, and we are completely helpless before them apart from God. The key is to draw on God's power when driving back satanic attacks and when launching our own attacks on his fortresses.

Knowing Our Enemy

Paul's next point is that "we are not fighting against flesh-and-blood enemies, but against evil rulers and authorities of the unseen world" (v. 12). It's all too easy to mistake our real opponents (evil spirits) for their human agents. Combative roommates, disagreeable spouses, tempting members of the opposite sex, or deceptive religious leaders can be persuaded and manipulated by Satan to do what they do. Unless we see the world-system for what it is, we will become hostile to *people* rather than the *leader* who has captured them. This would be a huge mistake—a mistake the church has made repeatedly throughout history and right up to the present day. Instead, we should cultivate compassion for people in the world and seek to release them from Satan's power.

Every Piece

Paul calls on us next to "put on every piece of God's armor" (v. 13). If we have some pieces in place, that's good. But our enemy is plenty smart enough to see which pieces are missing and strike there.

The Belt

First, "Stand your ground, putting on the belt of truth" (v. 14). The belt was important in an ancient set of armor. Sometimes called the girdle or the buckler, this piece was a wide leather strap with a sling under it, rather like a jock strap. Soldiers fastened the buckler firmly around their waists, and then used buckles on the belt to fasten the breastplate and the leather stranded skirt or thigh guards. The sword and scabbard also fastened to the buckler. In other words, the buckler holds the other pieces of armor in place.

In Rome, as Paul looked over at the fully armored soldier chained to him, he must have pondered how central the buckler was to all else and assigned it to stand for truth. It makes sense. If the enemy we face is Satan the liar, and the battlefield involves fortresses of falsehood, our stand against him must begin with and center on truth. We can also see why the rest of the armor attaches to the belt; we wouldn't even know about the rest of the pieces if God had not taught us about them in his revealed Word.

Christians are in a unique position in the world: We have a basis for knowing objective truth based on God's revelation. While other people have to guess what is true based on their own observations and interpretations, or trust their traditions to tell them, we know that "[God] has spoken to us through his Son" (Hebrews 1:1–3). We have here a supreme weapon that is truly "divinely powerful," as he says elsewhere.

However, the revealed truth of God has one "weakness": it has to be read and learned. Scripture doesn't teach itself to us—God expects us to step forward and take in the Word for ourselves. In oral cultures, people do this through public reading and recitation. They actually memorize large sections of the Bible. In literate cultures, people can read and learn for themselves, and this is a stopper for many Christians.

In chapter 21, we will examine in detail the story of when Jesus was confronted by Satan in the wilderness. In this battle he answered each satanic suggestion with the phrase "It is written" and quoted Hebrew Scripture. How easily he fired off statements from Scripture, each perfectly suited to the temptation! Jesus' knowledge of Scripture had amazed the rabbis in Jerusalem even when he was a boy. By now he was mighty in the Word. Paul also was a Bible scholar. What about us?

According to studies in America, the average evangelical's knowledge of Scripture today is negligible. As our popular churches continue to offer entertainment and light topical teaching geared to the lowest common denominator, the penalty is that Christians are not learning the Bible adequately. Most longstanding Christians today know some Bible stories and often a few pet proof-texts, but little more. Most don't even know basic Christian doctrine,[2] and few could declare the truth to Satan in the midst of spiritual battle. To know what God says about your situation or the concept with which you're dealing, you have to learn the Bible at a much deeper level than most Christians in the West have done.

The Body Armor

Next, Paul adds that we should put on "the body armor of God's righteousness" (Ephesians 6:14). The NLT has correctly suggested that the Greek text, which reads "the armor of righteousness," means God's righteousness. Some interpreters make a critical error here by suggesting that Paul means we should put on our own righteousness as protection against Satan.[3] But Paul would never say this; as he makes it clear in the previous letter, he aspires only to be "found in Him, not having a righteousness of my own derived from the Law, but that which is through faith in Christ, the righteousness which comes from God on the basis of faith" (Philippians 3:9 NASB). He is adamant that our only standing before God or men is grace, not works. Our righteousness is not our own but Christ's, imparted to us.

Under the faulty interpretation that we are to put on our own righteousness, Paul would be saying something like "Just be sure you're behaving so well that Satan can't accuse you." Ironically, that's just what Satan would love us to think! As long as we're trying to persuade ourselves that we are *relatively* righteous, we have placed ourselves directly on his ground—the ground of falsehood. In this case, we have to downplay our sins, which will often involve ignoring sins of omission like lack of love, failure to do what we should, and so on. We might rationalize some sins or minimize the seriousness of others, like inner attitudes, pride, unbelief, or lust. Soon we are behaving like Pharisees, pretending we are more righteous than we are.

Instead, repeatedly throughout the New Testament, God calls us to recognize that we have been united with Christ and have thus "become the righteousness of God in him" (2 Corinthians 5:21 NASB). Here Paul again calls on us to recognize the righteousness that comes from God on the basis of faith and to plead that no matter how much we have failed, we stand righteous before God.

Roman body armor was either a breastplate for officers or a chain mail shirt for most soldiers. This crucial piece guarded the vital organs in the chest and belly. Without it a battling soldier would be wide open to a deathblow. And this is never truer than in spiritual warfare.

Satan is the accuser. He tempts us into sin and then turns our failures back against us in burning accusation that we have failed God; that God is angry with us; that we are unworthy to serve him or speak for him. Satan strives with all his might to put every believer into a performance-based mindset where we try to see our behavior as righteous, usually compared to others, our own past, or what we *could* be doing. None of these is a true definition of righteousness; God is the only standard. When we try to define our own behavior as righteous, we are not agreeing with God. Jesus said no one is good but God (Mark 10:18). In our hearts we all know this is true.

By fomenting feelings of guilt, Satan tries to drive us away from God. Believers who base their standing with God on their own works feel so weighed down by shame that they have difficulty approaching him boldly. If they do approach him, they do so in a cowering, insecure way that does not reflect faith in what he has plainly told us. Intimacy with him breaks down. This is not the posture from which to wage spiritual warfare.

Conversely, we have to learn to put on our breastplate. We have to call out to God, saying, "Lord God, I come before you without a single plea of deserving or righteousness but solely on the basis of my position in Jesus." Likewise, when we try to speak for God or to minister, we say, "God, I'm asking you to empower what I do here, not because I think I'm righteous in any sense other than your imparted righteousness in Christ. I know I am completely unworthy to speak for you apart from that." We are to approach the throne of grace "with boldness" or "with confidence" (Hebrews 4:16).

When Christians take their seat with Christ, not based on their own good works, Satan loses his most potent weapon: accusation.

The Shoes

According to the NLT, Paul says next, "For shoes, put on the peace that comes from the Good News so that you will be fully prepared" (Ephesians 6:15). If this translation is correct, Paul is saying we should take our stand on the peace with God we received when we believed the good news, the gospel (Romans 5:1). This would make sense, even though it would be a bit redundant from the previous point. Certainly, we need to remember consciously that the gospel of grace is our only basis for peace with God and, hence, for inner peace with ourselves.

But the NASB translates Ephesians 6:15: "having shod your feet with the preparation of the gospel of peace." What is peaceful? The gospel? Or do we feel peace because of the gospel? Perhaps Paul is saying that knowing our mission and being ready to declare the gospel is our footing when we come into battle. If the NLT is saying that we feel peace *because* of the gospel, that would make sense as well. Both are true.

Shoes were important in ancient warfare. When fighting hand-to-hand, one of the worst things is to lose your footing. Once you stumble or slip, you become highly vulnerable to a jab from above. The Romans had a hob-nailed sandal with leather straps wound well up the calf for stability. They were excellent fighting shoes because they didn't slip or shift and gave good footing for pushing off in a lunge at the enemy.

Our footing has to do with the gospel. Once again, Paul is prescribing God's Word, which is the only place we learn the gospel. In spiritual warfare, we have to take our stand on what God has done for us (the gospel), not on what we have done for him. The gracious forgiveness we receive in Christ is the only basis on which we can stand against Satan. It is also what we offer the world, and in that sense the gospel is our footing in the face of Satan's fortresses. The gospel is what we have to hold up against the "things of the world," "the wisdom of the world," and "the spirit of the world."

The Shield

"In addition to all [or, *in* all], taking up the shield of faith with which you will be able to extinguish all the flaming arrows of the evil one" (Ephesians 6:16 NASB). I prefer to see the shield of faith as applying to all the pieces of armor, as the NASB margin reads. This makes sense, because even if we were to put on the shoes of the gospel, the belt of truth, and the breastplate of Christ's righteousness, none will do much good unless we believe they are real and effective. Faith is not something separate from the other things in this list. Rather, Paul is saying that real faith in what God says in his Word is essential. *Knowing* what God says means nothing if we don't *believe* it, and doubt creeps in for all of us at times. Here is the struggle. The believer has to come before God and ask for faith. We have to declare that we choose to believe what he says.

We find it hard to discern Christians with phony faith, but Satan knows exactly how real your faith is. When the sons of Sceva tried to cast out a demon using the borrowed faith of Paul, the demons fell on them and beat them severely, leaving them bruised and naked! (Acts 19:13–16). God expects us to struggle for our faith, and if we begin doubting, we need to take strong measures.

Never pretend you don't doubt. Be honest. But never flee from your doubts either. Face them and go after the answers and backing you need in order to believe. Do the study. Pray. Find mature Christians who can counsel and instruct you. Every time I've fallen into doubt, I've been able to study the thing I doubt, get help from others, pray, and eventually battle through to real faith. It helps when we live through spiritual experiences where God comes through repeatedly.

Remember that biblical faith is not mere mental assent; faith means active trust. It's all too easy to believe the truth about God in a mental sense but not entrust yourself to him. Many Christians who can articulate factual doctrine in great detail have lives that suggest they don't really entrust themselves to what they know. This trust has to do with deep interactions with God, where you commit yourself to live with confidence that his promises are true and that you can rely on them.

The Helmet

"Put on salvation as your helmet" (Ephesians 6:17). The helmet protects the head against potentially mortal blows. As believers, we have to cling to the knowledge that God is going to get the last word in our lives. Our security in Christ is the essential ground from which we can resist Satan's fearsome intimidation. In Romans 8:31, Paul asks the penetrating questions, "What shall we say about such wonderful things as these? If God is for us, who can ever be against us?" And in verse 33, "Who dares accuse us whom God has chosen for his own? No one—for God himself has given us right standing with himself." These are important points to meditate on in prayer and even to declare to Satan, as Jesus did. When you are feeling accused and insecure, say, "It is written . . ." and quote one or both of these verses. That's the best way to fight off satanic accusations.

As followers of Jesus, we are not just to hope we will inherit eternal life, but to *know* that we will. John says, "I have written this to you who believe in the name of the Son of God, so that you may know you have eternal life" (1 John 5:13). As we develop confidence that God's presence in our lives is real, we should also have increasing confidence that we will have eternal life. According to Paul, this is like a helmet guarding our heads. Our entire outlook shifts radically on all subjects when we believe this. Temptation becomes less attractive because we realize that acting in contradiction to who we are and who we will be forever with God just doesn't make sense. We realize that if we're going to be with God forever, we might as well start getting to know him and growing spiritually.

The Sword

Finally, Paul says we should "take the sword of the Spirit, which is the word of God" (Ephesians 6:17). Once again God's Word appears on the list. The shoes, the belt, and the sword all directly refer to the Word of God. Then there's the shield, which refers to faith in the Word: Clearly God's Word permeates the whole list.

This centrality of the Word makes more and more sense when we consider how important are the words of God in spiritual conflicts like the one in the garden of Eden and those we will study later in Daniel and with Jesus. It makes sense when we remember that the fortresses we're attacking are really ideologies and beliefs. The sword is an offensive weapon, unlike the earlier pieces of armor. And if you're going to attack false ideas, what better sword to have than the truth from God himself? Would I dare to launch out based on my opinion? My experience? The view of the majority? The things that seem to make the most sense? What has the most utilitarian outcome when believed? What sounds the coolest? Some of these could be used as supporting points, but the heart of the issue is what Satan asked Eve so long ago: *"Did God really say...?"*

Many Christians seriously underestimate the power of God's Word. If they didn't, they would learn more about it. They'd spend more time reading and meditating on it. Actions speak louder than words, and the actions of many Christians clearly suggest that they have never understood how powerful the Word of God is.

One who fully knows the power of God's Word is Satan. He will go to any length to keep people away from it. As mentioned earlier, he once succeeded in taking the Bible out of the hands of common people completely for a thousand years. During all that time, Christians had no way of knowing what was true in countless areas. They could only take the word of their priests, which often wasn't very reliable.

In modern times, Satan has continued to design one plan after another to get between believers and their Bibles. The higher critical movement in modernist scholarship demolished worldwide many people's confidence in the Bible. Entire seminaries were taken over by non-believing professors, who in turn filled pulpits with tens of thousands of non-believing preachers. Millions of Christians came under instruction that attacked the Bible as faulty folklore with phony authorship claims, out of date with the modern age. Other movements in the church today continue to undermine Christians' confidence and motivation to learn the Bible.

If Christian history teaches us anything, it's that Satan is desperate to keep us away from the Bible, or at least to undermine our confidence in it. Wouldn't you, if you were him? What an awesome accomplishment! Success in this area would mean getting those who are supposed to attack his kingdom to enter battle without their swords! Vast numbers of Christians today are entering spiritual warfare armed with rubber bands instead of "the sword of the Spirit, which is the word of God" (Ephesians 6:17).

PUTTING IT ALL TOGETHER

Having discussed the full armor of God, Paul concludes,

> With all prayer and petition pray at all times in the Spirit, and with this in view, be on the alert with all perseverance and petition for all the saints. (Ephesians 6:18 NASB)

Prayer is the language of spiritual warfare. Through prayer in the Spirit, we speak the words of faith in the truth God uses to guard our hearts and minds. It is usually during times of prayer that God gives us discernment about what Satan is doing. Through prayer we can also guard the hearts and minds of others, as Paul implies when he says to pray "for all the saints."

Chuck Smith has a provocative illustration in his book *Effective Prayer Life*:

> Suppose that someone attacked you on a dark street and started wrestling with you. If he were to pull a knife, the whole battle would suddenly be centered on one thing—control of the knife. All of a sudden, you'd forget about punching him in the nose. You'd be grabbing for his wrist and trying to knock that knife out of his hand, for you realize that it is the deciding factor in this battle.[4]

Here, we are the ones who produce the knife. Satan knows that prayer is the decisive weapon (especially when based on God's Word) and will do anything to keep us from praying. In a thousand ways he throws up interruptions, distractions, and reasons why prayer can wait until later. Our weapons remain unused until we wield them in effective prayer.

Another Twist

Roman practice in warfare provides an interesting historical side note. They often fought in maniples—square formations where the men in the rear fought facing backward to the men in front. The traditional phalanx, or line formation, was vulnerable to being pierced at one point, and the enemy could flow through and attack people from the rear, resulting in panic. But maniples could fight in all directions. This meant the individual soldier didn't need to worry about what was behind him—his brothers in arms would take care of that. He only had to fight straight ahead.

Did Paul have this in mind as he contemplated the Roman soldier? In the body of Christ, we can cover each other's backs through discernment and intercessory prayer. If we have the discipline to stand together, we become more able to stand our ground. Prayer, as Paul envisions it, is not an individual affair but something we do together and for each other.

Rather than cover the full scope prayer plays in spiritual warfare now, we will discuss it in the following chapters as we examine the specific areas where we confront the Evil One.

BINDING THE STRONG MAN

We earlier saw Jesus teach that you can only plunder the strong man's household after he has been bound (Matthew 12:29). He also told his disciples, "I have given you authority over all the power of the enemy, and you can walk among snakes and scorpions and crush them. Nothing will injure you" (Luke 10:19). We see Paul taking authority over a demon in Acts 16:18: "I command you in the name of Jesus Christ to come out of her." These passages all suggest that believers can issue authoritative commands that Satan must obey in the name of Jesus. Again, this ability to speak a word of authority is probably related to the notion of binding Satan.[5]

The authority to bind Satan is not, however, a blank check. For instance, we cannot simply pray that Satan will leave us (and those we minister to) alone for the rest of our lives. The power Jesus referred to must apply to specific confrontations in our lives or ministries where we can either drive Satan back from his intention or move into his territory with godly power that he cannot resist. Why else would Paul put such emphasis on prayer in ministry? He clearly felt that praying "constantly," "day and night" could make a difference (2 Timothy 1:3; 1 Thessalonians 1:2; Colossians 1:3; Romans 1:9). And it seems very likely that spiritual warfare, including wielding powerful weapons against Satan, was a big part of this prayer ministry.

Although we do not know all the boundaries on this power to take authority over Satan, I believe we can pray against him in the name of Jesus whenever we are speaking based on Jesus' authority as revealed in God's Word. We must pray within our authorized sphere of authority— the expressed promises of God. Too many books on this subject stress praying against Satan, but they leave out the part about God's Word. I visited one group who seemed to believe that if they shouted their prayers louder, Satan would be driven back. This has no effect on Satan whatsoever. For power in prayer against Satan, we need to pray the Word. J. Oswald Sanders explains:

> What could it mean to "tie up the strong man" except to neutralize his might through the overcoming power of Christ who came "to destroy [nullify, render inoperative] the works of the devil"? And how can that happen except by the prayer of faith that lays hold of the victory of Calvary and claims it for the problem at hand?[6]

CHAPTER 13

THE ARROWS OF SATAN: TEMPTATION

So far we have considered Satan's abilities, the broad outline of spiritual war, and some key passages on the subject. Now we're ready to examine the specific attacks we will face day in and day out and to think through practical countermeasures we can employ. We'll begin with those attacks we face in daily living and move to those we face in our ministries.

Satan lies and persuades. Since most of his tactics involve deception, this could be considered the overarching tactic that contains all the others. The first specific type of deception we will consider is temptation.

Most Christians are aware that Satan is "the tempter" (Matthew 4:3; 1 Thessalonians 3:5). Jesus taught Christians to pray, "Don't let us yield to temptation, but rescue us from the evil one" (Matthew 6:13). But not all temptation comes from Satan. Our sinful nature and the world present us with frequent temptation without any direct demonic intervention. Demons can, however, increase and intensify even natural temptations, in addition to those they launch directly.

REASONS FOR TEMPTATION

We argued earlier that Satan tempts non-Christians because the resulting sin habit may well keep them away from God. But why does he tempt Christians? After all, Christians are forgiven in advance for sins they commit (Hebrews 10:14; Romans 8:1); what does he gain by getting Christians to fall? For Satan, getting a believer to sin is never the end goal but the beginning of a process. He can use sin in a number of ways to break down and even destroy their spiritual lives, their message, and the quality of their churches.

Enslavement

Sin is very habit-forming. Jesus said, "I tell you the truth, everyone who sins is a slave of sin" (John 8:34). By convincing Christians they can just toy a bit in some area, Satan lures them into something much more powerful than they realize. Any fall into sin makes the next fall harder to resist and seemingly less significant. At the same time, rather than providing real satisfaction, the temporary pleasures of sin create a desire for more. As our resistance decreases and our desire increases, sin draws us into its enslaving power. Before long, Satan has established a destructive habit.

Sin habits can involve gross sins of the flesh like drug addiction or sexual immorality, but they can also involve more subtle areas like self-protective passivity in relationships, or giving in to laziness, or turning away from time in Scripture and prayer. Giving ourselves over to anxiety or self-absorption can quickly become sinfully habitual and directly violate God's Word. Considering that Jesus said loving God and loving others are of highest importance for his followers, many of our most devastating sin habits will likely be sins of omission, where we fail to do what we should have done (James 4:17). By capturing believers in more subtle habits, Satan can undermine their spirituality in a way that they can easily rationalize and perhaps not even notice. Outwardly well-behaved Christians who are spiritually stalemated satisfy Satan's goals. Materialistic greed, failure to seek out ministry, self-absorption, disengagement from true, loving relationships and the like are sufficient to guarantee believers will have little impact for God. Satan even convinces some that their sin is a good thing, such as when Christians become self-righteous, rejecting, or judgmental.

Seduction

Like a matador with a red cape luring bulls to their death, Satan often guides naïve believers into sin by causing them to focus only on avoiding gross sins of commission. But his most powerful temptations for Christians often involve nothing extreme. We have already seen that the *kosmos* is an elaborate system designed entirely to tempt people into living lives of self-indulgence and self-promotion. Herein the ultimate purpose is to keep people away from God, and we also saw that it traps Christians in a lifestyle that makes them ineffective for God. This is another goal in temptation: removing believers from God's service through sheer preoccupation.

Discrediting

As Satan enslaves Christians to habitual sin, he can use their lives to discredit the message of Christ. Sin-enslaved Christians create a poor picture of what following Jesus should be like. The watching world may see that we are just as bitter, materialistic, dishonest, and self-serving as anyone else. When Satan gets Christian leaders into gross sins of the flesh, he can break a big scandal, spreading their disgrace to millions.

I experienced this early in my Christian life. As a new believer, I was still occasionally falling into drug abuse. While working with another Christian friend, constructing a restaurant, we found a bottle of toluene— a powerful inhalant. Impulsively, we decided to get high. Returning later, we found that the plastic bag and the toluene were gone, but nothing happened. We were so intoxicated at the time that we wondered if we had simply misplaced our paraphernalia.

More than two years later, I was working at the same restaurant as a cook. One evening I was engaged in a spirited discussion with several employees who were eagerly questioning my Christian views. Just as I was getting ready to explain the difference between a grace-approach and a law-approach to God, my atheist boss walked by and overheard our conversation. At the perfect moment he interjected, "Well, Dennis, at least these guys don't hang out on the third floor sniffing glue!"

The rest of the conversation did not go well.

I couldn't believe this sharp anti-Christian guy had kept my sin secret until the perfect moment. In this case, my earlier yielding to temptation came back to haunt me, discrediting my witness. Fortunately, extreme situations like these are unusual for most of us, but poor marriages, materialism, pettiness, gossip, poor attitudes at work, and bitterness can be just as discrediting.

Satan also seeks to use the psychological and spiritual turmoil caused in the minds of sinning Christians to manipulate them, as we will see in our next chapter.

RESISTING TEMPTATION

In 1 Corinthians 10:13 Paul says,

> The temptations in your life are no different from what others experience. And God is faithful. He will not allow the temptation to be more than you can stand. When you are tempted, he will show you a way out so that you can endure.

This is a promise that God will prevent our being tempted beyond our ability to withstand it.[1] However, just because God protects us from overwhelming temptation doesn't mean temptation won't at times be severe. Temptation can be a powerful suffering experience for Christians, especially if we have recently been unsuccessful in resisting it.

DISCERNING SATAN'S PRESENCE

Temptation could be the result of a purely physical desire or reaction. Our sin nature is able to create regular, powerful temptation, so Satan may not even be involved. People who cast out "the demon of lust" or "the demon of pride" are in error. These are not demons but "the desires of your sinful nature" (Galatians 5:19). If deliverance from sins like these came from casting out demons, don't you think the Bible would tell us that? But Scripture never suggests this solution. *Victory over sin comes from walking according to the Spirit* (5:16).

But Satan can add the force of his influence to normal, fleshly temptation. When he gets into the act, temptation becomes more prolonged and more severe. Satan doesn't directly create our urges and reactions; those are ours by nature. Rather, he speaks to our minds, inflaming and justifying our sinful nature's impulses. We sense an increasingly powerful urge to sin, reluctance to act (in the case of sins of omission), or reaction (such as angry responses). These can build over minutes, hours, even days. You begin to sense that this is not a normal temptation. Thoughts in your mind continue to torment you even after you've surrendered the issue to God.

When this happens we often grit our teeth and try to resist, but we may never stop to think about why we continue to feel a growing urge to sin. Sometimes coordinated events just happen to come along, reinforcing the desire to sin. Just when a young believer has decided not to use drugs, a friend invites him over to try the newest batch. A student bemoans her loneliness only to receive a call from that ex-boyfriend she's been trying to avoid. At times like these, God may reveal that a demon is fueling the temptation. Other times we can't be sure that Satan is near, pressing us to sin. But if we suspect his involvement, we should play it safe and take measures suited to blocking his influence.

LIES AND TEMPTATION

To resist these demonically supercharged temptations successfully, we need to understand how Satan works in temptation. All temptations contain an implied lie even without his involvement. For instance, when people feel the urge to go on a buying spree, they assume that wasting money on self will make them happy. But "it is more blessed to give than to receive" (Acts 20:35). Those considering a sexual encounter usually believe that sexual stimulation will meet their inner needs better than the real love prescribed by God. With any temptation, we could extrapolate the implied false belief if we think about it for a moment.

Understood correctly, temptation is really a form of deception. We believe our false assumptions about the sin, and that makes it more appealing.

But when Satan comes in to fan the flames of temptation, he adds more lies and additional, powerful persuasion tailored to you and the situation. When tempting Jesus, he even generated an argument using Scripture (Luke 4:9–11). These arguments work together in interlocking systems that weaken our resistance, especially if we fail to answer each one explicitly with truth from God's Word, as Jesus did.

Let's examine some typical arguments Satan uses to weaken Christians' resistance to temptation, and then compare them with what God says about each case. As you read these, remember that Satan may combine several at once or give several in succession.

Deserving

A favorite argument of Satan goes, "After what you've been through lately, it's hard to see why a little of this [sin] couldn't be justified. You deserve a little relief right now." Or "You've given out enough. It's your turn to receive for a change." He's suggesting that it's time to balance the scales. Whether through self-sacrifice or mistreatment, you are in a deficit position, and therefore you deserve a little break with some enjoyable sin. The overeater may sit down with a box of ice cream and some homemade cookies; the materialist may buy another gizmo; someone else might reach for the bottle or some pills. An "omitter" might decide she deserves a full night in front of the TV instead of going to her women's group.

Threats

Fear can be a potent motivation. An affluent couple suddenly receives a million-dollar inheritance. They know they should give most of this money to God's work or to the poor rather than hoard it, because they already have more money than they need. But they begin to imagine all kinds of dangers that could develop. What if the stock market crashes? What if a long-term illness strikes? What if the house burns down? What if our company goes belly-up? Before long, they decide the only prudent thing to do is invest the money, "just in case."

Many commit sins of omission based on fears. "If I let myself get too involved in this small group I won't have enough time to stay organized, or to stay fresh for work, or to hang out with my family." Some people fear that if they go down the path of developing a ministry, it will become a slippery slope, and they soon will be broken through overexertion. Others are afraid to share their faith because they imagine negative reactions.

Secrecy

Satan threatens you with ruin unless you keep your sins secret. He can produce terrifying visions of what will happen if anyone finds out how bad your problem is. Besides, they wouldn't have anything positive to offer anyway, so what's the point? Most such visions are lies intended to keep you wrestling with your problem in the isolation of secrecy. Satan knows believers who keep their sin secret will not be able to draw on the strength and counsel of the body of Christ and are unlikely to gain victory. He can use the guilt you feel from lying about your sin to further alienate you from God and other believers. Even though you know you are to "confess your sins to each other and pray for each other so that you may be healed" (James 5:16), your fear of rejection can make it seem impossible to disclose the problem. To leaders, Satan points out that "you might cause others to be disappointed and stop following God—keep quiet for the sake of your people!" He knows if he can keep you quiet you'll probably fall further and further into your habit, requiring even more secrecy and dishonesty. He knows that if you open up and come into the light, the power of your sin habit will likely be broken.

Superspirituality

Christians may read or hear that they should live their spiritual lives in a goal-oriented way. They have goals in other areas of their lives, but none when it comes to spirituality. Frequently, though, they think that setting goals would be fleshly. Wouldn't it be more spiritual to just follow the Spirit's leadings as they come, rather than try to bring in human control by forming a plan? After all, "The wind blows wherever it wants" (John 3:8)—why should we try to orchestrate a certain outcome? Satan knows that Christians with no spiritual goals are drifting in a poorly motivated state. Believers who through prayer, study, and reflection gain a sense of God's will for their lives are not afraid to aspire to spiritual goals.

Just This Once . . .

When you feel a strong urge to sin in a particular area, you usually recognize it would be wrong, but a persuasive thought enters your mind: "Just a little bit wouldn't hurt much." Or you may decide you're going to check out an event you know could put you in a position of temptation or compromise, but you're not really going to do anything. This is how most sin episodes begin. You rarely intend to give yourself over to a big session of wallowing in the mud. You usually intend only to relieve the urge to sin a bit by engaging in some minor compromise. We call it toe-dangling because it's like dangling your toes over the edge of the cliff, just to feel the air out there, while ignoring the risk of falling. Of course, toe-dangling never lessens the sin urge; just the opposite is true.

Fatalism

When temptation succeeds and you form a habit, Satan is zealous to persuade you that your case is hopeless. Once you believe your kind of problem never changes, you will never seek help. You are disbelieving God, which substantially cuts off his liberating power. Fatalism denies God's power to change lives and makes any effort to seek help seem pointless.

Overconfidence

Christians sometimes act in baffling ways. Why would a dating couple struggling to resist immorality go on a weekend camping trip together? In some cases it's because they have already decided to have sex, but surprisingly often one or both of them actually believed they could do this without getting into trouble. Satan tries to persuade believers they can handle situations he knows they cannot. This works well with people who've had a measure of victory over habits that used to enslave them, like alcoholism, drug use, or promiscuity.

Excuses

Christians in sin often need help developing excuses in order to deflect the Holy Spirit's conviction, ease their own minds, and pacify other believers. Excuses are important for deflecting responsibility, and Satan is often there to offer creative help. He persuades omissive Christians (who for years haven't lifted a finger to share their faith or serve) that the reason is their inability: "Someone like me just can't do things like that." Bitter Christians usually are convinced that their bitterness is because of what others did to them, or the way certain people are. The real reasons—their own lack of forgiveness and their immature reactions—may play no part in their thinking. Christians held in the grip of greed often point to others greedier than they as examples of "real" greed; their own extravagance is just so they can identify with their "mission field" among the successful. A believer ruining his witness and health by overeating observes sadly that some people just have gland issues and bad genes as he dives into his corn chips and soft drink. Another believer who still hasn't developed a habit of spending daily time with God in prayer and the Word observes that he's just not a morning person. Of course, he isn't an evening person either.

Rationalization

A heavy-drinking student shrugs and reminds himself that at least it's not cocaine anymore. A dating couple walks away from a groping session observing that "at least we didn't have sex" . . . and besides, "we're basically committed." A lazy believer who just spent the whole day lying around and indulging self feels like nothing else could be expected from someone who feels a little down. A mother who's just screamed in rage at her kids and husband muses that the people in this household only understand strong language: "It's a shame, but you do what you have to do."

Rationalizing and minimizing sin is when we manufacture reasons why this kind of sin doesn't really count, or may not even be sinful if you understand the situation. Even if it's somewhat sinful, it's one of the less important sins and probably won't do much harm.

Self-Righteousness

A pastor shudders in revulsion as he watches his lesbian neighbors walk into their house arm in arm. His "occasional" problem with pornography is *nothing* like that. A wife points out in disgust that her husband is about as spiritual as a frog. Her coldness toward him is just a natural, unavoidable response. Jesus taught that self-righteous judgment is a dodge people use to avoid looking at their own sin. These critical attitudes really amount to looking at the speck in your brother's eye and failing to notice the log in your own (Matthew 7:3).[2]

REFUTING

All of these and many others are mental fortresses we erect to protect our "right" to sin. Without them, temptation would lose much of its power in our lives. Satan knows that mere sinful urges aren't enough to enslave Christians thoroughly; we also need belief systems that effectively prevent us from appropriating God's deliverance. We must see that *a key reason we are often defeated by sin is that we believe a falsehood.* Although all people are capable of generating false interpretations of their behavior and attitudes, Satan can persuasively suggest good additions. This is Satan at his best—not in causing sinful desires themselves but in helping us to construct the belief systems that perpetuate and strengthen those desires.

Time in prayer and God's truth are powerful antidotes to temptation at precisely this point. Christians who view their own sin problems the same way God views them are poised to make real progress, while those who believe the lies of Satan are doomed to ongoing failure.

When he was tempted, Jesus repeatedly replied to Satan's temptations: "It is written. . . ." He knew that much of the battle with sin is really a battle over truth. It's not enough that we try to *ignore* lying suggestions from the Evil One; we have to learn to *refute* them using the power of God's Word. We lose spiritual standing and power if we leave these suggestions unanswered. In the spiritual realm, claims and counterclaims regarding what is true cause power to shift.

Consider how you could pray, using these Bible passages to refute each of the lies itemized above.

Fortress	*Scripture*	*Application*
Deserving	"The Lord ordered that those who preach the Good News should be supported by those who benefit from it. Yet I have never used any of these rights. . . . And you should imitate me, just as I imitate Christ" (1 Corinthians 9:14–15; 11:1). "What do you have that God hasn't given you? And if everything you have is from God, why boast as though it were not a gift?" (1 Corinthians 4:7).	Paul uses this example (where he deserved to be paid for his ministry but gave up that right for the good of others) to urge people to imitate him by not insisting on "rights." Instead, we should focus on what we can give to others. The idea that we deserve anything implies that we have earned what we have, but Scripture teaches that all we have is a gift from God.
Threats	"Don't love money; be satisfied with what you have. For God has said, 'I will never fail you. I will never abandon you' " (Hebrews 13:5).	People turn to money to give them a sense of security when they feel threatened. The same could be true of relationships. But our security is supposed to be in God.

Fortress	Scripture	Application
Secrecy	"Confess your sins to each other and pray for each other so that you may be healed. The earnest prayer of a righteous person has great power and produces wonderful results" (James 5:16). "When I kept silent about my sin, my body wasted away through my groaning all day long. For day and night Your hand was heavy upon me; my vitality was drained away as with the fever heat of summer" (Psalm 32:3–4 NASB).	Healing from sin problems is often contingent on our bringing them into the light. Sin's power lies in the darkness, where Satan rules. Satan's threats that honesty will destroy us are lies. We may be seriously underestimating the agony we are causing ourselves by hiding our sin. We think it will hurt us to confess, but according to Scripture the opposite is true.
Super-spirituality	"Don't you realize that in a race everyone runs, but only one person gets the prize? So run to win! So I run with purpose in every step. I am not just shadowboxing" (1 Corinthians 9:24, 26).	Paul didn't believe pursuing goals was fleshly. He considered it part of good stewardship to take careful aim in life and develop spiritual goals.
Just this once . . .	"I tell you the truth, everyone who sins is a slave of sin" (John 8:34; see also Romans 6:16).	All thoughts that a little bit of sin will ease the urge are foolish. The pleasure of sin guarantees only one thing: We will want more. A little taste of sin is never the end of it.
Fatalism	"I am certain that God, who began the good work within you, will continue his work until it is finally finished on that day when Christ Jesus returns" (Philippians 1:6).	Jesus changes lives, and fatalism is pure unbelief. No matter how gross our problem is, God is greater than our sin.

Fortress	Scripture	Application
Over-confidence	"If you think you are standing strong, be careful not to fall" (1 Corinthians 10:12).	Confidence in self blocks the grace of God. We should become deeply and powerfully suspicious of our own flesh nature.
	"The human heart is the most deceitful of all things, and desperately wicked. Who really knows how bad it is?" (Jeremiah 17:9).	If we believe our own heart's assurance that we can handle situations, we are listening to a source that cannot be trusted.
Excuses	"The temptations in your life are no different from what others experience. And God is faithful. He will not allow the temptation to be more than you can stand. When you are tempted, he will show you a way out so that you can endure" (1 Corinthians 10:13).	We always have ample excuses for our failures, and none of them matter. Instead, we should admit our fault frankly and without qualifications. Only agreeing with God breaks the power of sin. Making excuses only means we will fall again— and soon.
Rationalization	"This is the way of an adulterous woman: She eats and wipes her mouth, and says, 'I have done no wrong'" (Proverbs 30:20 NASB).	In our ingenuity, we can justify virtually anything. Grace, not rationalization, is the answer to guilt feelings.
	[God speaking to Job] "Will you really annul My judgment? Will you condemn Me that you may be justified?" (Job 40:8 NASB).	This is really what we are doing when we rationalize sin. God says it's evil, but we argue that it's not so bad.
Self-righteousness	"Therefore you have no excuse, everyone of you who passes judgment, for in that which you judge another, you condemn yourself; for you who judge practice the same things" (Romans 2:1 NASB; see also Romans 14).	When we judge, we condemn ourselves, not only because we too are guilty but also because the act of self-righteous judging is a serious sin in and of itself.

In each category, these are only one or two of many passages we could use appropriately. We can pray, "God, I know I've been thinking this, but I'm going to believe what you say in this passage." When we learn to assault the fortresses Satan is building in our own minds with scriptural truth, temptation loses much of its power.

REPLACEMENT

Battling the negative thought patterns fostered by Satan is important, but it's not enough. We also have to work at replacing the enjoyment of sin with the true joy God intends for our lives. *Only when we build lives adequately founded on real love will the lure of sin significantly diminish.*

Christians have the unique opportunity to experience the love of God. Deepening in our knowledge of God's love results in a unique love for others as well: "We love each other because he loved us first" (1 John 4:19). Healthy, growing Christians have something to enjoy that goes beyond anything the world-system can imagine. The one true cry of our hearts is for a life of real love. For this we were created, and God wants us to learn to love as Jesus loved us (John 15:12).

Building a life of real love is not easy. It requires that we draw near to God and learn from him how to love others. Then we have to practice loving others. Finding a group of believers in community who are serious about learning to love is difficult. Even if we do find such people, only those who pursue love with determination and perseverance will ever experience the fullness of what God has planned for us.

Christian love is serving love. In Scripture, the word for service is *ministry*. In ministry, we practice serving love toward both believers and nonbelievers. As we become servant ministers in God's great purpose on earth, we gain a remarkable sense of significance and purpose in our lives. The ecstasy of being used by God to effect lasting, meaningful change in the lives of others can easily dwarf the passing pleasures of sin. Many Christians have only succeeded in shedding stubborn sin habits when they realized they had to if they wanted to continue being used by God.

When believers succeed in building communities of love that are afire with the thrill of being used by God, they finally find a permanent and healthy substitute for sin. Our battle in this life never ends because Satan can shift his approach from tempting us with sins we have conquered to luring us with more subtle sins that fit our new situation. But we will find growing victory over temptation when we fight it according to God's pattern.

FIFTEEN PRACTICAL IDEAS FOR RESISTING TEMPTATION

Simple solutions are usually inadequate when it comes to temptation. However, after carefully considering the above, these ideas should help.

1. Face your temptation and identify it clearly. What are you thinking about doing, or not doing, and why? Admit this to God.

2. Ask yourself and God what you are being tempted to believe about your sin. What mental processes are making temptation harder to resist? What does God say about that in his Word?

3. Discuss the temptation with God in prayer. Talk to him about it—thanking him for his grace, pleading for his power and help, acknowledging that even if you fell into sin he would still love you, and going over why you don't want to fall again.

4. Ask God to reveal a vision of how your life could be if you were free from this sin habit. What does Scripture promise? Longing for God's positive vision for your life is more powerful than focusing on the dreadfulness of ongoing failure. But consider also: What are the possible consequences of falling? Do you really want to pay that price for something that won't satisfy anyway?

5. Admit to one or more friends or your spouse that you're being tempted. Ask for prayer and counsel. Don't wait until you fall into sin. Draw on the support and wisdom of Christ's body. Pray together. If possible, ask advice of someone who has won victory in the same or a similar area.

6. Remember when you fell to this sin before? Did it really deliver the pleasure and satisfaction you were seeking, or did it leave you even more miserable? Declare to God your willingness to endure suffering under temptation rather than believe the lie that giving in will make things easier.

7. Look to external, environmental helps. Agree to get online accountability software or blocking software if you are struggling with pornography, and give someone else the password. Avoid parties where people are drinking or using drugs until you gain more control. Set goals with a friend if you are struggling with apathy or aimlessness, and check back regularly on how things are going. Agree with your dating partner that you aren't going to go out alone to places where sin is possible, or maybe decide to quit making excuses about money and get married. Once you gain enough victory in this area of sin, some external constraints may become unnecessary, but make certain you truly are free before removing them.

8. Remember the power of habit. Use habituation to your advantage. First, realize that by occasional, even rare or partial compromise with sin, you are keeping a negative habit alive. This is one of the great dangers of falling to temptation. On the other hand, time and distance weaken negative habits, so every success in resisting temptation brings us closer to release from future temptation. If you don't want to suffer under temptation, you must begin winning these struggles consistently enough to break the habit. Believe those who have gained victory in an area like yours—they often state that they no longer feel much temptation in a key area where once they were habitually enslaved. You can gradually replace negative habits with positive ones.

9. Find one or more verses that address your area of sin and memorize them. You might place these on a card and look at them periodically. When you read or recite these passages, pray that God will help you truly believe them.

10. Don't toe-dangle! If you move the slightest bit closer to sin,

whether sampling something similar or even spending time thinking about it, you make an inner decision to compromise, and already you are sliding down the slope. If this happens, admit it frankly to a friend along with the context: why you are afraid and what might happen next.

11. Immediately find something redemptive and fun to do with your time to keep you out of trouble. Who can you contact for the purpose of building *them* up? What might you read that could help in this area?

12. Don't stay by yourself. Temptation works best in isolation.

13. Predetermine that if you fall into sin, you are definitely going to admit your failure, and be specific about who you will admit it to (ideally, someone responsible who won't just pat you on the back). Deciding that you won't hide your sin will help you avoid it.

14. Remember what preceded this temptation episode. Were there triggers that set it off? Consider how you can avoid one or more of those in the future.

15. If this area of temptation keeps coming up, tell a friend about it, and ask him or her to pray for you and to ask you occasionally how it's going. In other words, *establish accountability.*

CHAPTER 14

THE ARROWS OF SATAN: ACCUSATION

Causing Christians to sin is the beginning, not the end, of Satan's plan. As suggested earlier, one of his key goals is to exploit the psychological and spiritual turmoil sin causes in us. Deception goes into high gear if he succeeds: By planting accusations in the minds of believers who fall into sin, Satan can take events that should be resolved easily and turn them into highly destructive episodes. These episodes demonstrate that what we believe can be just as important as what we do.

FOUR DIRECTIONS OF ACCUSATION

When people sin, Satan fires accusations in at least four directions.

Accusing Humans to God

Revelation 12:10 says, "The accuser of our brothers and sisters has been thrown down to earth—the one who accuses them before our God day and night." And Zechariah gives us a fascinating vision of such accusation going on in heaven:

> Then the angel showed me Jeshua the high priest standing before the angel of the Lord. The Accuser, Satan, was there at the angel's right hand, making accusations against Jeshua. And the Lord said to Satan, "I, the Lord, reject your accusations, Satan. Yes, the Lord, who has chosen Jerusalem, rebukes you. This man is like a burning stick that has been snatched from the fire" (3:1–2).

We also see these kinds of accusations in Job. They have to do with legal controversies in heaven, and the Bible never fully explains them. We know we don't need to worry about them, because Jesus is our intercessor (Hebrews 7:25; 1 John 2:1).

Accusing God to Humans

We saw how Satan accuses God when we studied Genesis 3: By causing Eve to believe God didn't have her best interests in mind, Satan weakened her ability to resist temptation. Satan continually strives to break down Christians' faith by suggesting that God hasn't come through, will never come through, is only interested in restricting and taking things away, and doesn't love us. When he's not portraying God as distant and uncaring, he suggests God is harsh and dangerous. Always he portrays God as bitterly disappointed and unhappy with us.

All these accusations have one core effect—breaking down our relationship with God—but only if we believe them. Think of how awkward you feel approaching someone who knows you did him wrong—especially if this is the umpteenth time you've done so. These can be some of the most uncomfortable experiences in life.

For example, when my son was in grade school, he had difficulties with one of his subjects. We had a good relationship and usually enjoyed talking with each other. But when I brought up this problem, I saw in my son what God must often see in us: This normally talkative boy got sullen and quiet. I could only extract one-word answers, and his discomfort was all over his face; he even began to walk out of the room in mid-conversation. All I wanted was to discuss ways I could help, but his shame was a barrier. He clearly perceived me as very disappointed and dismayed (which was not true). I was amazed at how hard it was to move into good communication about his problem and how difficult it was to reassure him of my love and desire to help. Only later did I realize that I act the same way with God when I fail.

Satan knows that in our dealings with God, relationship is central, and he is a master at creating distance in relationships. Just as his sin distanced him from God, he knows how to manipulate the psychology of sin to make us feel like we can't draw near to God when we sin. We feel uneasy toward God because we harbor suspicions about his character.

Satan especially urges us to doubt the grace of God. The mystery of God's grace is so hard to grasp and so easy to doubt that only concentrated, conscious review of it can restore us to intimacy in difficult times. Believers who succeed in their walk with God must learn to gather Scriptures that speak of his grace and love and cling to them with both hands during bouts of satanic accusation. Eventually we learn to face God squarely and begin with thanksgiving for his gracious view of us even when we fail miserably. Thanksgiving for grace is the best way to break through the icy distance we feel during times of shame over our failure. Quoting key passages is a good idea.

Every time victims of a constricting snake exhale, the snake's coils tighten, preventing the lungs from expanding as much as before. In the same way, believers who inwardly accept any part of Satan's portrayal of God find themselves losing ground in a way that quickly suffocates the relationship. We must aggressively oppose these subtle suggestions, using the Word with faith and thanksgiving, each and every time Satan tries to plant such lies in our minds.

As we evaluate and respond to satanic accusation, we also need to take note of a key transition between the Old and New Testaments. Readers of the Old Testament see God often expressing anger and disappointment with his people. But have you noticed this is absent in the New Testament? God fully expended his righteous anger upon Christ at the cross. God sees his people now as "the righteousness of God in Him [Jesus]" (2 Corinthians 5:21 NASB). Realizing how totally he accepts us under his New Covenant is crucial to overthrowing Satan's accusations about God being angry with us.

This is why Paul says, "Sin is no longer your master, for you no longer live under the requirements of the law. Instead, you live under the freedom of God's grace" (Romans 6:14). In a more legalistic relationship, God would be angry with us when we failed him, and this anger would make us afraid to draw near to him. As a result, we would lose relational intimacy with him and sin would more easily follow. We must see the connection between being under grace and freedom from sin. And we must refute Satan's portrayal of God with the truth about his grace.

Accusing Believers to Each Other

Satan is the *devil,* which means "accuser." He sows suspicions in an effort to erode relationships. Just as he tries to foster suspicion of God, he diligently sows suspicion of our fellow Christians as well. Many of us are suspicious by nature, often based on our life experiences. Satan fans the flames of our suspicion with well-aimed accusations. Closeness between Christians is almost as dangerous in his view as closeness between believers and God. Breaking down relational closeness in the church is one of the best ways to destroy its witness. Married people should also be aware that he vigorously accuses spouses to each other in order to destroy intimacy in marriage.

In 2 Corinthians 2, Paul was addressing lack of forgiveness in the church when he said they should forgive "so that Satan will not outsmart us. For we are familiar with his evil schemes" (v. 11). Division in the church is Satan's business: " 'Don't sin by letting anger control you.' Don't let the sun go down while you are still angry, for anger gives a foothold to the devil" (Ephesians 4:26–27). Both of these passages directly connect human relational alienation with the activity of Satan.

Accusing other believers is easy for him because people often *are* guilty. We will never be in a church, Bible study, or family where other people don't wrong us; some suspicion is often warranted in these situations, and sometimes later events confirm our suspicions. But we should recognize Satan's spin: It's not only that a person has done something wrong, but as a result he is fundamentally untrustworthy. It's not just that she said something wrong, but she said it deliberately, with the intent to hurt you. Satan strings patterns of historical failure together into a scenario that suggests permanent distrust and avoidance. Rejection and separation seem to be the only reasonable responses.

Many of these supercharged suspicions are based not only on people's actions but also on their motives. This is one of the key reasons Scripture calls us to stop judging people's motives. In a passage responding to people questioning Paul's motives, he says,

> I do not even examine myself. For I am conscious of nothing against myself, yet I am not by this acquitted; but the one who examines me is the Lord. Therefore do not go on passing judgment before the time, but wait until the Lord comes who will both bring to light the things hidden in the darkness and disclose the motives of men's hearts; and then each man's praise will come to him from God. (1 Corinthians 4:3–5 NASB)

Notice that Paul isn't claiming we can never judge or discern something about another. In the very next chapter he says of one who was found in flagrant sin: "I have already passed judgment on this man" (5:3). Rather, in context, he is saying we shouldn't judge people's intentions. We are ill-equipped to know people's motivations, and our weakness in this area opens the door to satanic accusation. Much unrighteous judgment in marriages, friendships, and churches begins with judging people's motives.

Satan is very persuasive when arguing a case against fellow Christians, so we should be wary anytime suspicion of another believer comes to mind. Anytime you begin to reflect on the failings or betrayals of another believer, learn to ask questions that can prevent unrighteous judgment:

1. Is my suspicion based on objective, factual knowledge, or is it based on hearsay, my own imagination, or circumstantial evidence?

2. Have I taken the time to suspend judgment until I hear the other side of the story from the one I suspect?

3. Even if the wrongdoing I suspect is real, is it significant? Or is this a common failing and not important enough to make a big deal out of?

4. Am I being self-righteous? Am I upset about sin that's no different

from what I do all the time? Can I recall times when I struggled with a similar problem? Should I show more grace?

5. Am I judging motives? Is it the deed or the suspected motivation that upsets me?

6. If the problem is real and serious, am I prepared to help the person? Am I an armchair critic, or am I an engaged believer prepared to extend loving discipline or advice?

7. How do I know Satan isn't speaking to me right now? Have I prayed and asked for God's view of this situation?

Careless, immature Christians rarely ask any of these questions. Instead, they run with reckless abandon on suspicions Satan suggests. They can't wait to share their newly discovered betrayal with other believers. The thought that the voice in their head might be Satan's never occurs to their self-centered minds. No wonder Satan finds it easy to break down unity in Christian groups and families. If only we could remind ourselves that Satan is the accuser, perhaps we'd be a little more cautious before jumping to negative conclusions about others.

Accusing Me to Myself

We already saw how, when we sin, Satan accuses God to us by suggesting that he is disappointed in us and angry with us. Satan also uses these occasions to launch attacks on our view of ourselves. According to Satan, I am a hopeless case, a worthless being, fated to continue in sin until my dying day. God, on the other hand, frequently stresses the importance of seeing ourselves as he sees us. He often urges us to focus consciously on our new identity in Christ:

> Since you have been raised to new life with Christ, set your sights on the realities of heaven, where Christ sits in the place of honor at God's right hand. Think about the things of heaven, not the things of earth. For you died to this life, and your real life is hidden with Christ in God. (Colossians 3:1–3)

Paul even assured the carnally minded Corinthians: "He will keep you strong to the end so that you will be free from all blame on the day when our Lord Jesus Christ returns" (1 Corinthians 1:8). Those who present themselves to God are to "consider [themselves] to be dead to the power of sin and alive to God through Christ Jesus" (Romans 6:11). The more we see ourselves as God sees us, the more freedom we gain from a life lived in contradiction to that picture. Freedom from sin results when we adopt God's view as our own.

Satan wants us to see quite a different picture. According to his accusing voice, I'm not the kind of person God can use. My unfaithfulness guarantees futility in spiritual matters.

Christians who believe these accusations drift into discouragement and fatalistic depression that result in apathy and despair. Continuing to pursue God and spiritual growth seems pointless to someone with such a bleak future. A Christian in this condition spreads gloom and unbelief to other believers and cannot convincingly share the gospel.

This is absolute defeat. How urgent it becomes at such times to recognize the voice of Satan! Would God suggest these thoughts? Not if we can believe the Bible, where we read, "God, who began the good work within you, will continue his work until it is finally finished on the day when Christ Jesus returns" (Philippians 1:6); "God is working in you, giving you the desire and the power to do what pleases him" (2:13). From one end of the Bible to the other the message is clear: *God changes lives.*

When we believe Satan's condemning charges, we may think we're being humble. We say we doubt ourselves, not God. But this is *not* humility. We really *are* doubting God. If our identity and future depended on our own efforts to perform and improve, such negative representations would be appropriate. However, when God declares our true identity is in Christ, and he calls us to view ourselves that way, our fatalistic views amount to a direct denial of his Word. We're saying, in effect, "My problems are greater than God."

If you are under accusation, you need to recognize who is talking to you and immediately enter into a spiritual battle for the truth. *Passivity in the face of accusation is the same as agreeing with Satan.* That thought shocks some people, but it's true. Simply trying to shake off negative thoughts when you're under accusation has little or no effect; you have to in faith refute those claims from the Word of God.

Here is where thinking and praying Christians begin to distance themselves from careless and subjective believers. Reading, praying, and pondering key passages about our identity has to be a regular part of the growing Christian's discipline. We are so used to assessing ourselves based on our performance or our characteristics compared to other people that we find it counterintuitive to begin basing our view of ourselves on what God says is true. Intense inner struggle is common when we set about reviewing God's clear statements about our identity and realize we haven't believed what he says. This is what the Bible calls "struggling" or "striving" in prayer (Romans 15:30; Colossians 4:12). In prayer, we don't struggle against God, who is on our side, but against Satan's lies and our own unbelief.

When you wrestle with accusation, begin by affirming the truth about your guilt. Don't make the mistake of trying to justify or minimize your own shortcomings. When we begin to argue, "Well, it isn't as bad as it was a couple of years ago" or "At least I'm not doing the other thing now," we put ourselves on Satan's ground—the ground of falsehood.

Instead, we should acknowledge our poor performance. "Yes, I'm covered in sin and failure. But I was never standing on my own works to begin with." *The point isn't what I have done for God but what he has done for me.*

Who dares accuse us whom God has chosen for his own? No one—for God himself has given us right standing with himself. (Romans 8:33)

If anyone is in Christ, he is a new creature; the old things passed away; behold, new things have come. (2 Corinthians 5:17 NASB)

I take my stand where Paul took his:

[That I] may be found in Him, not having a righteousness of my own derived from the Law, but that which is through faith in Christ, the righteousness which comes from God on the basis of faith. (Philippians 3:9 NASB)

If God grants us discernment that we are being actively accused by an evil spirit, we may need to speak a word of authoritative rebuke: *Depart from me, Satan, in the name of Jesus.* "If God is for us, who can ever be against us?" (Romans 8:31). As we actively confront Satan's lies with truth and the shield of faith, his burning accusations will eventually melt away and we will regain our spiritual equilibrium and sense of closeness to God. But we may have to argue for some time—perhaps even hours in some cases—before we reacquire inner peace. We also can safely assume that even after victory, the devil may return for another attack later, and we must remain just as persistent in refuting his lies. This is what Paul means when he says the shield of faith can stop the fiery arrows of the devil (Ephesians 6:16).

CHAPTER 15

SATAN AND YOUR MINISTRY: DIVERSION

We've already seen that God has given his people a mission, the same one Jesus himself pursued, of reconciling the world to God. Naturally, this involves evangelism, but the ministry of reconciliation involves more. After people meet Christ, they need to grow spiritually, continuing their reconciliation by becoming closer to him. For this, he provides Christ's body, with its ability to nurture, build up, equip, and heal broken people.

We need the full range of ministry described in the New Testament to accomplish our task. Every believer is called to play a part in accomplishing this purpose, through which the leadership is to "equip God's people" to do the work of ministry (Ephesians 4:11–12). We are to be "with one mind striving together for the faith of the gospel . . . united in spirit, intent on one purpose" (Philippians 1:27; 2:2 NASB). The gifts, ministries, and effects given by God are to "each of us" (1 Corinthians 12:7), an expression that means "each and every one of us."

The Greek word translated *minister* in English means "to serve." Every believer is called to be like Jesus, who came "not to be served but to serve others" (Mark 10:45). Satan knows he can safely ignore millions of Christians who see their faith only as something that meets their own needs. When we understand that we are in the body of Christ for what we have to *give* rather than what we can *take*, we're ready to step up to the true field of spiritual battle. Satan cannot ignore these believers, and if we intend to contribute to the mission God gave the church, we'd better be ready to withstand Satan's best. Satan is a strategic enemy who knows enough to focus the weight of his attack on those who are causing the most damage to his kingdom. He also goes after those who might do damage in the future. Satan knows he must derail people and groups intent on building the kingdom of God.

DECEPTION IN MINISTRY

Satan's powers of deception are never more impressive than when he works on dismantling people's ministries. He's clearly capable of interfering with the field in which you serve, as we'll see, but often this is unnecessary if he can divert you in such a way that your ministry poses no threat. When the Evil One convinces Christians to expend effort in directions that do not contribute to our true mission, they can work their hearts out and never pose a serious threat to his kingdom. This is *diversion*. He diverts Christians' efforts from what would result in victory to what is doomed to failure. Satan is so good at this we hardly know where to start when describing his work.

In the early twentieth century, according to church historian Justo Gonzáles, virtually the entire American church joined together for one grand purpose. Over a period of twenty years, liberal and conservative denominations enjoyed a unity of purpose never seen before as they labored to accomplish their goal: prohibition. Here we had the largest church in the world, joined and working two decades to accomplish something that has nothing to do with our mission, is not mentioned in the Bible, and ultimately did nothing to advance God's kingdom. Instead of leading people to Christ, this resulted in an upsurge of crime and probably left lingering bitterness toward the church. Remember: These were not fringe crackpots or nutcases but good-hearted, sincere servants of God doing what in their hearts they truly believed was his will. Today, few Christians believe this was a good idea, regardless of their view on drinking.

We talked earlier about Satan's masterful deception of the church as a whole. Satan deceives leaders, not just for personal pleasure but mainly in order to divert them from their mission. Christian history is littered with examples of the church devoting itself to projects that have nothing to do with our central mission and that actually discredit it. Diversion is his plan for you also. He may not be able to talk you into doing something crazy (like burning people at the stake or publicly whipping sinners), but if he directs your efforts toward ineffective pursuits, he wins.

No Need to Change

This deceiving work continues unabated in our day, especially in the West. How else could we explain why the church in one of the world's most Christianized nations is declining, and why most growing churches get more than 90 percent of their growth by rustling believers from other churches?[1] Clearly, the Western church is moving in directions that do not result in people being reconciled to God in meaningful numbers.

How can this be? What good are our theological studies, strategies, and millions of person-hours and dollars expended in ministry if they do not result in people being reconciled to God? Interestingly, recent studies demonstrate that believers in churches that are stagnant or declining usually believe their churches *are* winning many people to God.[2] Other studies demonstrate that leaders of growing churches are completely unaware that their growth is nearly all based on transfers from other evangelical churches; they regularly overestimate the percentage of converts in their churches by *five to fifteen times* the actual figure.[3] How likely is it that churches will face the pain of seeking out new directions when they already believe they're on the winning track? When Satan convinces Christians that their ineffective and misdirected efforts are successful, he guarantees they'll continue in those same ways. To overthrow his deception, we must be willing to withstand the pain of looking honestly at our own failures.

Individual Christians have just as much trouble facing their own failures as do churches. How many believe they are faithfully serving God but haven't led anyone to Christ or discipled anyone in years, and have actually stopped trying? Facing our own ineffectiveness for God requires a strong grasp of grace. Only believers operating under the grace paradigm will be emboldened to admit they haven't found the way. Grace gives us both the courage to admit we're failing and the strength to succeed. If we're soft on grace, looking at our failure will only result in demoralization.

Facing our failure is also a voluntary act of sacrificial suffering. The agony of soul caused by looking squarely at failure is one aspect of bearing the cross. How many times have you been brought to tears before God over your inability to advance his mission in this world? Not often? Never? What's wrong with this picture? Only those willing to suffer the pangs caused by honestly assessing their own ineffectiveness will have the necessary drive and creativity to discover successful paths.

God granted my own church the opportunity to practice this last year. For multiple complicated reasons that we don't fully understand, we had a miserable year with hardly any growth, and that's not our usual experience. Even our thriving student ministry was stalemated to an alarming degree, and a number of other signs were negative. Of course, the picture is always cloudy; it was a good year for world missions and social service ministry. We've had years like this before, but when thousands of people have trusted your leadership, this is an agonizing experience.

Our top leadership was doomed to spending weeks of painful questioning and analysis. Was God just giving us a chance to consolidate the gains of earlier years? Or was it one of the far more likely reasons: sin in the church, ineffective ministry methods, a hardening field of ministry? Anyone who has engaged in a lengthy assessment like this knows how painful it is to care from the deepest part of your heart but face an overall gloomy outlook. I got the duty of breaking the news at our big annual "state of the church" meeting. How I longed to be encouraging and positive! But that's not what the facts warranted. I hope my call to trust in God's power and love and try again was at least somewhat encouraging.

God often calls Christians to serve in failure. Nearly every servant of God in the Bible had to withstand profound failure at times. Some, like Jeremiah and Isaiah, had to withstand failure *all the time*. Nobody ever listened to these men of God, and all the consequences they warned people about eventually came to pass. This could happen to us. But are we willing to become weeping prophets over our failure like they were? Or will we comfort ourselves by buying in to Satan's delusion that we're doing fine?

Results in ministry are not our first calling. Servants of God "must be faithful" no matter what (1 Corinthians 4:2). God is more interested in faithfulness than in results. But Paul also says, "Therefore I run in such a way, as not without aim; I box in such a way, as not beating the air" (9:26 NASB). He explains, "Though I am free from all men, I have made myself a slave to all, so that I may win more" (9:19 NASB). Paul saw faithfulness as the first priority, but results also do matter. After all, Jesus told us to "make disciples of all the nations" (Matthew 28:19), not merely to have good intentions.

By breaking our overall ministry goal down into smaller parts, we can see more clearly how Satan uses diversion to misguide our efforts.

Evangelism

Satan knows he must divert our efforts away from effective means of reaching people for Christ. For most believers today, he does this through intimidation, accusation, and deception. We will discuss intimidation and accusation later. Here, we want to think about deception. What are Satan's main lies in this area?

Large numbers of Christians in the West today believe in an extreme form of fatalism that makes sharing their faith irrelevant. Fatalism is the view that all things are fated to be a certain way, so it's pointless to try to "change the future." While Christians who assume fatalism also know God commands us to share our faith, they lack the motivation to do so because they feel the command makes no sense. This error has nothing to do with belonging to a Calvinistic tradition. Calvinist interpreters teach that when God ordains the ends, he also ordains the means to those ends. In other words, God knows who the elect are, but he also knows who will present his call to them, so our witnessing *does* matter.

When you believe in fatalism, you think that if you don't share the gospel with someone, God will see to it that someone else does, or maybe he will win the person himself, without human agency. In any case, little is at stake when you turn away from testifying under this kind of thinking. This is the view one leader hurled at William Carey in 1786: "Young man, sit down; when God pleases to convert the heathen, he will do it without your aid and mine." If Carey had listened to this counsel from J. R. Ryland, he never would have launched the modern missionary movement God has used to reach millions around the world.

If you've had such thoughts, have you recognized this as the voice of the Evil One? Such thoughts are not the voice of God: he says, "How can they believe in [Christ] if they have never heard about him? And how can they hear about him unless someone tells them?" (Romans 10:14).

Fatalistic people direct their efforts toward things other than evangelism. The sad truth is that in the West, millions of fatalistic Christians rarely if ever lift a finger to share the gospel with anyone. But this is not necessarily the fruit of soft commitment and worldliness. Many of these believers are highly active in church music, acts of service, counseling, and political agitation. They're not necessarily do-nothings, but they have been diverted from the most important work. When enough believers conclude that evangelism doesn't matter much, the entire church grinds to a halt in its mission.

Satan also diverts Christians from good evangelism by convincing them to use strategies that will never work. Partly because of the ghettoization caused by fortress theology, Western Christians seem largely out of touch with how non-Christians think and perceive the world. When you live in isolation from those with whom you hope to communicate, you have to guess at what would be appealing or meaningful to them. You are not in a position to use your own sensitivity in relationship to see when you're getting through with your message. In short, you have a poor understanding of non-Christian motivation and thought.

In my view, several of the top evangelistic methods Christians trust today are actually diversions from effective approaches. I think these include worship evangelism, public spectacles, and accommodation (to postmodernism or to lust for health and wealth). Not only are these approaches alien to the Bible, but evidence cited in the footnotes also shows they simply do not work.[4]

Where can we turn for effective evangelistic ideas? In my opinion, *Becoming a Contagious Christian,* by Bill Hybels and Mark Mittelberg, offers a well-balanced and effective approach to personal evangelism. You need not agree with the whole seeker approach advanced by Hybels' church, but studies show that Willow Creek Community Church significantly exceeds most other churches in conversion composition. I believe this is because they teach their people how to reach out to non-Christians in realistic and biblical ways.

Discipleship

The New Testament church practiced personal disciplemaking widely and apparently developed all of their leadership through this approach.[5] We should remember that Jesus didn't call us only to make *converts* but to make *disciples* of all nations. Somehow, though, after the second century, Satan has virtually eradicated personal disciplemaking from the history of the church. Today we see some resurgence of disciplemaking in the West, and a good deal on various mission fields, but studies show that very few American Christians ever try to disciple a younger believer.[6] Instead, we trust "new believer" classes and other programs to do this task, even though evidence is all around us that such programs are largely inadequate.

If over 95 percent of all Western Christians see no need to try to make disciples, Satan has accomplished an astonishing feat of diversion. Again, we're not talking about uncommitted believers who never think about ministry in the first place; this includes committed Christians who spend significant time in ministry.

Healing and Nurture

God calls the body of Christ to be a place of healing and spiritual nurture for lost and broken people. He wouldn't give gifts like healings (the plural implies different kinds of healing—physical, emotional, and spiritual), encouragement, teaching, and wisdom if Christians weren't supposed to have ministries in these areas. Good ministry involves "admonishing every man and teaching every man with all wisdom, so that we may present every man complete in Christ" (Colossians 1:28 NASB).

The church does a better job in the area of nurture than it does in other areas, even though most Christians take no hand in the work. Christians today often believe that only professional pastors or counselors are qualified to work with people's lives. Too many fail to see that nurture and healing should include a move away from self-oriented *receiving* help to effectively *giving* help to others. Leaders have not convinced their members that they should pursue building their own ministries. If we leave broken people feeling better but still focused on themselves, we have not really healed them. In some churches, being neurotic and unstable is the best way, and maybe the only way, to get attention. We tend to people while they are in crisis but frequently don't guide them into maturity.

Serving the Poor and Disadvantaged

The ethics of generosity in helping the poor is rooted in the person and work of Christ himself:

> You know the generous grace of our Lord Jesus Christ. Though he was rich, yet for your sakes he became poor, so that by his poverty he could make you rich. (2 Corinthians 8:9)

Jesus' example should lead us to see our responsibility to use the wealth God has entrusted to us to glorify him by sharing with the poor.

John draws the connection this way:

> We know what real love is because Jesus gave up his life for us. So we also ought to give up our lives for our brothers and sisters. If someone has enough money to live well and sees a brother or sister in need but shows no compassion—how can God's love be in that person? (1 John 3:16–19)

Caring for the physical needs of others is an essential part of what it means to love others as we love ourselves (see the parable of the good Samaritan in Luke 10:25–37; see also Matthew 25:34–40). Church historians say that the Western evangelical church drifted away from social ministry after the 1800s, but they also see a resurgent interest in recent years. Our biggest concern today is not only that the church continue to take seriously God's call to share with the poor and disadvantaged; we also have to make sure we direct our energy into projects that result in real, lasting life change for poor communities. Just as in other areas, Satan will divert any new interest in social justice into ineffective channels. The most common diversion we see today has been called "gingerbread" social ministries.

A gingerbread house is carefully decorated for appearance, and sometimes it looks quite cute. But you wouldn't want to try to live in one! Gingerbread houses are just for show or for having some fun doing a craft with the kids.

A gingerbread ministry is analogous because such ministries don't change people's lives in any lasting way and may be more for the show or for the enjoyment of the one doing the ministry. I remember as a kid how my church would have the youth group take turkeys or fruit baskets to shut-ins or poor people just before Thanksgiving. It always bothered me to walk up to one of these houses with my basket (although the people were always grateful). I wondered to myself, *What about the rest of the year? Why are we just taking something to them at Thanksgiving? Who are these people, and is this really meaningful help?*

Unfortunately, too many social ministry programs are only temporary handout programs that will have little or no lasting effect on the lives of the poor. In fact, studies show that handout ministries may do more harm than good, creating dependency and demeaning people's sense of significance. Teaching the poor how to work their way out of poverty in a lasting way is far more daunting than providing a turkey once a year.

We can be thankful for some outstanding examples of in-depth social ministries in America today, and even more in other countries. However, far too many churches have been diverted into gingerbread social ministries. Food pantries, soup kitchens, and homeless shelters could all be legitimate parts of a thorough community development strategy. But by themselves they do little to change the long-term cycle of poverty holding people in its grip.

Equipping

Again, the New Testament is clear that the church is to equip its members for the work of ministry (Ephesians 4:11–12), but somehow Satan has diverted efforts away from this project to an amazing degree. While most churches have some sort of equipping ministry, only a small minority in the church attends, and such equipping classes tend to be superficial. Objective studies show that regular attendees of many evangelical churches are painfully ignorant and ill-equipped.[7] A few weeks of leadership training classes can hardly be expected to present people "complete in Christ," especially when members believe that equipping is up to the staff alone. If we hadn't lost the New Testament emphasis on personal disciplemaking, people would be far more successful in learning how to wield the Bible and other spiritual weapons in real life.

CONCLUSION

If major studies today are demonstrating that most Western Christians aren't effective in evangelism, don't believe in personal disciplemaking, engage in little community development, and haven't equipped people in the church to serve God, what are they doing with their time and money?[8] For many, the answer is "nothing." Too many Christians have never been convinced that the church is anything other than a place we go to have our own needs met. One church in our area recently put up a question on their church sign: "Is your church still meeting your needs?" Such a message probably calls to many self-centered Christians in the church's quest for transfer growth.

Leaders are often squeamish about asking for time and commitment from people who are committed to the world-system as their first priority. Many other Christians realize they should serve God and expend significant time and effort each week, trying their best to do so. Yet the Western church continues to decline, remains shallow, does not build real community, and has not equipped its members—all because of successful diversion. The church does a great deal of good. But we could do so much better if we discerned Satan's tactics to divert efforts into areas doomed to failure from God's perspective.

Changing the situation cannot mean we simply add more work and ministry to the schedule. Instead, we have to be prepared to assess and eliminate ineffective and unbiblical ministries in favor of more effective ones. Any ministry can be ineffective at times, and we don't want to be quitters just because the going gets tough. We must ask the hard questions:

1. Am I sure that what I am doing is called for in the Bible?

2. Has this approach ever had success? How do I know? How recently? (An approach that had success in the '50s or '60s won't necessarily work today.)

3. Am I aware of anyone else who is succeeding using this approach? Are they doing anything differently?

4. If others are succeeding using other approaches, should I consider changing mine? (Make sure their success is real and not merely apparent. It should also be biblical and ethical.)

5. Should I try to think outside the box and devise an approach we haven't thought of before?

CHAPTER 16

SATAN AND YOUR MINISTRY: OPPOSITION

If the Evil One is unable to divert Christian efforts into useless projects, he still has options for derailing ministry that include intimidation, temptation, interdiction, and failure. He can be especially successful in this endeavor if believers are unaware of his schemes. In fact, those engaged in fruitful ministries can expect, more than anyone, to meet up with Satan along the way.

INTIMIDATION

Satan uses accusation to intimidate those trying to serve God. He constantly tries to convince servants that they should quit what they are doing or they will do more damage than good. Because we're so imperfect, Satan often has good material to work with when convincing Christians they don't belong in ministry.

Incompetence

The devil tries to persuade servants of God that they are too incompetent to do what they hope to do. This is usually a relatively easy sell; most of us know we lack competence and wonder if someone with our level of proficiency should really even try to serve. But while our basic competency comes from God (2 Corinthians 3:5), it's developed and enhanced through practice as well as equipping (training). I remember how incompetent I felt as a young Christian worker, and others were eager to point it out from time to time; however, I'm glad my spiritual counselors urged me to pursue competency while continuing in ministry rather than quitting, as I sometimes wanted to do. During the years since, God has allowed me to be a part of a movement that has reached thousands for Christ and that hopefully will continue to expand in the future. Now, nearly forty years later, I find myself still feeling incompetent, sometimes more than ever.

When feeling a lack of skill or knowledge, we should consider some important questions that Satan never brings up: Though I may be lacking in some areas, where would the church be if I quit? Are there others more competent who could step in and take my place? Does a semi-incompetent ministry give way to no ministry? Also, if I am truly incompetent now, how can I become competent? Have I considered that most Christian workers feel this way from time to time?

Even the greatest New Testament church planter felt inadequate at times. In 2 Corinthians, Paul discusses an episode of inner anguish he experienced in the Roman province of Asia. He recounts, "I had no rest for my spirit" (2:13 NASB), but goes on to speak of how he resolved his feelings: "Not that we are adequate in ourselves to consider anything as *coming* from ourselves, but our adequacy is from God" (3:5 NASB).

Here is what Satan, who wants us to quit, doesn't want us to think about: *God uses incompetent people!* As long as we have God's Spirit working through us, even the least competent servant can do amazing things. We should use our felt incompetence as motivation to pray more. This is an opportunity to develop dependency on God. Yes, we would probably be more effective if we became more competent. But God can teach us while we continue serving.

Hopelessness

Sometimes Satan argues against the feasibility of our task. This is different from arguing against the competency of workers (although he can certainly combine the arguments). Christians suffering this kind of attack have thoughts like: *The mission you are pursuing simply can't be done. It's too difficult under present conditions. Nobody wants to hear this. Nobody's interested in this. People hate what you're saying. Your expectations of commitment, servitude, and spirituality from today's people are unrealistic. People won't accept this. Too many factors are stacked against you. Nobody's moving. Nobody's changing.*

Underlying all these charges is the same conclusion: *Give up!* If Satan can convince believers that their job is too difficult to be realistic, demoralization and discouragement set in. Motivation drains away. Who feels excited about exerting themselves on a project they know will never work?

Notice how these thoughts batter your mind right before trying to teach the Word or share your faith. The afternoon before a Bible study may regularly be filled with depressing thoughts about how pointless your effort is. Like clockwork, the Enemy shows up ready to rain down punishing, discouraging thoughts during the hours and even days before workers go forth to serve. In any normal group, Satan has more than enough negative factors from which to make his case. What are we to do?

First, realize that this is a good sign. Satanic opposition is a hallmark of all healthy, fruitful ministries. Leaders in particular must accept that feeling such awful inner dread and despair is inevitable if they want their prayers for fruitfulness answered. Rather than being worried that we feel battered by inner doubts, we should feel worried when we *don't* feel these accusing voices. Merely realizing that Satan is speaking to your mind is one of the best defenses. Ask yourself, "Would God say this to me?"

Second, watch for micro-movement in your ministry. Every small positive change in people is a refutation of the lying claims that you're ineffective, that God isn't going to work, and that the situation is hopeless. Maybe the large-scale changes you desire haven't happened, but change comes slowly among fallen people. Cultivate patience. Of course, if ineffectiveness goes on too long, we need to reconsider our methods and perhaps our whole direction; just don't jump to this conclusion.

When I'm under attack like this, I find relief by reviewing my calling. When I remember God's call to serve, I can draw comfort from knowing

I'm being faithful to it. Remembering God's faithfulness in earlier years as he made it clear that I should serve him helps me deflect the negative thoughts tormenting my soul.

But one defense is far more important than any of these: *We must learn how to claim the scriptural promises given to ministering Christians.* God repeatedly makes it clear that building his kingdom is not impossible or hopeless. He put his own personal power on the line in these promises, making it clear that he is able to do this task and that he will use us in this process.

For example, "Thanks be to God, who always leads us in triumph in Christ, and manifests through us the sweet aroma of the knowledge of Him in every place" (2 Corinthians 2:14 NASB). Jesus said, "Upon this rock I will build my church, and the powers of hell will not conquer [withstand] it" (Matthew 16:18), and he said this without qualifications. Believers should realize there is no chance he will fail to do as he says, regardless of temporary setbacks. "The entire body, being supplied and held together by the joints and ligaments, grows with a growth which is from God" (Colossians 2:19 NASB). Paul describes Christ's power in the church this way:

> [Christ] from whom the whole body, being fitted and held together by what every joint supplies, according to the proper working of each individual part, causes the growth of the body for the building up of itself in love. (Ephesians 4:16 NASB)

Jesus said, "You will receive power when the Holy Spirit comes upon you. And you will be my witnesses, telling people about me everywhere— in Jerusalem, throughout Judea, in Samaria, and to the ends of the earth" (Acts 1:8). In the words of Paul: "I am not ashamed of this Good News about Christ. It is the power of God at work, saving everyone who believes" (Romans 1:16). If we believe God's Word is true, how plausible do Satan's demoralizing charges sound? Learn to recite passages like these to him when he attacks with thoughts of hopelessness.

Unworthiness

Satan also accuses serving Christians of being unworthy to serve. In this case, unworthiness refers to the inconsistency between the ideal of mature faith and our own selfish, undisciplined, sinful lives. Satan has only one solution: Quit.

Of course, some believers fall into such serious sin that they should step aside and seek restoration. Continuing to serve in ministry when you have unresolved serious sin can bring disgrace onto God. Recent scandals involving adultery, homosexual activity, drug abuse, divorce, and theft of church funds should never have happened. Anyone struggling with something like this should immediately come clean to colleagues who will decide how best to resolve the problem. When discussing the qualifications for leaders, Paul stresses elements of character more than anything else (1 Timothy 3:1–13; Titus 1:6–9). Even though these are for elders and deacons, the principles should apply to most areas of service.

But we also see many home group leaders, teachers, and evangelists thinking they should quit merely because they're struggling with things like a poor prayer life, lust, pride, laziness, an injured marriage, or a disorganized family. Dropping out of ministry in such scenarios is questionable. For one thing, if we bring only those with no such issues into ministry, the church will have no ministers at all. Do we really believe some Christians are so mature they don't have problems? If so, I wonder why we can't attract any to our church!

It would be great to have such super-believers in key ministry roles, but we have to serve in the real world. Without justifying sin in any way, we must insist that God calls sinful people into ministry. Too often Christians who present themselves as those who have conquered sin either are faking it or have a weak doctrine of sin—ignoring sins of omission or inner sins that nobody sees. We are constantly amazed at how God builds his kingdom using defective, damaged people. God's army attacks the enemy line bandaged, hobbling on crutches, and with arms in slings.

When Satan hurls the burning javelin of accusation that you are unworthy to serve God, remember the following:

1. *Choose Transparency.* Part of Satan's lie when accusing us of unworthiness is that if others found out how sinful we are, they would turn away with horrified faces and instantly hurl us out of ministry. But this is rarely true. More likely they will admit they have a similar problem or at least one just as significant. Satan is desperate to keep us in the bondage of secrecy about our sins. He knows that if we keep our problems secret, (1) we will be unable to draw on the help of others for deliverance, (2) we will likely reach the conclusion that our struggles are unique and worse than anyone else's, (3) we will grieve the Holy Spirit because we are deceiving our colleagues, and (4) we will keep sinning, because in so many areas the key to progress is bringing the sin into the light. Tell fellow workers in the church, including your leaders, that you are having a problem, and be specific.

2. *Embrace Grace.* Not only are we justified by grace and grow by grace, but we also minister by grace. No Christian is worthy to minister for God, including you. But the question is what should we do about it? Quit? Disbelieve that God will use us? Shut our mouths? This is what Satan hopes. Instead, in ministry, just like in other areas, we must learn to approach God purely on the basis of his grace—his undeserved favor.

3. *Draw Close to God.* "Resist the devil, and he will flee from you. Come close to God, and God will come close to you" (James 4:7–8). Christians struggling with accusation often find themselves alienated from intimacy with God. Accusation is serving as a wedge to drive them away; they feel too guilt-ridden and ashamed to approach God with boldness. Only the breastplate of his righteousness and the shield of faith will deflect these arrows of accusation.

4. *Continue to Work on Your Problems.* Instead of rationalizing and hiding sin, strive to trust God more with your struggles. Don't stop seeking help.

5. *Use Scriptural Truth to Refute Satan's Charges.* God is clear that all ministry depends on his power, not on our worthiness. Christians

withering under constant demonic reminders of their own unworthiness should remember passages like these:

I can do everything through Christ, who gives me strength. (Philippians 4:13)

We have this treasure in earthen vessels, so that the surpassing greatness of the power will be of God and not from ourselves. (2 Corinthians 4:7 NASB)

[The Lord] said, "My grace is all you need. My power works best in weakness." So now I am glad to boast about my weaknesses, so that the power of Christ can work through me. (2 Corinthians 12:9)

Threats

Christian servants often live with an impending sense of doom. Even when things are going well they may feel like all their work is a house of cards that could collapse any minute. These feelings usually signal Satan's threatening voice, especially when they are irrational and persistent.

When Paul was in the middle of a significant spiritual awakening in Corinth—when numerous people had come to Christ, and they had moved out of the synagogue and into homes, becoming not a small group, but a budding movement—how was Paul feeling as he lay in bed at night? Exhilarated? Gratified? Content? No. Jesus had to visit him in person one night and say, "Do not be afraid any longer" (Acts 18:9 NASB). Paul was scared. I find it strangely comforting to read that this bold and courageous apostle was so overcome with fear that Jesus brought him words of encouragement.

Facing fear is often the lot of those who serve God. Satan blusters, threatens us with destruction, and usually with much more than he can deliver. But for those who have seen his blows over the years, these threats carry weight. Less experienced servants of God may become even more frightened. Our fears can become downright irrational.

Many Christians report experiences of sensing the presence of a demon, perhaps in their bedroom at night, encounters that frequently are extremely frightening and sometimes have a lingering effect. When these experiences do involve the activity of Satan, he is again threatening and persecuting believers, often in an effort to deter them from potential acts of service for God.

Understood properly, Satan is sticking his thumbs in his ears while flapping his hands and saying, "I'm going to huff, and I'm going to puff, and I'm going to blooowww your house down!" But our houses are built with brick. In actuality, believers are profoundly secure in Christ. We have to learn to draw all security from faith in our position in him and his watch-care over his church. When walking in the Spirit, Christians face nothing from Satan that God can't handle: "Greater is He who is in you than he who is in the world" (1 John 4:4 NASB).

Satan's intent in these threats is to create stress and distraction. One could easily spend the whole day worrying rather than creatively and prayerfully thinking about how to proceed. Instead, we should point out, "It is written":

> Now all glory to God, who is able, through his mighty power at work within us, to accomplish infinitely more than we might ask or think. (Ephesians 3:20)

> God has not given us a spirit of fear and timidity, but of power, love, and self-discipline. (2 Timothy 1:7)

> Don't worry about anything; instead, pray about everything. Tell God what you need, and thank him for all he has done. Then you will experience God's peace, which exceeds anything we can understand. His peace will guard your hearts and minds as you live in Christ Jesus. (Philippians 4:6–7)

> Jesus came and told his disciples, "I have been given all authority in heaven and on earth. Therefore, go and make disciples of all the nations. . . . And be sure of this: I am with you always, even to the end of the age" (Matthew 28:18–20).

Even when I walk through the dark valley, I will not be afraid, for you are close beside me. (Psalm 23:4)

God is protecting you by his power until you receive this salvation, which is ready to be revealed on the last day for all to see. (1 Peter 1:5)

Christian workers who take up the sword of the Spirit and believe God's powerful promises for protection and fruitfulness consistently turn back Satan's threats. These inner battles may go on for hours or even days, but if we battle through and show up ready to serve, Satan loses.

TEMPTATION

Satan has special temptations for those who minister. During times of success he tempts them to pride and carelessness. During times of failure he tempts them to discouragement and unbelief. At the root of both is the effort to make spiritual workers see ministry as depending mainly on human effort rather than on God's power. The more he can get believers to view their ministry humanistically, the more he can drive them toward a host of mistakes that will undermine the ministry's spirituality.

When believers fall to Satan's temptation to put self at the center of ministry, their temperaments begin to take over. Aggressive people become impatient, pressuring others, losing their temper, and overextending. Passive people become pleasers, being soft in their dealings and cowering in fear of making strong calls for action and change.

INTERDICTION

In military terminology, interdiction refers to delaying, disrupting, or destroying enemy forces or supplies en route to battle. Paul tells his friends in Thessalonica, "We wanted very much to come to you, and I, Paul, tried again and again, but Satan prevented us" (1 Thessalonians 2:18). How did Satan prevent Paul from visiting? We don't know. But we know he does sometimes succeed in interfering with our plans in a variety of ways. He has agents he can mobilize. He can cause companies to make decisions about your people. We mentioned earlier the classic case of the new Christian who hasn't been able to get a date for a year being suddenly confronted with someone showing attraction. Satan can cause accidents, make lights go out during a teaching, and flight connections to fail. Anything constituting part of the world-system is under his control (1 John 5:19).

One of Satan's most dangerous types of interference involves his effort to carry believers in your ministry away from good spiritual nutriment, including involvement with fellow Christians. He can lure young believers away from God by having friends show up with free drugs, illicit sex, or the like. He frequently brings young believers into contact with false teachers.

As servant-workers, we not only have to withstand Satan's attacks on our own minds, we also have to learn how to protect God's flock from attacks on them. When we anticipate these enemy moves we have opportunity either to block his plans through prayer or to render them ineffective through instruction, encouragement, and counseling. Paul said to his friends in Corinth,

> I fear that somehow your pure and undivided devotion to Christ will be corrupted, just as Eve was deceived by the cunning ways of the serpent. You happily put up with whatever anyone tells you, even if they preach a different Jesus than the one we preach, or a different kind of Spirit than the one you received, or a different kind of gospel than the one you believed. (2 Corinthians 11:3–4)

I know this feeling all too well. How aggravating it is to work patiently in bringing a guy to Christ, only to have some extremist or cultist move in with falsehood. In their excitement for the things of God, young Christians often have little resistance to novel perspectives; Satan knows that spiritual infancy is the time to get them off track.

Knowing how vulnerable people are to the Evil One's manipulation, we need to anticipate, watch for his activity, and be ready to protect. God often compares leaders of his people to shepherds, and one of the main points in having shepherds is protection. Jesus describes how "a hired hand" will run away when a wolf threatens the sheep, but the good shepherd lays his life down to protect them (John 10). We know how Jesus laid down his life, but in what sense will we have to lay down our lives to protect God's people from the wolf? While we can never protect our people completely, we can prevent many attacks if we're willing to pay the price.

First, there is a sacrifice involved in learning how Satan works. Through study and personal experience, we must come to know our enemy in a deep way.

Next, there is the sacrifice of constantly praying for our people by name and allowing God to show us areas of vulnerability and likely avenues of satanic attack. The burden of constant watchfulness is heavy. While others zone out before their systems of entertainment, effective Christian workers spend the time and effort to bear their friends before God in prayer, asking for discernment. Then they develop strategies for heading off or countering attacks from Satan. Observant and prayerful leaders often recognize the clues of impending attack. At other times, God may reveal things they had no way of knowing, along with ideas for how to respond. God empowers such attentive and alert leaders to turn back one attack after another.

No wonder Peter stresses the need for alertness and a sober spirit (sharp thinking and sound judgment) in leaders.

> Be of sober spirit, be on the alert. Your adversary, the devil, prowls around like a roaring lion, seeking someone to devour. But resist him, firm in your faith. (1 Peter 5:7–9 NASB)

Unless leaders are prepared to pay the price of continual watchfulness in prayer for their people, Satan will dismantle their ministries one person at a time. Because of the sheer burden of watching out for all the sheep, we should have many shepherds over small flocks in the church. Churches organized only in large groups are at the mercy of Satan, and we can expect no mercy from him.

FAILURE

Satan may or may not be able to cause failure in your ministry. But no matter what, you will experience ministry failure. God calls every one of his servants to minister in failure at times, and maybe many times.

Facing significant failure presents believers with a fork in the road. For some, failure is the occasion for creative thinking, new learning, deepening convictions, and a new appreciation of grace. For others, failure signals a turn to demoralization, recriminations, bitterness, and quitting (or even a shift to cheating, lying, and manipulation). One of the key factors determining which way people go is whether they recognize Satan's voice in times of failure.

The Evil One has a battery of arguments ready for any Christian he sees failing. Often, Satan argues that failing in ministry (or in other areas of life) is a sign that God has forsaken you, usually out of disappointment in your lack of spirituality and commitment. At other times, failure must mean you are ill-suited for such work (even though it's hard to imagine any kind of sophisticated work you can master without ever failing). Sometimes Satan claims that your failure just points to how unreasonable you are for thinking this kind of work is possible. All the possibilities add up to the same conclusion: Give it up!

Satan is also an expert at pressing how embarrassing failure is: "What must people be thinking? What a fool you look like!" He plants these thoughts in your mind to stir up a fever of self-protectiveness. Under this manipulation, you may decide not only to quit but also to make doubly sure you never get into a similar position again. Whether the failure involved witnessing, discipleship, or group leadership, you may join the ranks of those who have permanently un-volunteered for further vulnerability in ministry.

Embarrassed workers may also seek to off-load responsibility by firing angry accusations at others. Languishing ministries are notorious for division. Christians working from an ego-driven base cannot handle failure, making them highly vulnerable to Satan's suggestions that they should attack fellow believers, blaming them for spoiling everything, failing to help, or putting them in a situation where they would fail.

CONCLUSION

With opposition, just as with Satan's other main avenues of attack, the biggest danger is believing his lies and accepting his interpretation of events. We have so much more to fear from Satan's convincing suggestions than we do from anything else he can hurl at us. Our own apathetic lack of alertness and prayer are big problems as well. Only believers who daily, prayerfully watch for satanic moves are in position to anticipate his schemes in time to do something about them. Once God alerts us to a probable move, we can use prayer and proactive counseling and instruction to provide safety for our people.

CHAPTER 17

SATAN'S POWER MOVES

In the Western world, Satan most often prefers to work in stealthy ways. After spending centuries fostering a materialistic mindset, he apparently feels it would be a mistake to contradict that with obvious displays of spiritual power. If Westerners saw demon possession and other acts of naked satanic power, they might begin watching for him instead of slumbering in comfort-driven, self-centered apathy.

In other regions, where people are already convinced that spirits are real, he usually takes a very different approach. Instead of counting on their lack of awareness of the spirit world, he uses their spiritualism against them. In these cultures, he doesn't lull people to sleep with continual entertainment and greed but instead lures them into the realm of the occult. There, practitioners openly summon the power of demons to give people what they want. These "blessings," though, aren't without a price. Satan never gives anything away. His intention isn't to heal or protect but to degrade and destroy.

Recent developments suggest this situation may be changing, especially among the postmodern generation. Western young people are increasingly open to spiritual solutions to their problems as they feel science and materialism have let them down and left them empty. But as the biblical worldview falls into eclipse, people frequently turn their openness toward the occult and nature religions. At the same time, people in developing countries are progressively more interested in taking their turn at materialism. To respond appropriately, Christian workers in both worlds have to become more versatile and knowledgeable.

OCCULT POWER

Demonic subjection usually relates to the occult. The word *occult* means "hidden" and refers to a collection of practices and beliefs known from the most ancient times. Herein people hope to obtain healing, protection, or even revenge against enemies, all with the help of spirit beings. They often think these beings are gods or benevolent spirits, but according to the Bible, they are accessing demons. Throughout human history, occult practice follows a remarkably uniform pattern. Key principles and practices betray this similarity regardless of the names and the stories in which they appear.

Instead of helping people, Satan gives blessings or favors (real or apparent) in exchange for *influence*. He obtains this ability to take control of people's lives because they've come to him for something. They may not realize what they are doing or with whom they are dealing, but that doesn't matter to him—he won't hesitate to seize control without his victims' knowledge. His control can range from intermittent influence to the extreme of demon possession. Although the term *demon possession* is a questionable translation of the Greek (which means "to have a demon" or "to be characterized by a demon"), we will use the socially accepted term. In possession, a person is inhabited by an evil spirit and apparently loses freedom of choice to a greater or lesser extent.

Human Vulnerability

Occult thinking begins with human fear and insecurity. People have basic needs, and they worry that these needs will not be met. They need food. They need protection from disease, enemies, infertility, and disaster. They need to know what's going to happen so they can adjust their plans. Without access to medical and scientific solutions to these problems, people often turn to the spirit world. Personal need and perceived danger are the primary motives for seeking out occult spiritual power.

Once people reach the conclusion that they are in danger and that the spirit world holds the solution, the question becomes how to access that power. Historically, the most common means for accessing spirit power are shaman figures and magic.

Shamanism

Shamans are intermediaries with the spirit world and channelers of spirit power. Known under many names—medicine men, witch doctors, priests, psychics, wizards, witches, wise men, mediums, and healers of various types—they all serve the same purpose and follow a similar pattern of operation. The person in need of healing, protection, or fertility approaches the shaman figure for help. The shaman usually goes into a trance or a ritual (sometimes with drugs), intended to signify his or her contacting the spirit world, and then invokes spirits to give insight, heal, or otherwise bless the person or curse his enemy. These could be animal spirits or spirits of departed people. Disease may be "healed" by exorcizing the demon causing it.

Both the seeker and the shaman figure will often actively seek spirit possession during these sessions. People may go on vision quests where they meet their spirit guide or protector in life. Sometimes, in group ceremonies, whole villages seek spirit possession together.[1]

Magic

Traditional magic is intimately connected to shamanism but also may be practiced without the aid of a shaman. The underlying concept behind traditional magic is, again, accessing the power of spiritual beings to heal, protect, give fertility, or to curse.

In this magic (unrelated to sleight of hand), pieces of bark, animal parts, rocks, or other natural objects are collected and used in ritual ways to affect the future. People believe these objects can channel associated spirits. So a woods spirit can be summoned by a piece of bark from those woods. These "medicines" can be made into a poultice (to smear on the body), a spirit-trap, a talisman worn around the neck, eaten, or in a thousand other ways applied to the supplicant. Normally, along with the magical material, people recite incantations and perform rituals intended to invoke spirits.

At other times magic involves using designs, rhythms, word sequences, body movements, tattoos, or star patterns to tap into natural forces through understanding spirit power. Certain words chanted in a rhythm, for instance, might repel spirits or summon them. Astrology is based on the belief that the stars and planets are spirit beings that come into varying degrees of power during different times of the year.

THE OCCULT IN THE BIBLE

The Old Testament

Not surprisingly, God says that any involvement with the occult is a serious sin. He doesn't want his people accessing Satan's power for any reason.

> When you enter the land the Lord your God is giving you, be very careful not to imitate the detestable customs of the nations living there. For example, never sacrifice your son or daughter as a burnt offering. And do not let your people practice fortune-telling or use sorcery, or interpret omens, or engage in witchcraft, or cast spells, or function as mediums or psychics, or call forth the spirits of the dead. Anyone who does these things is detestable to the Lord. (Deuteronomy 18:9–12)

So disgusted is God by the occult that he said, "I will also turn against those who commit spiritual prostitution by putting their trust in mediums or those who consult the spirits of the dead. I will cut them off from the community" (Leviticus 20:6). Any doubt that this entails capital punishment disappears in verse 27: "Men and women among you who act as mediums or who consult the spirits of the dead must be put to death by stoning. They are guilty of a capital offense."

Contemporary readers are often shocked and offended when they read that God would have punished religious practices by death. But this is mostly a reflection of a materialistic mindset in which spiritual things don't matter much. It also reflects our relativism, which holds that nothing is really objectively true or false. For those who believe in the objective reality of God, Satan, and hell, however, things look different. If destroying a person's physical life is worthy of capital punishment, why wouldn't destroying their soul deserve the same? The severity of the penalty shows how seriously God views occult involvement. Israel was surrounded by nations that thrived on the occult, and they were tempted to imitate dangerous spiritual practices. Many of the measures prescribed in the law were to guard against the Israelites' weakness for idol worship and the related occult practices and beliefs.

Even the strict measures God prescribed were not always successful. Scattered throughout the Old Testament are indications that both idol worship and the occult penetrated Israel at many points. The evil king Manasseh practiced nearly everything mentioned in the passages above:

> [Manasseh] built these altars for all the powers of the heavens in both courtyards of the Lord's Temple. Manasseh also sacrificed his own sons in the fire in the valley of Ben-Hinnom. He practiced sorcery, divination, and witchcraft, and he consulted with mediums and psychics. He did much that was evil in the Lord's sight, arousing his anger. (2 Chronicles 33:5–6)

The prophets often expressed bitter frustration at the widespread occult practices in Israel. Isaiah cried,

> Stand fast now in your spells and in your many sorceries with which you have labored from your youth; perhaps you will be able to profit, perhaps you may cause trembling. You are wearied with your many counsels; let now the astrologers, those who prophesy by the stars, those who predict by the new moons, stand up and save you from what will come upon you. Behold, they have become like stubble, fire burns them. (Isaiah 47:12–14 NASB)

He also wondered, "Shouldn't people ask God for guidance? Should the living seek guidance from the dead? [It seems] people who contradict [God's] word are completely in the dark" (8:19–20). Jeremiah warned, "Do not listen to your false prophets, fortune-tellers, interpreters of dreams, mediums, and sorcerers who say, 'The king of Babylon will not conquer you.' They are all liars, and their lies will lead to your being driven out of your land. I will drive you out and send you far away to die" (Jeremiah 27:9–10).

Here we see a key feature of most occult practitioners: lying. Both observation and Scripture confirm that the vast majority of apparent occult miracles are pure deception. Science generally has been unable to duplicate telepathy, premonitions, telekinesis, and other occult tricks in the laboratory. Many occultists are charlatans, using sleight of hand and illusion to bilk money from the foolish.

The real problems come when occult power is real. Engaging in occult practices is like playing Russian roulette: You never know when the barrel is going to be loaded. People playing occult games or engaging with mediums or charmers for fun may suddenly find themselves confronted with actual spiritual power. Satan uses the occult to obtain control over people's lives, or what God calls "ensnaring their souls":

> Now, son of man, speak out against the women who prophesy from their own imaginations. This is what the Sovereign Lord says: What sorrow awaits you women who are ensnaring the souls of my people, young and old alike. You tie magic charms on their wrists and furnish them with magic veils. Do you think you can trap others without bringing destruction on yourselves? (Ezekiel 13:17–18)

Overt spiritual phenomena such as demon possession and lesser forms of demonic influence are associated with the occult. God doesn't prohibit the occult to needlessly restrict freedom but to protect people from Satan's power.

When you consider Paul's revelation that those who worship idols are really worshiping demons (1 Corinthians 10:20), the Old Testament Scriptures can be seen in large part as a story of the struggle against demonic religion and the occult. Israel's inability to resist this invoking of demons is one of the biggest themes in preexilic Old Testament literature. However, demon possession is hardly mentioned.

The prophets of Baal carried on in a way that suggests they were seeking spirit possession, although this is not mentioned in the text (see 1 Kings 18). King Saul lost God's Spirit and instead received "an evil spirit from the Lord" (1 Samuel 16:14; 19:9 NASB), but that was an unusual case having nothing to do with the occult. His visit to the medium of Endor happened later (28:7), and some think this was not actually a demon but tormenting conviction and guilt—the spirit, while not evil in itself, had an evil effect on Saul.

We have enough knowledge of this era's pagan religions (in service to Baal, Asherah, Molech, Teraphim, et al.) to know that their worship included occult themes (divination, healing, fertility, etc.), probably leading to spirit possession. But the Bible does not focus on this aspect. This is in line with the Old Testament's shunning attention to the demonic,[2] which we discuss in chapter 19.

Jesus' Ministry

We also saw that satanic activity, including demon possession, rises to a crescendo during Jesus' ministry. It probably makes sense that neither before Jesus came on the scene nor after his death do we detect the same concentration of overt demonic activity. Satan no doubt knew that a key battle was at hand at that time and in that place.

Liberal commentators and non-Christians claim that the high frequency of demonic phenomena in the gospels is just a reflection of that culture's superstition—i.e., ancient people explained every illness or problem as demon possession. But this is wrong; other cultures did blame all illness on demons, but the gospel writers knew the difference between illness and possession:

> News about him [Jesus] spread as far as Syria, and people soon began bringing to him all who were sick. And whatever their sickness or

disease, or if they were demon possessed or epileptic or paralyzed—he healed them all. (Matthew 4:24)

Here we see that even epilepsy, often misdiagnosed as demon possession, is viewed as a distinct condition.

Jesus cast out many demons, but the most dramatic case was that of the so-called Geresene demoniac:

When Jesus climbed out of the boat, a man possessed by an evil spirit came out from a cemetery to meet him. This man lived among the burial caves and could no longer be restrained, even with a chain. Whenever he was put into chains and shackles—as he often was— he snapped the chains from his wrists and smashed the shackles. No one was strong enough to subdue him. Day and night he wandered among the burial caves and in the hills, howling and cutting himself with sharp stones.

When Jesus was still some distance away, the man saw him, ran to meet him, and bowed low before him. With a shriek, he screamed, "Why are you interfering with me, Jesus, Son of the Most High God? In the name of God, I beg you, don't torture me!" For Jesus had already said to the spirit, "Come out of the man, you evil spirit."

Then Jesus demanded, "What is your name?"

And he replied, "My name is Legion, because there are many of us inside this man." Then the spirits begged him again and again not to send them to some distant place. There happened to be a large herd of pigs feeding on the hillside nearby. "Send us into those pigs," the spirits begged. "Let us enter them." So Jesus gave them permission. The evil spirits came out of the man and entered the pigs, and the entire herd of 2,000 pigs plunged down the steep hillside into the lake and drowned in the water. (Mark 5:2–13)

This case of possession is so extreme that it serves as an example of nearly every known symptom of demon possession.

- Nobody could bind him, and he had crushed chains. This seems to indicate extraordinary strength (vv. 3–4).

- His "howling among the burial caves" (v. 5) indicate paroxysms or fits.

- He cut himself with stones (v. 5), which points to a self-destructive tendency.

- He demonstrated hyperesthesia, an ability to know things about others you have never met and which you have no way of knowing. He immediately recognized Jesus as the Son of God. Having telepathic or other occult powers is a sign not found in other mental illnesses or conditions (vv. 6–7).

- He also immediately cried out to Jesus, "Don't torture me!" (v. 7). This aversion has been called spiritual resistance. Demon possessed people are repelled by Jesus and the gospel, unlike psychotic people, who are often fascinated by Jesus. (Note the same features in another case, in Luke 4:33–35.)

- In verse 9, the man spoke with a voice not his own. The presence of different voices or other tongues or personalities could suggest possession. When shamans seeking possession fall into trances, they often speak in strange tongues, which they interpret as the languages of animals.

- In verse 12, the demons pleaded with Jesus to send them into some nearby pigs. This desire and ability to transfer from one victim to another may characterize some demons. (Jesus referred to this danger in Matthew 12:43–45.)

Some of these symptoms could be caused by other conditions. Christians should always check for medical causes before assuming someone is possessed. Careless believers can confuse schizophrenia or epilepsy with demon possession.

A final case recorded in Mark 9 and its parallels elsewhere reveals additional information. A man approached Jesus and said, "I brought my son so you could heal him. . . . I asked your disciples to cast out the evil spirit, but they couldn't do it" (vv. 17–18). This was different from their experience earlier, when they returned from their mission saying, "Lord, even the demons obey us when we use your name!" (Luke 10:17). Jesus cast the demon out, and when his disciples later asked, "Why couldn't we cast out that evil spirit?" Jesus replied, "This kind can be cast out only by prayer" (Mark 9:28–29).

Here we learn that not all demons are alike. This spirit being apparently had more power than those the disciples previously had expelled. Some demons must be able to refuse commands for a time and have to be compelled in a more prolonged spiritual battle. The additional words *and fasting* (found in the King James Version) were later additions to the text. [3] While fasting probably wouldn't hurt, we have no biblical warrant for thinking that fasting facilitates spiritual deliverance.

The Early Church

The Greco-Roman world was awash in the occult. Like other cultures where the occult was widely practiced, spirit possession phenomena were common according to extra-biblical texts. While demon possession seems to fade into the background after the ministry of Jesus, it still appears at times.

Paul confronted a fortune-telling girl in Philippi and cast a demon out of her, saying, "I command you in the name of Jesus Christ to come out of her" (Acts 16:16–18). This is an interesting case, because we learn that the girl had been following Paul for days and crying out, "These men are servants of the Most High God, and they have come to tell you how to be saved."

Here is a clear case of satanic infiltration or counterfeit. Her message seems outwardly true but was probably highly inappropriate in tone and manner (just like today's counterfeits). It caused Paul to feel "exasperated," and in any case he felt no need to have Satan advertise his mission. This story also confirms the linkage between fortune-telling and demon possession.

Paul cast out demons in Ephesus as well (Acts 19:1–12). His success caused the sons of Sceva to imitate him, with disastrous results (vv. 13–16). Their misfortune demonstrated that merely using the name of Jesus in some magical way was ineffective. Only true believers are authorized to speak with his authority.

Perhaps the most remarkable and important Acts story dealing with the occult is in 19:18–19:

> Many who became believers confessed their sinful practices. A number of them who had been practicing magic brought their incantation books and burned them at a public bonfire. The value of the books was several million dollars.

This example of early church practice suggests that occult practitioners who meet Christ should confess their involvement publicly and destroy their paraphernalia. This is a prayer of renunciation, where the believer renounces his or her former involvement, and any known or unknown agreement with Satan, in order to sever any lingering satanic influence and gain freedom.

The account is also interesting because of the incredible value of the book pile. The actual value given is fifty thousand pieces of silver. Considering that a grown man would earn only one of these pieces of silver for a day's work, you can imagine how large this heap must have been. It implies the group in Ephesus was very large and that they were deeply invested in the occult.

CONFRONTING OCCULT PHENOMENA TODAY

Interestingly, the epistles contain no specific teaching on how to cast out demons or deal with related demonic phenomena. In light of how extensive the epistles' teaching is on all phases of Christian ministry, this is a striking void. We have the narrative examples of Paul in Acts and Jesus in the Gospels, but the complete silence on this subject in all subsequent books demands an explanation. The Old Testament doesn't discuss demon possession or deliverance either—this, despite the fact that possession must have been common in the demon-cults followed around and within Israel. What are we to think?

For one thing, I think it suggests exorcism must not be a central part of Christian ministry. Surely if deliverance from possession was integral on the level of preaching the Word, discipleship, evangelism, or prayer, we would have some instruction or reminders. How could Paul, Peter, and the rest fail to mention a central key to ministry success? Instead, their letters focus on dealing with Satan's deception, temptation, and accusation. These more covert or hidden tactics are front and center because we will see Satan acting in these ways far more often than in overt acts of power, like possession.

Leaders of some "deliverance ministries" that center on exorcism as the key to victory in the church and victory over sin must be embarrassed by this silence. Some answer that nothing is said of exorcism because early Christians were so familiar with it that they didn't need any more instruction. But how many other important areas of teaching are missing from the Bible because people "didn't need it"? In addition, how would we ever know if this were true? That dubious claim is an excuse for emphasizing what the Bible does not emphasize. The result will be unbiblical extremism.

Leaders should not jump to the conclusion that people are possessed—especially Christians. Too often this has been a shallow and false solution to complex problems in the church. I've seen many people supposedly delivered from serious sin habits through exorcism soon demonstrate that the problem isn't gone at all. Of course, deliverance ministers can always claim that the demon has returned, thus dismissing the issue. In my thirty-eight years of observation, Christians having demons cast out so they can be delivered from sins only leads to spiritual immaturity and false belief in shortcuts that disappoint.

This should hardly be surprising, considering that *the practice is not biblical.* The New and Old Testaments are clear that our sin problems are the result of our own fleshly lust, not demon possession. If you subscribe to the teaching of a deliverance ministry like this, ask yourself: If pride, lust, or bitterness were the result of possession, why wouldn't Paul advise people to cast the demons out? Why would he instead attribute these to one's own sinful desires? (Galatians 5:19; see also James 1:14–15). The Bible gives no warrant for casting demons out of believers.

Possessed people are usually quite noticeable. When I was preaching at a village church in India, an elderly woman suddenly began to cry out and gesticulate in an unnatural way. I asked my translator what she was saying, and he translated, "I am more powerful than any of you! She has been mine for thirty-five years! There is nothing you can do!" Four men carried her out of the meeting to a nearby hut with a covered front porch where they prayed over her. Amazed, I asked if we shouldn't stop and pray for her, but the other Christians made it clear they wanted me to continue with my teaching. They did not seem surprised by the experience.

Later they explained that this was a common occurrence there. They also noted that this was the first time this woman had ever attended a Christian meeting, which I thought was significant. In a village without electricity or access to TV, radio, or other media, a peasant woman like this had probably never seen such a gathering in her life. Unlike many meetings where people know how the demon-possessed are supposed to act, this woman had no pre-learning. I believe this was an authentic case of possession. Unfortunately, I had to leave for another meeting before I could find out how the prayer session ended, but my translator was confident she would be delivered.

If we are confronted with a possessed person, we should follow the pattern we see in stories of Jesus and Paul and command the demon to depart, using the name of Jesus. Practitioners familiar with possession also recommend forming a prayer group at the time and during the days and weeks to follow that can intercede for the possessed person. People delivered from possession are in a vulnerable state and should immediately be confronted with the gospel; if they receive it, they should be counseled, trained, and supported while establishing their Christian walk.

LESSER FORMS OF DEMONIC CONTROL

Satan can exert lesser forms of control over people, including Christians. I agree with most interpreters that demons cannot possess Christians in the same way they do non-Christians. The idea that the "temple of the Holy Spirit" (1 Corinthians 6:19) could be taken over by Satan is too implausible. Still, his control can at times be extensive.

Mind Control

Satan's most common means for capturing believers is to gain control over their thinking by so deceiving them that they no longer think like believers. This must have been the case with Ananias and Sapphira. When Peter confronted them he said, "Ananias, why have you let Satan fill your heart? You lied to the Holy Spirit" (Acts 5:3). Peter was not suggesting that Satan possessed Ananias but that Ananias was so deceived he gave his heart to a project inspired by Satan.

In another passage, Paul warns Timothy that he should oppose certain opponents in the church:

> Gently instruct those who oppose the truth. Perhaps God will change those people's hearts, and they will learn the truth. Then they will come to their senses and escape from the devil's trap. For they have been held captive by him to do whatever he wants. (2 Timothy 2:25–26)

Some think these must be non-Christians; otherwise they wouldn't have been so completely under Satan's power. But if that were true, why wouldn't Paul recommend exorcism? I think both the language and the context—Timothy's work within the church at Ephesus—suggest these people may well have been believers, or at least indistinguishable from believers. Again, Paul is not saying they were possessed in the same way a non-Christian could be. Instead, they had bought into Satan's lies to such an extent that they had effectively come under his control. Notice the antidote that Paul prescribes: teaching the truth. This treatment wouldn't do any good for a demonized person, but it would help one who was deceived.

In other cases, Satan gains control of members by using their own sense of guilt about sin in their lives and then turning it into accusations against fellow believers. Already sensing their own guilt, such people shift blame to others in order to convince themselves *no one* is sincerely following God. Thus Satan doubly attacks the church—taking control of individual believers' minds and pitting them against one another.

We see this happen in our own day. Satan is able to take control of Christians' thinking anytime they start believing him. One church after another has been torn apart from within by believers operating under his direction. They don't know this is happening, and in fact they usually believe they are acting for God, or at least acting reasonably. We saw earlier that those who lead divisions are usually sinning and self-condemned, suggesting satanic manipulation through accusation (Titus 3:10–11). At the same time, Satan may send those into the body who are not really believers but have come to exploit. These are the "false brethren" Paul considered so dangerous (2 Corinthians 11:26 NASB).

When we believe Christian friends are coming under Satan's influence, we should try to counsel them. We should warn them, teaching or reminding them how Satan works. Through patient, loving admonition, we can often turn people back from this fate. I like to warn believers that they may be underestimating the importance of the inner struggle they're having with Satan's lies. They need to see that if they believe the first lie, it won't just be a mistake but an entry point for Satan. When they yield at one point the danger increases dramatically. Satan never lets people off with isolated cases of deception; he will press the case with one point after another until he gains control of their thinking.

I recently counseled a brother who was under temptation to believe that others in the church, especially leaders, were dealing wrongly with him. He was judging motives, and his recollections were very inaccurate. All of his commentary sounded like it could have come from the mouth of Satan. I warned him that he was under deception, and that if he didn't make a clear choice to dispel these accusations he would fall further under deception and completely lose control of his thought life. He didn't believe me, apparently concluding that I was counseling with self-serving motives. Within a few months, his Christian walk had deteriorated and his alienation increased to the point he left the church. I wasn't surprised to hear soon after that he had begun to openly question the Bible's reliability. Believing Satan is a deadly, slippery slope.

Failure to Separate

Christians who were formerly occult practitioners occasionally report experiences of extreme darkness, inability to pray, compulsions to curse Jesus, hallucinations, and other symptoms, sometimes years after being converted. Cases like this could result from a failure to break ties with the occult; that's most likely why Paul led a prayer of renunciation and the destroying of all occult objects at Ephesus (Acts 19:19), and we should imitate this practice today. People from occult backgrounds need to renounce the occult and destroy their paraphernalia in the presence of witnesses. These objects should include all books having to do with New Age, astrology, spiritual healing, fortune-telling, or Wicca, as well as charms, talismans, sacred objects, tarot cards, or Ouija boards. One reason we should destroy these rather than just throw them away is to keep them from falling into the hands of others.

A friend of mine met Christ and sometime later revealed that he had studied a couple of books by medium Edgar Cayce. I told him he should renounce that interest and destroy the books, preferably bringing them to our men's group where we could burn them together. A week later, he told me he had decided instead to throw them into the trash. Two days afterward, while going up the alley to his house, he saw two teenage girls standing by his Dumpster, looking at the discarded books they had pulled from the trash. He instantly realized he should have destroyed the books. Fortunately, he was able to share Christ with the girls and steer them away from the occult.

We should also teach our people to studiously avoid any further contact with the occult. Galatians 5:19–20 includes idolatry and sorcery among the deeds of the flesh. Revelation 21:8 names sorcery as one of the sinful themes of the last days deserving judgment in the lake of fire. While forgiven Christians don't have to expect that fate, we should never think we can deal on Satan's ground without consequences.

A Christian is not in danger if he merely handles a book of magic or an idol. Paul didn't hesitate to visit temples and closely study the idolatry at Athens. He told them he "looked carefully at [their] objects of worship" (Acts 17:23 NIV). We are not highly vulnerable to demonic influence through incidental contact, and we shouldn't be superstitiously fearful. The danger comes when we approach the occult like other practitioners— with the *intent* of gaining favors.

With the rise of nature religion and the occult in Western culture, leaders will likely see more overt demonic events in the lives of those coming to their churches. Leaders elsewhere in the world already face a continual struggle against occult involvement. Possession and related problems are common in many of these cultures. For *all* leaders, strong warnings against occult involvement should help to cut down on such events. So too should clear separation and renunciation of past occult involvement. If demonic influence is evident, we must be ready to speak a word of authority, commanding the spirit to depart in the name of Jesus.[4]

CHAPTER 18

GOING FORWARD

Is your Christian life a struggle? Do you wonder why things aren't easier? Have you faced repeated disappointment? Does your ministry seem ineffective? Because Satan is real and his world-system is powerful, all these feelings are normal. As long as an enemy as awesome as Satan is here to challenge the progress of Christians, our lives will include battering. Temptation, accusation, confusion, depression, loss, and death are common in a fallen world. Paul comforted his new converts with the words, "We must suffer many hardships to enter the Kingdom of God" (Acts 14:22).

Should we cover up and try to protect ourselves? Should we pad our lives with comfort and diversion? Or should we selflessly attack Satan's fortresses? God is looking for followers who will heroically step up and offer themselves freely to rescue the dying world around us. Jesus called us to learn to love as he loved us, and his love included self-sacrifice. When we give up our peacetime mentality and brace ourselves for spiritual war, we will be ready for God to use us in the ways he wants to. Thank God we aren't called to wage this war alone! We should seek out a group of like-minded believers with whom we can take our stand.

Christians who refuse to face up to spiritual war gain no safety for themselves. Like ostriches with their heads in the sand, these believers become civilian casualties—unarmed and clueless people who have wandered into the middle of a battlefield.

OUR FOCUS

If you've read this far, you've been thinking about Satan for some time, and you realize there is a lot to consider when it comes to the primary enemy of God. But remember, the center of our attention should be Christ. A Christ-centered perspective certainly includes awareness and alertness to the Evil One's actions, but the fact is that some Christians focus too much on demons.

The best thing we can do is "set [our] hearts on things above, where Christ is seated at the right hand of God" (Colossians 3:1 NIV). Because of our position in him, we are ultimately invulnerable to Satan despite any damage he may do in the short term. Experienced believers know that we don't need to spend lots of time wondering what Satan is up to. Instead, once we know how he thinks and works, we mainly need to focus on drawing near to God, who will alert us when necessary to any demonic activity in our lives or our ministries.

In addition to drawing near to God, we need to focus on our mission. Wouldn't it be unfortunate and ironic if reading a book about Satan resulted in Christians becoming less energized and more distracted from our mission? That would suit him beautifully. Millions of people need to know what Jesus has done for them. Young Christians need to be built up, instructed, counseled, and healed. Love relationships need to be strengthened. These are the tasks God calls us to accomplish.

As we pray for the people we serve, we can trust that God will call our attention to the ways Satan may be interfering. In fact, now that you've devoted this time to reading about him, you probably will start noticing his work more often. Recognition is important, because then we know how to answer and resist him, especially if we're deepening our understanding of God's Word.

So humble yourselves before God. Resist the devil, and he will flee from you. (James 4:7)

The God of peace will soon crush Satan under your feet. May the grace of our Lord Jesus be with you. (Romans 10:20)

Section 3

FOR FURTHER STUDY

APPENDIX 3. JESUS' TEACHING ON HIS OWN MISSION

APPENDIX 4. ASSESSING GOD'S SECRECY

CHAPTER 19

SATAN IN THE OLD TESTAMENT

WHY IS THE OLD TESTAMENT SO QUIET ABOUT SATAN?

Although we meet Satan in the Old Testament, references to him or demons are rare, especially compared to other literature of the time. Ancient Middle Eastern religious texts dwell constantly on demons and spirits. These include instructions about incantations, talismans, fetishes, and spells to protect people from demons.

In some Old Testament passages, Satan's presence and work are implied but not directly stated. The book of Job and the prophets discuss Satan in a way that assumes their readers were already familiar with him. However, the absence of any mention of Satan or evil spirits in one book after another is striking.[1] Unlike any other religious text of the time, the Old Testament never gives a single incantation to use against demons, never a single healing or exorcism technique, never an instruction on self-protection against menacing spirits. How can this be, and what does it mean?

Liberal Theories

Some liberal scholars have suggested that belief in a personal Satan and demons was a later development in Jewish religion. Seventeenth-century scholars theorized that this late-developing belief was useful for dating the Old Testament books and strata. Texts mentioning demons must be of late origin (after 400 BC), they argued, because Israelites didn't know about Satan early in their history.[2] Even when Satan is mentioned, they claim, he is not against God but merely does God's will as a prosecutor.[3] They think the fallen-angel concept came later, perhaps in the 200s BC. These views ignore the data of the Old Testament text. Aside from the serpent in Genesis 3, Christians who believe the Bible is inspired recognize demons as early as Genesis 6:1–2, where the "sons of God" are fallen angels, according to Jude 6–7. And this act, along with others, provokes the judgment of God in verse 7, so the demons were *not* doing God's work. Psalm 106:36–37 teaches that idols are demons to which people made human sacrifice (see also Leviticus 17:7), and in 1 Chronicles 21:1 (NASB) we read, "Then Satan stood up against Israel and moved David to number Israel."

Daniel 10–11 makes clear reference to demons opposing God's purposes; Zechariah 3:1–2 shows Satan as the accuser of a righteous man, and receiving God's rebuke, so again it is clear that he is opposed to God's viewpoint, not serving him. He appears in Job 1–2, accusing both man and God. Satan *does* appear, and he is shown as fallen and evil.[4] We already saw that Ezekiel says Satan was a cherub, which is an angel.

The theory that ancient Judaism evolved the idea of Satan and demons late in their history lacks credibility for other reasons as well. In Near-Eastern literature far older than the Old Testament, demons abound. If Israel's religious vision was a matter of religious evolution, as liberal scholars claim, demon spirits should have been the *first* development, as they were everywhere else. Universally, the more primitive and ancient a religious complex is, the more it focuses on spirit beings—especially evil spirits.

In spite of occasional references, the Bible is exactly the opposite. Without question, most information on Satan comes from later in the Bible; once again, the near silence on this subject is deafening in the early books. Even relatively liberal scholars admit this; for instance, G. Earnest Wright, of Harvard, says, "In the Old Testament clear references to demons are rare." Wright goes on to observe,

> When we examine the world of polytheism more closely, we find beneath the surface a vast, dark, and uncomfortable world. . . . That is the world of demons, magic, and divination. By contrast, the first

and most obvious thing which we can say about Israel is that, comparatively speaking, her religious life is most astonishingly free of this sort of thing, at least in ideal. . . . The surprising thing is not that the cult of magic and divination was known in Israel, but that it should be so definitely forbidden in the law and associated by the prophets with an idolatry which destroyed rather than saved.[5]

The Real Reason

Here is the likely reason Old Testament revelation offers little information about demons: The ancient obsession with demons and magic probably caused God to exclude lengthy discussion on the topic. The Israelites, not universally indwelt by the Holy Spirit and prone to imitate their polytheistic neighbors, needed to focus on God. The danger of fascination with demons, leading to magic and the occult, is always near. While angels and demons are present in the Old Testament, and not just in the later books, the spotlight is firmly on God. As Wright correctly observes:

> So radical was the wholehearted concentration on Yahweh and so exclusive was the demand of Yahweh that loyalty and attention be directed to him alone, that the world of lesser beings simply dropped out of conscious sight. . . . The man who possessed such fear and faith had nothing in the world to be afraid of, except his own sin and the sin of his people. That faith was an extraordinary thing in the ancient world.[6]

We have already looked at several Old Testament dealings with Satan. For the sake of completeness, we will look at two other key passages before surveying the New Testament information.

SATAN IN JOB

Scholars disagree on the date of the book of Job. They generally conclude that it is very early or very late in the Old Testament's development.

It presents itself as a very early story because it never mentions anything Jewish. While people can debate when it was committed to writing, I think it is probably a very early book.

Confrontation in Heaven

In Job, chapter 1, we read,

> One day the members of the heavenly court came to present themselves before the Lord, and the Accuser, Satan, came with them. "Where have you come from?" the Lord asked Satan. Satan answered the Lord, "I have been patrolling the earth, watching everything that's going on." Then the Lord asked Satan, "Have you noticed my servant Job? He is the finest man in all the earth. He is blameless—a man of complete integrity. He fears God and stays away from evil." Satan replied to the Lord, "Yes, but Job has good reason to fear God. You have always put a wall of protection around him and his home and his property. You have made him prosper in everything he does. Look how rich he is! But reach out and take away everything he has, and he will surely curse you to your face!" (vv. 6–11).

Notice several interesting things in this description. First, we see Satan showing up in heaven. He apparently is able to go into God's presence, even though he no longer lives there. This passage confirms that Satan's abode is the earth.

Satan's Accusations

Satan was acting in the role of accuser, in this case against both Job and God. Job, allegedly, is only following God for ulterior, selfish motives. In typical satanic logic, the only reason to do anything is to gain advantage for self.

However, Satan's version of reality also implies that God is delusional or dishonest in his claim that a valid relationship exists between himself and Job, involving loyalty and obedience. He thought it was obvious that God had been buying obedience from Job by giving him material blessing. Considering God's obvious great knowledge and wisdom, this could even be a deliberate, deceptive show—an effort to create the impression that some people love him and voluntarily follow him, when he knows that nothing but threats or bribery lead others to follow.

God's Passivity

The most intriguing question is why God seems to cater to Satan's accusation, even letting him terrorize Job in extreme ways. Does he care what Satan says? Could it be that Satan made this accusation in front of the other angels, and God didn't want to leave the accusation unanswered? We know from the end of the book that God had plans to use these trials for Job's spiritual growth and ultimate benefit. But this may not be the only reason. God seems to entertain Satan's accusations at a surprising level. Why not just blow Satan away, hurling him back to earth? Instead of simply dismissing the claims, God allowed people to suffer and even die to disprove Satan's lie.

This story is a fascinating glimpse into spiritual warfare, fitting the larger picture unveiled in the rest of the Bible. God was clearly reluctant to use force against Satan and his lies. Instead, he gave wide latitude and eventually let events refute what the Evil One said. God didn't ignore Satan's lies (which had already persuaded a third of the angelic host to rebel); they had to be treated seriously. They had to be refuted.

Much must be at stake in this struggle over what is true, if God is willing to allow suffering and death rather than leave Satan unanswered. What could possibly matter so much? Why not simply laugh off these lies? Why not silence Satan forever? These questions, so similar to those arising from Ezekiel 28, are not answered in Job. Satan soon disappears from this story, but the rest of the Bible provides startling and satisfying answers to all these queries, as we saw in the mystery hidden for eons past.

DEMONS IN DANIEL

Daniel is a book of visions and history, mostly recalling God's remarkable dealings with Daniel and his friends during their captivity in Babylon. But one section, in chapter 10, pulls the curtain back to reveal a fascinating glimpse of spiritual warfare.

A Visitation

After Daniel was in mourning for three weeks over the fate of exiled Israel, he had a vision in which a "man" stood before him. But this was no ordinary man.

> I looked up and saw a man dressed in linen clothing, with a belt of pure gold around his waist. His body looked like a precious gem. His face flashed like lightning, and his eyes flamed like torches. His arms and feet shone like polished bronze, and his voice roared like a vast multitude of people. (Daniel 10:5–6)

He was an angel from God who recounts his journey:

> Don't be afraid, Daniel. Since the first day you began to pray for understanding and to humble yourself before your God, your request has been heard in heaven. I have come in answer to your prayer. But for twenty-one days the spirit prince of the kingdom of Persia blocked my way. Then Michael, one of the archangels, came to help me, and I left him there with the spirit prince of the kingdom of Persia. Now I am here to explain what will happen to your people in the future, for this vision concerns a time yet to come. (10:12–14)

He later adds:

> Do you know why I have come? Soon I must return to fight against the spirit prince of the kingdom of Persia, and after that the spirit prince of the kingdom of Greece will come. Meanwhile, I will tell you what is written in the Book of Truth. (No one helps me against these spirit princes except Michael, your spirit prince. I have been standing beside

Michael to support and strengthen him since the first year of the reign of Darius the Mede.) (10:20–11:1)

What Were They Doing?

This dialogue reveals that angels and evil spirits fought with each other for weeks at a time. Both apparently identify with various nation states, and it sounds like a demon associated with Persia tried to prevent this angel from bringing his message to Daniel. Michael, an "archangel," had come to hold off that demon while the angel completed his mission, but just as Michael arrived, another demon (associated with Greece) was coming to reinforce the one from Persia, thus compelling the messenger to talk quickly. The angel needed to get back to fight alongside Michael, whose assistant he had been for some time.

What an amazing picture! What do these spirit beings do when they fight? Reformation artist Albrecht Durer made a famous woodcut showing how he imagined it, though this fine work of art certainly is not an accurate portrayal of spiritual warfare. For one thing, he shows the demons looking like reptilian monsters (see following page). As we have seen, Satan and his followers are actually majestic, beautiful beings. Also, Durer has the angels and demons fighting with swords and spears, stabbing each other, or shooting arrows. What good would it do to stab a spirit being with a sword?

No, this is a projection of human warfare onto the angels. Real spiritual battle must be very different. Hollywood versions are no more plausible. Firing jets of flame would have no more effect than arrows. Although Daniel doesn't give us the details, we can make an educated guess at what these beings were doing for three weeks. Considering the warfare cases we've already seen in Genesis and Job—and what happened when Jesus confronted Satan in a forty-day battle (discussed in the upcoming chapter)—we can guess what they were doing: They were probably *arguing.*

In every confrontation between Satan and God or his people, we see Satan doing the same thing: stating his propositions, making his suggestions, pushing his view of the situation. In several cases, God the Father, Jesus, or others respond. The statements and the answers are important,

"Saint Michael Slays the Devil" by Albrecht Durer

for these are the grist of spiritual warfare. *Ideas, claims, counterclaims, and denials, all centering on the question of what is true—these cause power to shift in the spiritual realm.*

The Nature of Spiritual Warfare

Again, although we don't know all the rules that govern spiritual warfare, we can infer some. In all likelihood, the angel that came to Daniel couldn't leave the battle with the demon from Persia because if any of that evil spirit's claims went unanswered, God's angel would have forfeited spiritual power. Only when Michael came to answer the lies could this angel break away long enough to come to Daniel. As strange as it may seem, this is the best guess for what these powerful beings were doing during those three weeks.

We have seen clear biblical evidence that our own struggle with Satan takes the same form. As he makes his claims and accusations, we must answer them with biblical authority or we will forfeit the power and position that should be ours.

Territorial Spirits?

These two demons were named after empires or countries (Persia and Greece), and we saw a similar reference earlier in Ezekiel about the city-state of Tyre. Recently, some Christians have taken this to mean that evil spirits typically associate with locations on earth—a view that agrees with much occult literature. This in turn has led to new spiritual exercises known as "spiritual mapping" and "strategic prayer." Under these theories, people study crime records in a particular city in order to determine where that town's strongest demons live. Then they go and try to exorcise the controlling demons during "prayer walks."

These conclusions aren't warranted from either passage. While demons apparently may associate with nation-states or empires, we have no indication here that they're assigned to particular parts of town or that we're supposed to fight with them in this way. We should avoid reading into biblical passages more than they say. If demons were located in certain areas, we'd have no way of knowing it and no biblical instructions on what to do about it. If this kind of spiritual warfare were important, we can rest assured God would have said something about it in Scripture. Of course, praying for cities or peoples makes sense. The point is, don't read in more than the Bible teaches.[7]

CHAPTER 20

SATAN IN THE NEW TESTAMENT

The contrast between the Old Testament shortage of teaching on Satan and the extensive teaching in the New is remarkable. The wealth in the latter begins with Jesus. God clearly entrusted his Son to communicate most of the key information people would need about the Evil One, and Jesus spoke more about him than any other voice in Scripture. God may have felt that one who supremely knows Satan should impart this knowledge.

Jesus created Satan, was there when he fell, and faced him personally in the wilderness. Jesus knows Satan in a way no one else ever has. He not only taught us about Satan, he also taught his apostles, who in turn wrote the New Testament books.

A DIFFERENT AUDIENCE

We can also deduce another likely reason for increased revelation about Satan in the New Testament. Believers after Christ's first coming enjoyed greater spiritual strength than did Old Testament believers. John 7:39 says that prior to this "the Spirit had not yet been given, because Jesus had not yet entered into his glory." From this and other passages, we see that the Holy Spirit unleashed new ministries because of Jesus' work. Because spiritual baptism, universal indwelling, etc., provide us with a new identity in Christ, we, in contrast to Old Testament believers, can "live new lives" and be "set free from the power of sin" (Romans 6:4, 7).

After Pentecost, the Holy Spirit permanently indwells all believers.

The Spirit was present in the Old Testament, and he would "come upon" some people at times, but not like our indwelling. Paul says, metaphorically, "We were all made to drink of one Spirit" (1 Corinthians 12:13 NASB), adding that "the one who joins himself to the Lord is one spirit with Him" (6:17). Referring to this difference between the Old and New Covenants, Jesus said the Spirit "lives with you now and later will be in you" (John 14:17). God's Spirit within us gives us guidance, power to live for God, and authority over evil spirits.

As for the sole or even main reasons for God's choice of timing, we can't be sure. However, these capabilities given to believers probably account for why God waited until the New Testament period to reveal the fuller truth about Satan. In the earlier era, God was concerned to preserve his covenant people from Satan's attacks through the neighboring nations; the emphasis was on defense. With Jesus, though, the emphasis shifts—as we've seen, New Covenant believers are to take the offensive against Satan by invading his kingdom. Believers operating under an offensive posture require a higher level of understanding about the kingdom of darkness.

JESUS ON SATAN

The Accusing Enemy

Jesus often referred to Satan using the term *diabolos*, or "devil" (e.g., Matthew 4:1), literally meaning "one who hurls against." From pre-New Testament times, though, this is one who hurls accusations and slander. The Bible uses this term of both humans and of Satan regarding accusation, complaint, and slander; Jesus uses it nearly always in reference to Satan (once referring to Judas, in John 6:70). In his very title, Satan is an accuser, or a slanderer.

At other times Jesus calls him another name: Satan. The word *Satanas* comes from Aramaic and means an adversary or enemy; it doesn't always refer to Satan himself. In Mark 8:33, Jesus calls Peter "Satan," either because he was thinking in self-serving terms, like Satan does, or because he was unknowingly acting as an opponent to God's direction for Jesus' life. Likewise, in the Old Testament, the Hebrew version of this word can refer to human opponents or accusers.

The Murdering Liar

Jesus also stressed Satan's violence and deceit:

> He was a murderer from the beginning. He has always hated the truth, because there is no truth in him. When he lies, it is consistent with his character; for he is a liar and the father of lies. (John 8:44)

Satan lives in a world of falsehood. When Jesus says there is no truth in Satan, is he suggesting Satan speaks falsehood because he believes his own lies? Or is it that Satan's determination to propagate falsehood is so consuming that he has driven all truth from himself? Clearly, Satan is a constant and continual opponent to all that is true. And the results are lethal—murder is his ultimate aim.

We have already observed how Satan worked on Eve through deceiving claims, especially about God. He worked on Jesus the same way, and we too can expect him to approach us with his most powerful weapon: the lie.

The Ruler of This World

In John, Jesus repeatedly called Satan the "ruler of this world" (*kosmos:* e.g., 12:31; 14:30; 16:11), and he was the first to reveal this about Satan. Although Daniel and Ezekiel referred to demons as national leaders, this title for Satan shows that the whole order is somehow under his power. Of course, as ruler of the world-system, Satan manipulates humans in a way calculated to keep them separated from God.

The Destroyer of Humans

In Matthew 13, Jesus told several so-called "kingdom parables." In the parable of the sower, the birds eat the seed sown by the roadside. Jesus later explains,

The seed that fell on the footpath represents those who hear the message about the Kingdom and don't understand it. Then the evil one comes and snatches away the seed that was planted in their hearts. (v. 19)

Here Jesus reveals Satan's central intent in spiritual warfare: keeping the hated humans from knowing God's grace through the gospel. In another passage, Jesus said of Satan, "The thief's purpose is to steal and kill and destroy. My purpose is to give them a rich and satisfying life" (John 10:10).

In the parable of the soils, Jesus reveals that Satan has the ability to snatch the good news from people's hearts, which means he can work within a person's mind to oppose Jesus' mission of rescue. In Matthew 13:24–30, we see him opposing it another way. In the parable of the wheat and the tares, Jesus explains that after the owner of a wheat field sowed his crop, "that night as the workers slept, his enemy came and planted weeds among the wheat" (v. 25). The enemy wanted to ruin the harvest by infiltrating it with plants that bear no grain. The owner's response is relatively passive: He tells his servants to let both plants grow together, and they will separate them at harvest time.

Again, we see Satan trying to foil God's purposes on earth. This agrees with all we know about Satan—he doesn't engage in pointless acts of terrorism or displays of power (contrary to some tall tales). His actions are carefully calculated to block God's purposes and to destroy human beings by guiding them to hell.

Demon Possession

Jesus cast demons out of possessed people numerous times. Possession was very common during his ministry but is rarely mentioned elsewhere in the Bible. In all likelihood, Satan knew this was a time and a place where God was executing his strategy, and he concentrated his forces accordingly.

People were amazed at the authority Jesus wielded against evil spirits (Mark 1:27). But his enemies charged that he cast them out by the power of Beelzebub (the prince of demons, according to Jewish tradition;

Matthew 12:24 NIV). Jesus rebuked them, pointing out that Satan and his followers are too strategic to fight among themselves.

> Any kingdom at war with itself is doomed. A city or home divided against itself is doomed. And if Satan is casting out Satan, he is fighting against himself. His own kingdom will not survive. (vv. 25–26)

This comment clarifies that Satan has a kingdom (the *kosmos*) he guards against incursion, and his followers are well disciplined and unified.

Jesus also imparted his authority to cast out demons: "One day Jesus called together his twelve disciples and gave them power and authority to cast out all demons and to heal all diseases" (Luke 9:1). This same authority is ours today, as you can see from the activities of Christians recorded in Acts.

Apart from Jesus' teachings on Satan, some of the most important revelations came during his confrontation with Satan in the wilderness.

CHAPTER 21

JESUS AND SATAN: CONFRONTATION

One of the most fascinating revelations of Satan comes when he tempted Jesus. Jesus was alone when this battle occurred, so we must assume that the gospel accounts are the part he chose to tell his disciples. He probably relayed these parts of the struggle because they were the most instructive and probably typical of the whole episode. Using Luke's account, let's read this prototypical confrontation and observe the dynamics of the struggle.

THE SETTING

> Then Jesus, full of the Holy Spirit, returned from the Jordan River. He was led by the Spirit in the wilderness, where he was tempted by the devil for forty days. Jesus ate nothing all that time and became very hungry. (Luke 4:1–2)

Jesus lived as a man, not as God. Paul explains in Philippians 2:6–7 that Jesus emptied himself, meaning that in some way he set aside the use of his divine attributes. This must be the case, because God cannot be tempted by evil (James 1:13), whereas Jesus was tempted. We should realize that he defeated Satan in this episode not by using special power available only to him but through the same power we have—the power of the indwelling Holy Spirit and the Word of God. That means his battle approach is a fitting example for us to follow.

We see that the Spirit led Jesus to confront Satan and be tempted by him, which suggests he will let us face such temptation as well. Learning to withstand these attacks strengthens believers; after this trial, "Jesus returned to Galilee, filled with the Holy Spirit's power" (Luke 4:14).

AUTONOMY

> The devil said to him, "If you are the Son of God, tell this stone to become a loaf of bread."
>
> But Jesus told him, "No! The Scriptures say, 'People do not live by bread alone' " (Luke 4:3–4).

Most first-time readers have the same reaction when reading this first temptation: "What's wrong with this? Is God saying there's something wrong with eating bread? If Jesus is hungry and has the power to create bread, why shouldn't he?"

The answer has to do with Jesus' sensitivity to God's provision and leading. His reply points to the principle involved. The passage he cites is from Deuteronomy, where Moses explains why God gave the children of Israel manna to eat during their journey in the desert.

> He humbled you and let you be hungry, and fed you with manna which you did not know, nor did your fathers know, that He might make you understand that man does not live by bread alone, but man lives by everything that proceeds out of the mouth of the Lord. (8:3 NASB)

Moses was saying that God taught the people humility and dependence by supplying manna. They had no other sustenance in this extremely barren desert. If God didn't provide daily, they would starve. By putting them in a position of complete dependency, God was trying to teach them how to trust him instead of resorting to a favorite human sin: autonomy. Autonomy means self-rule, or self-sufficiency. We want to make our own decisions, set our own direction, and meet our own needs so we won't have to depend on God.

By citing this Scripture, Jesus implied that Satan was tempting him to autonomy; he instead would choose dependency and faith in God. The underlying thought could be, "If God wanted me to eat bread, why hasn't he provided any?" or "I have no instructions from God to make bread."

We face the same temptation when we feel our needs are unmet and the opportunity comes to take matters into our own hands by handling the situation in some way not prescribed by God. A believer who feels lonely may meet a romantically interested non-Christian. Another might decide not to endure circumstances beyond his control and run away from the problem. A depressed believer may turn to drugs or drink or go on a buying spree. Autonomy is the root cause of many spiritual maladies.

Jesus shunned autonomy at all times:

The Son can do nothing by himself. He does only what he sees the Father doing. (John 5:19)

I do nothing on my own but say only what the Father taught me. (John 8:28)

Satan loves autonomy. He lives that way and thinks everyone should. He views any desire to follow God's lead or to depend on him as servile, restrictive, and degrading. In Satan's mind, the only one who can meet my needs is me. People who wait around for God to meet their needs are chumps and fools.

But waiting on the Lord is important for us as followers of God. If we could just clap our hands and have our needs fulfilled, the result would be disastrous. Instead of growing in faith, we would become spoiled brats: no gratitude, no need to move deeper with God, just taking everything for granted. Instead, God calls on us to live with unmet needs at times in order to strengthen our faith. The pressure we feel on our faith when waiting on God brings us to a point of decision: Can I trust God to come through? As we struggle with this question, we have the opportunity to begin trusting God at a new level. On the other hand, making our own decisions without consulting God leads to a lifestyle of self-reliance that kills true spirituality.

So this temptation certainly is important, and we should be able to identify with it. We also should note that Satan's call to autonomy contains an implied lie: "God isn't going to meet your needs. He can't be trusted. You have to provide for yourself." Underlying each and every satanic temptation is a lie—a direct challenge to the truth of God's Word. Our underlying beliefs about what's true will influence our ability to resist temptation. Jesus' reply from God's Word ended this temptation.

PRAGMATISM

> Then the devil took him up and revealed to him all the kingdoms of the world in a moment of time. "I will give you the glory of these kingdoms and authority over them," the devil said, "because they are mine to give to anyone I please. I will give it all to you if you will worship me."
>
> Jesus replied, "The Scriptures say, 'You must worship the Lord your God and serve only him' " (Luke 4:5–8).

Here Satan makes an extraordinary claim—that he owns all the kingdoms of the world and all their glory. Interestingly, Jesus doesn't challenge the claim. This is the first clear allusion to the important New Testament teaching that Satan rules this world-system.

Jesus had come to take the world back for God by establishing his kingdom. When Satan offered Jesus ownership of the world, his offer was in accord with God's purpose and Jesus' goal. Of course, the means for attaining the goal were completely unacceptable; Satan was really suggesting that Jesus do God's work in the world's way. Satan's lie therefore was not that he owned the world but that one could possibly accomplish God's work through sinful means. Again Jesus' citation of God's Word from Deuteronomy laid the question to rest.

Once more those of us interested in serving God should be able to identify. We too will find ourselves being tempted to reach God's goals, or ours, through Satan's means. This temptation has been prominent in church history. Leaders frequently have used deception, manipulation, greed, and even coercion to build the kingdom of God.

PRIDE

Finally,

> Then the devil took him to Jerusalem, to the highest point of the Temple, and said, "If you are the Son of God, jump off! For the Scriptures say, 'He will order his angels to protect and guard you. And they will hold you up with their hands so you won't even hurt your foot on a stone.' "
>
> Jesus responded, "The Scriptures also say, 'You must not test the Lord your God' " (Luke 4:9–12).

After Jesus rebuffed him twice by citing Scripture, Satan showed he can also use the Bible. His citation from Psalm 91 promises divine protection, and who would God protect more than his Son? Clearly he is challenging Jesus' faith. But why jump from the temple? There are plenty of cliffs in the desert. No doubt it was because the temple was the most public place in Israel. What a statement, what an outstanding promotional event this would be! Jesus could prove his authenticity to the people in a moment. We see here both issues in the previous temptations. Satan is challenging Jesus to take his ministry advancement into his own hands. Will he turn to autonomous decision making? Will he attempt to advance his ministry through unethical behavior?

Again Jesus responded with Scripture. His citation of Deuteronomy 6 (within Luke 4) perfectly goes to the heart of what's wrong with Satan's suggestion. Jumping from the temple would put God in a position where he has to act. Instead of humbly following God, this would be a naked attempt to manipulate him.

In the third temptation, we see Jesus and the Evil One both using the Bible like a weapon. Satan's citation was appropriate in a narrow sense, but Jesus' rejoinder went beyond proof-texting to balancing what we might call "the whole counsel of God." Jesus was practicing sound interpretation—not interpreting one passage so as to contradict another. Satan must have hoped he could bait Jesus into shallow opportunism.

The lying nature of temptation is again evident. Satan's suggestion implies that we need to pressure God: "You can't wait on him to come through. He's too self-interested to keep an eye on what's best for you."

THE LAST ADAM

In 1 Corinthians 15:45, Paul writes, " 'The first man, Adam, became a living person.' But the last Adam—that is, Christ—is a life-giving Spirit." Just as Adam begot a fallen race of humans, separated from God, Jesus gave birth to a new humanity, united with God.

Many other contrasts are also possible. Consider their situations when tempted. Adam was with his wife, in full strength and perfect health; Jesus was alone and isolated, feeling weakened and hungry at the end of a long fast. Adam was tempted in a lush, beautiful garden where all his needs were met; Jesus faced Satan in a stark, hot, and dry desert. Adam's temptation was to do something obviously wrong; Jesus was tempted to act in ways that seemed morally neutral.

In some key ways, however, the two incidents are quite similar. Adam and Eve's temptation centered on the Word of God; Jesus' temptations centered likewise. Satan appealed to Eve based on the lust of the flesh (the fruit was good for food), the lust of the eyes (the fruit was beautiful), and the boastful pride of life (the fruit was able to make one wise like God). With Jesus, he stuck to the same strategy, appealing to the lust of the flesh (making the stones into bread), the lust of the eyes (all the beauty and grandeur of the world), and the boastful pride of life (showing off by jumping from the temple). As we've noted, John teaches that these three avenues of temptation comprise the heart of the world-system (1 John 2:15–16). The predictability of Satan's approach becomes a major advantage for believers who learn his ways.

Of course, the biggest contrast was the outcome: with Adam, failure; with Jesus, victory. "When the devil had finished tempting Jesus, he left him until the next opportunity came" (Luke 4:13). Satan didn't have infinite pitches he could throw, only a few. Once he had thrown his favorites, he had nothing more to say; he could only withdraw. Jesus won this battle, but temporarily. The last phrase, "until the next opportunity came" reminds us that Satan is relentless and tireless. He would be back.

HOW DO WE KNOW
IF SATAN IS REAL?

Studies show that while over 90 percent of Americans believe in God, only 41 percent believe in Satan.[1] What evidence do we have that Satan is real?

MY OWN DOUBTS

I began following Christ as a college student. For some years before that I didn't believe in the supernatural; I saw belief in gods and religion as features of ancient superstition and psychological self-deception. I'd adopted an existential/modernist worldview that had no place for primitive concepts like demons.

During an episode in jail for drug dealing, God broke my prideful heart and drew me back to following him, as did the rest of my family. I truly repented, and I told God I would serve him because I was sick of my life of selfish hedonism.

After a miraculous release, I went back to college and began trying to figure out what spiritual growth entailed for someone like me. At area Bible studies I heard stories of the supernatural—miracles, spirits, even demons. Although I'd surrendered to God in my heart, my mind still stumbled at these accounts. The speaker would go on about the Red Sea parting, and my mind would wander into a state of fear and questioning. Did God really expect me to believe such things? Was I setting out on a path of self-deception? Was I going to pretend I believed things when I really didn't?

One area of painful doubt was Satan and demons. All the historic foolishness bound up with belief in evil spirits rose up in my mind like a dark cloud. People have always attributed anything they didn't understand to demons. Throughout history, and still today in many cultures, people have believed that spirits are the cause of physical illness, mental problems, even storms and earthquakes. Did God really expect me to believe in the reality of such beings?

Though reluctant at first, I became a strong believer in Satan and demons within a relatively short time. Key philosophical and biblical realizations, as well as personal experience, convinced me that nothing could be more real than Satan. For those who doubt that Satan and demons are real, I am including a discussion of the evidence that won me over. If you have no doubts about Satan, you could skip this part, but consider whether these points might be useful when defending the reality of Satan to younger believers who do have doubts.

PHILOSOPHICAL REASONS FOR BELIEVING IN SATAN

1. Evidence From the Existence of God

We have good reasons for believing an infinite, personal God exists. Only such a God accounts adequately for creation. Only such a God accounts for the personhood, morality, and spirituality of humans. Only such a God accounts for the remarkable predictive prophecy found in the Bible. If you are not familiar with these reasons, please read one of the many good books on the subject.[2]

One huge body of evidence creates problems with the notion of an infinite, personal God: The world contains incredible levels of evil. If a good God created the world, why is it encumbered with so much evil? Doesn't this suggest that God has left his creation to its own devices, or perhaps that he himself is evil? If God were all-good and all-powerful, wouldn't he put a stop to evil? This is the problem of evil—the primary argument used by non-theists against the biblical account of God.

The problem of evil is a serious challenge to the reality of a loving, all-knowing, all-powerful God. Even though most biblical interpreters believe human free will and our historic fall from grace adequately account for evil, any reading of Genesis shows that something was already wrong. The serpent approached Eve with all the marks of satanic psychology even before humans fell into sin.[3] Clearly, if we accept a real Satan who fell from God, that fall must have happened *before* the fall of humans.

Here, then, is the real source of evil on earth. The more I thought about this as a young Christian, the more sense it made that there would be symmetry of sorts between God and Satan. God is the almighty, loving, righteous, personal source of all goodness. Satan is a powerful, bitter, and dangerous source of evil. *This is not dualism*—the belief in equal and opposite forces of good and evil—because Satan is a created, finite being.

Unless such a being exists, we are left with no supernatural source for evil but God himself. That's why atheists and others claim God must be evil. If Satan is real, though, we can identify a different source for evil. And I think the existence of Satan is a reasonable corollary to belief in God for this reason alone.

However, doesn't seeing Satan as the source of evil merely move the question back one step? After all, whether God created people who fell or angels who fell hardly seems like an important distinction. In either case, God created conditions that led to evil, and if he is omniscient, as the Bible claims, he did so with the full knowledge of all that would follow. How then can the existence of Satan in any way distance God from ultimate responsibility for evil?

Answering this legitimate question is complicated, but the answer is powerful. Earlier we saw that the Bible's account of Satan's career and the course of his conflict with God contain a remarkable answer to the dilemma of a good God and an evil world. God had good reasons for allowing Satan's revolution to develop: a once-and-for-all demonstration of the futility of rebellion, and his own grace. Because God let it develop to its logical extreme and solved our problem at his own expense, the universe will forever be safe for free-choosing beings, and hence for real love.

Without a real Satan we would be left with huge gaps in our understanding of the biblical worldview. Only the conflict between God and

Satan adequately accounts for the course of human history as we see it. The more we understand the big picture, the more we see that the existence of a personal Satan is a necessary part of the biblical explanation of reality.

2. Argument From Human Nature

Before I believed in God, I expended a lot of mental energy trying to rationalize how humans were just like other animals. I wrote off various human behaviors as the herding instinct, territoriality, or the breeding instinct. But even then, some features I saw in myself were troubling. My own depth of abstract thought and self-awareness seemed profound. I sometimes found it hard to believe such complexity could arise without help of some kind. Obviously, humans had developed larger brains, but even that seemed strange. Sometimes when I pondered human intelligence I doubted my own atheism.

Imagine a graph plotting the relative intelligence of every organism on earth, from the amoeba to the highest primates. In a million species of animals, only an expert could tell the difference in intelligence between any two adjoining points on the graph. The discrepancy is so slight that scientists dispute which animals have greater intelligence. For instance, today there's debate over whether chimpanzees, orangutans, or dolphins have the second-highest intelligence. But human intelligence is dramatically higher. Why would one species so completely outstrip the nearest species in intellect? And why are humans everywhere on earth all at about the same level? Wouldn't we expect to find some populations midway between a chimp and a human?

I searched in vain for a similar extreme difference between any single species and any other species in intellect, in behavior, or in any other capability. There are always species with nearly similar capability in any area, but not with human intelligence. I often found myself contemplating my own life history and wondering whether macroevolution or special creation better explained my ability to so reflect. These were troubling thoughts to an atheist!

After surrendering to Christ, I could admit to myself what I had always sensed: Humans have something that defies explanation through pure natural selection. Intelligence is only part of the picture. Human creativity and love of artistic expression—whether producing art or enjoying it—are also unique in the animal world. Pondering how many hours I spent alone happily enjoying music when I could be out gathering food or building shelter—something that enhances survival—pointed to a dimension within that no other animal possesses.

Spiders or bowerbirds might produce beauty also, but always for some functional reason like catching prey, attracting a mate, or storing food. To my eye, humans were unique in this very central feature, and this pointed to something within humans that we simply cannot find in any other animal. Then there is the human belief in mortality and the afterlife. Why don't we see some shred of these in any other species? Multiple characteristics in humans point to the reality of a spiritual dimension.

Why do humans crave a sense of significance? Why will humans with all their needs for food, shelter, sex, comfort, even fame and adoration, sometimes voluntarily kill themselves because they feel a void of love or meaning? Could I really believe that love is nothing but a chemical reaction in the brain? Something completely explained by the interaction of matter and energy?

I realized even at that young age that the implications of materialism pointed directly to determinism. The idea of free choice is incompatible with a world that is a vast physical machine. Why would my mind be the only exception to the cause-and-effect sequence driving the universe? Yet I couldn't escape the sense that I sometimes made free choices that were not conditioned in any way. I wanted to be the kind of person that was honest with myself, but such realizations made me feel dishonest, and I would look away from what I was contemplating.

Now, as a Christian, I no longer struggle with the sense that I'm fooling myself. I realize that all these points and many more accord perfectly with the biblical revelation that I am a person created in God's image, not an object floating in an endless stream of pointless cause and effect. I'm not pretending I'm a spiritual being with a dimension far beyond the material; rather, I was pretending back then, when I claimed we could explain everything based on a materialistic worldview.

Still, it took months for me to connect the dots between the nature of humans as spiritual beings and the existence of angels. I eventually realized that as a human I have the body of an animal but also a spirit that reflects God's image and personhood. I even believed that my spirit or soul would survive the death of my body. At some point I realized I was being arbitrary in doubting that angels exist. If I already believed humans are spirit beings and could live without a body, why did I find it so far-out to think that God had created other spiritual beings that have no bodies? I still remember the night when the realization hit me: *We* are probably the strange ones, because we have both spirit and body. I saw that if I was prepared to admit that humans are spiritual beings, I had no reason to doubt that God could have, and probably would have, created other spiritual beings without physical bodies.

It took no time to move from this point to believing in Satan and in demons. After all, not all humans we meet are good; some are as evil as can be. Why wouldn't other spiritual beings be the same way?

No one who believes people are spiritual beings, or that God is a spiritual being, has any good reason to dismiss the existence of other spiritual beings, including evil ones like Satan.

THE BIBLICAL STAKES FOR DENYING A PERSONAL SATAN

As a young Christian I began my personal encounter with the Bible. For a variety of reasons I was thoroughly convinced that only the Bible was a legitimate candidate for divine revelation. Only the Bible advances an infinite, personal God who adequately accounts for what we see in the world and within ourselves. I thought it was very significant that earth's three monotheistic religions (Christianity, Judaism, and Islam) all go directly back to the Bible. What a remarkable book indeed! And I also saw that only the Bible presents grace as the cornerstone of God's dealings with humans—a portrayal of God as righteous, just, and loving.

These points, my own encounter with God, and the remarkable

predictive parts of the Bible all combined early on to give me a high view of Scripture. I was certain that unless God had spoken in some direct way, we had no hope of ever discovering enough about him to answer our basic questions, let alone how to have a relationship with him, and the Bible was the only credible candidate I could see for genuine divine revelation. Studying history of religion and reading other scriptures (of other religions) only strengthened my conviction that the Bible is in a class by itself. Even though I still struggled with some parts of Scripture, I knew it towered over any other claimed source of revelation.

Within this formative period I also realized that the reality of Satan is a take-it-or-leave-it proposition that includes taking or leaving the Bible itself. From one end to the other the Bible is a story about Satan. Yes it's also a story about God and humans, but none of it makes any sense without the other player. Without a real Satan, the Bible loses a main character and a key part of its plot. Furthermore, we would have to consider large sections to be flat-out lies.

As Christians we see Jesus at the linchpin of the Bible's story. And he spoke of Satan and demons more than all the other authors put together. He believed in, met, and warned about Satan. We saw the key reasons why the Old Testament teaches comparatively little about Satan and angels, but demons clearly surface in multiple books. The New Testament, loaded with teaching about Satan and spiritual warfare, sees the whole Christian life and mission as a battle with Satan.

Anytime people suggest that Satan is not real, they lay waste to the whole biblical story. If God is the only supernatural force in the universe, then he actually is orchestrating both sides in the struggle. Instead of a spiritual war, we would be confronted with a pseudo war, wherein God is fighting against himself.[4] All biblical theology collapses into nonsense without a personal, literal Satan.

PERSONAL EVIDENCE FOR THE REALITY OF SATAN

Considering these and other arguments, I realized I could no longer deny Satan's reality. But soon other experiences added even more conviction to my beliefs. Growing Christians soon encounter the reality of Satan in a very personal way. Just as I began to experience God's presence in my life, I began to experience something else—very powerful, very persuasive, and very evil. New voices began to speak to my mind, suggesting conclusions with such power that I recognized them as outside myself. Other Christians helped me realize these were the voices of Satan and his fellow evil spirits.

Such voices would intensify incredibly during times when God was using me to minister to others. As my own faith grew I began sharing it with others. Several friends came to faith; they in turn reached others. Within a couple of years I found myself teaching and leading a small group of friends, and here is where I met Satan in a way I had never imagined. The inner battering I would experience every time I tried to prepare a teaching or share my faith was out of this world.

The way Satan could sow discord and suspicion in groups of Christians was impressive. Through these experiences, I not only came to know Satan but also to respect his power and intelligence. New Christians sometimes doubt Satan, but mature ones, especially those who serve God in ministry, rarely do. Believers who serve seem to be well aware of Satan's work, as he opposes everything they try to do for God, often with amazing effectiveness.

Those who acknowledge and surrender to Jesus as their Lord have every reason, philosophically, biblically, and experientially, to believe that Satan is a being just as real as God. Much depends upon our understanding and practical ability to use the weapons of spiritual warfare effectively. Not only our own happiness and growth, but also the survival of other people's spiritual lives may depend largely on our ability to win this struggle.

DIFFICULTIES IN OLD TESTAMENT PREDICTIONS OF THE SUFFERING SERVANT

Old Testament prophecy predicts the coming of Messiah in two roles: as the servant of the Lord, and as the reigning king. These mainly correspond to Christ's first and second comings even though Jesus already reigns in a partial way. The prophecies of Messiah's first advent are less numerous than those foretelling his return; they are also more confusing when studied in their context. Realizing that these roles correspond to two comings of the same person would have been virtually impossible until after Jesus lived and explained the connection. Let's examine some of the key passages on the servant, noticing the problems in each.

ISAIAH'S SERVANT SONGS

Probably the best body of prophecy concerning Jesus' first coming is the "Servant Songs," in Isaiah 42:1–9; 49:1–13; 50:4–11; and 52:13–53:12. We could summarize Isaiah's portrayal of the servant as follows: One day a servant of the Lord will come who will be filled with God's Spirit. He will begin his ministry in obscurity rather than with the majesty people might expect. He will teach the ways of God and live a sinless life. His own people will reject him. He will suffer persecution and torture; his body will be marred horribly. His contemporaries will believe God has forsaken him. Finally, the servant will be killed, but in dying he will pay the price that the human race should have to pay for sin. Then he will rise from the dead, and multitudes, both Jews and Gentiles, will be brought into close relationship with God because of his work. This description conforms to Christ's life to an amazing degree. The New Testament makes it clear that early Christians knew these passages referred to Jesus (see Matthew 8:17; 12:17–21; Acts 8:32–33). However, critics have raised a number of objections against this "Christian reading."

First, the passages never call the servant *Messiah*, which would have created serious difficulty in connecting the two. The descriptions of King Messiah and the servant seem in utter contradiction. Instead of being a king, the servant "has no stately form or majesty" (Isaiah 53:2 NASB). Instead of commanding respect and honor, he is "despised and rejected—a man of sorrows, acquainted with deepest grief" (v. 3). He doesn't banish his foes; instead, "He was oppressed and treated harshly. . . . He was led like a lamb to the slaughter" (v. 7). King Messiah lives and rules forever, but this servant is "led away. No one cared that he died without descendants" (v. 8). Rather than empowering his reign, "it was the Lord's good plan to crush him and cause him grief" (v. 10).

Second, the four passages are spread out in a section of Isaiah dealing with God's faithfulness to Israel and his future dealings with her. When moved away from the text and set next to each other, a remarkably consistent picture emerges, but when viewed in original context, these passages are far less clear. Jewish readers have argued that Christians are performing a cut-and-paste textual surgery that ignores context.

Third, in the same section of Isaiah, God calls Israel herself "my servant Jacob" and "my servant Israel." Jewish readers claim these "anonymous servant" passages also refer to Israel as the Lord's servant. They think the seeming references to a suffering individual are metaphorical allusions to Jewish sufferings. Even within one of the Servant Songs he uses the term *my servant Israel*, referring apparently to the "anonymous" servant as a namesake, similar to the way Ezekiel calls him "my servant David" (Isaiah 49:3; cf. Ezekiel 34:23–24; 37:24–25). Christians reply that these passages can't be about Israel as the Lord's servant, because the career of the servant is completely different from that of Israel, and he is said to be sinless (Isaiah 53:9). Also, in more than one case, Israel is contrasted with the Servant of the Lord (Isaiah 42:6; 52:14; 53:2–6). Jewish readers retort that the passages may not well fit Israel but neither do they fit King Messiah.

All of these problems result in considerable confusion, especially to anyone who doesn't already know the history of Jesus' life.

> It is of greatest importance to know that Judaism before Christ never interpreted this passage [Isaiah 53] as referring to the sufferings of the Messiah. An expert in Jewish literature [Joseph Klausner] says, "In the whole Jewish Messianic literature of the Tannaitic period [before 200 AD] there is no trace of the 'suffering Messiah.' " . . .
>
> This is the point: it was completely hidden from the disciples that the Son of Man must fill the role of the suffering servant of Isaiah 53 before He comes in the power and glory of God's kingdom. . . . [A] suffering and dying Messiah or Son of Man was unheard of and seemed to be a flat contradiction to the explicit word of God.[1]

This, of course, contrasts with the clear predictions of the Messiah as reigning king. Such predictions, which, according to Christians, refer to his second coming, were universally recognized as referring to Messiah before the time of Christ.

QUESTIONS RAISED

These observations lead to an interesting question: Why would God break the servant prophecies into four pieces and intersperse them with passages about a different servant? If they were all together, the pattern would be so much plainer. Surely God must have realized the confusion that would arise because of this strange layout. Identifying the suffering servant with Messiah would be difficult, especially when we note another striking omission: The Old Testament never states or even hints that Messiah will come twice. Without this crucial piece of information it is virtually impossible to see the servant and Messiah as the same person. Readers who knew that King Messiah would live forever, that he would destroy his enemies, that he would have both stately form and majesty, were compelled to see some different person in these descriptions of the suffering servant.

How odd that God would not mention that the servant and Messiah are the same person. How odd that he would leave out the crucial detail that Messiah will come twice. Without these two missing pieces, the whole section becomes difficult if not impossible to understand for readers before and during the life of Christ.

PSALM 22:6–18

The twenty-second psalm describes Jesus' crucifixion—centuries before the mode of death was conceived. The details include that his hands and feet were pierced (v. 16), that he was naked (v. 17), that his bones were being pulled out of joint (v. 14), that his thirst was so intense his tongue stuck to the roof of his mouth (v. 15), that he was encircled by taunting persecutors as he died (v. 12), and that men gambled for his clothing while he watched (v. 18).

Jesus quoted verse 1 while on the cross: "My God, my God! Why have you forsaken me?" No doubt, he was calling people's attention to notice that the well-known psalm was being fulfilled in their presence. In addition, God literally was forsaking him at that moment as the judgment for human sin fell upon him.

We can only marvel at such a remarkable prophecy today, especially in light of our knowledge about Christ's crucifixion. However, if we imagine ourselves reading this psalm before or during Jesus' life, we get quite a different picture. It uses poetic language and speaks in the first person. It seems to describe the author's miseries in metaphorical terms. One would hardly conclude that it refers to the fate of King Messiah until after Jesus spotlighted it on the cross. The psalm never mentions Messiah. Further, since it says the victim is laid in "the dust of death" (v. 15 NASB), a pre-Christian reader would hardly conclude that it referred to Messiah, since related passages make it clear he lives forever. The missing point, that there are two messianic comings of Messiah, compels any reader to conclude that this is about someone else.

ZECHARIAH 11:12–14

Zechariah predicts Judas's betrayal of Christ, portraying God as a shepherd. For the purpose of communication, Zechariah enacts the betrayal and actually mentions "thirty pieces of silver." God remarks with sad irony that this "magnificent sum" (the price of a slave) was the value his people placed on him.

The New Testament teaches that this divine drama was referring to Judas's betrayal (Matthew 26:15). Notice that the passage also predicts that the money would finally be thrown into the temple and given to a potter. This was fulfilled as the priests used it to buy land from a local potter after Judas's death.

This astounding prediction is not without difficulties. The highly metaphorical nature of the shepherd requires interpretation; a careful contextual study reveals that the shepherd is God, and therefore Christ, as God, was sold for thirty pieces of silver. However, this would in no way be clear before the event occurred. Again, too, the passage mentions nothing about Messiah.

MICAH 5:2

Most of us know Micah 5:2 from Christmas readings:

> But you, O Bethlehem Ephrathah, are only a small village among all the people of Judah. Yet a ruler of Israel will come from you, one whose origins are from the distant past.

The Jews in Christ's time knew this referred to Messiah, as witnessed by the scribes quoting it to Herod the Great when arguing that Messiah would be born in Bethlehem (Matthew 2:5–6). Have you ever wondered, though, why we only focus on the first aspect (his birth in Bethlehem) and not on the fact that he is to be ruler in Israel? This passage clearly refers to a reigning king whose throne lasts forever and is worldwide, as the context makes clear:

> He will stand to lead his flock with the Lord's strength, in the majesty of the name of the Lord his God. Then his people will live there undisturbed, for he will be highly honored around the world. (Micah 5:4)

None of this fits Jesus' first coming, so it's hardly surprising that Jewish interpreters refuse to see this passage as referring to him. The passage is also an example of what some call the "prophetic gap": Messiah's birth in Bethlehem occurred during his first coming, according to Christians, while the rest of the passage refers to his second coming. But Micah never mentions the time-gap between the prediction's two parts; we're expected to believe that the passage would skip over two millennia without a word to indicate it. Skeptics argue that this is nothing less than a clear break in historical context that renders the interpretation suspect. Christians should ask themselves why God would fail to mention this passage of time.

ISAIAH 61:1–2

Jesus quoted Isaiah 61 during his first public sermon:

> The Spirit of the Lord is upon me, for he has anointed me to bring Good News to the poor. He has sent me to proclaim that captives will be released, that the blind will see, that the oppressed will be set free, and that the time of the Lord's favor has come. (Luke 4:18–19)

Unlike some of our earlier examples, people knew this passage was a messianic prediction long before the time of Jesus. When he read the passage, he stopped reading in the middle of verse 2 (Isaiah 61), where it refers to "the time of the Lord's favor." He left out the part about "the day of God's anger" and, rolling up the scroll, he said, "The Scripture you have just heard has been fulfilled this very day" (Luke 4:21). He stopped reading in the middle of a rhyming couplet! The rest of the Isaiah passage goes on to predict that Messiah will bring lasting peace and blessing to Israel. Today, we realize he didn't read the rest because that part hadn't been fulfilled yet; it will be fulfilled at his second coming.

The problem again is the prophetic gap. Why would God craft a messianic prediction so as to suddenly skip from one coming to another without mention of the intervening millennia? Even if he did inspire such a prophecy, why wouldn't he at least mention somewhere that there are two comings? The omniscient God surely would know that such omissions could only cause confusion. No wonder Jewish interpreters scoff at the Christian reading, which involves a break of context without any textual cue.

OLD TESTAMENT TYPOLOGY

The extensive Old Testament ceremonial law—the sacrificial system (especially the Day of Atonement), the tabernacle, and the festival calendar—also point directly to the work of Jesus, who was crucified on Passover. Looking back today, we see the ceremonial system as a remarkable prefiguring of Christ's atoning and intercessory work.

Even so, put yourself in the position of the first-century student of Scripture: How would you know there was any connection between Messiah and this system? No passage prescribing it ever mentions any messianic connection. Once again, only after Jesus' death (and probably after his explanation) did it become apparent that he was this elaborate system's fulfillment. Ancient Jews never had any idea of what they were acting out.

THE PATTERN

Although the list of messianic prophecies could go on and on, the pattern remains the same. In every single case they fail to mention Messiah, are metaphorical and obscure, contain prophetic gaps, or in other ways require two messianic comings in widely different roles. In every case, too, missing information compels the reader to reach the wrong conclusion: that these passages have nothing to do with Messiah.

However, while honest reading of these prophecies reveals a pattern of missing information, confusing contexts, and hard-to-interpret language, the lack of clarity is not universal: Actually, many predictions of Messiah are crystal clear. A closer look reveals that all the clear predictions refer to his return, and all the obscure or confusing predictions refer to the Advent. This is not just a generalization. *All* predictions of the second coming are clear, and *all* predictions of the first coming contain one or more of the issues mentioned above.

The complete uniformity of this pattern leads to only two conclusions: Either Jesus was not Messiah and all these passages mean something else entirely, or God purposely arranged to hide Messiah's mission in his first coming. As appendix 3 explains, Jesus, during his ministry, did little to ease the confusion.

JESUS' TEACHING ON HIS OWN MISSION

In Jesus' teaching, we see many comments that seem to perpetuate the confusion about the two messianic comings. For instance, when he began his ministry, Mark says,

> After John had been taken into custody, Jesus came into Galilee, preaching the gospel of God, and saying, "The time is fulfilled, and the kingdom of God is at hand; repent and believe in the gospel" (1:14–15 NASB).

To his audience, this could mean only one thing: that Jesus was proclaiming himself King Messiah and that the announced kingdom would be the one where "the wolf and the lamb will live together" (Isaiah 11:6). Although Jesus later qualified his proclamation as being different from the Old Testament representation of a worldwide compulsory rule of God, he did so in a veiled way, like in his "kingdom parables."

THE KINGDOM PARABLES

In Matthew 13, Jesus gave the parables of the kingdom, each one stressing the difference between what people were expecting (based on Old Testament prophecy) and the kingdom he'd actually come to establish. They anticipated a sudden takeover; instead, the kingdom would grow gradually from obscure beginnings (parables of the mustard seed and leaven).[1] Instead of "ruling the nations with a rod of iron" and banishing all sinners, believers and nonbelievers would live side by side in the kingdom Jesus brought (parables of the soils, dragnet, wheat and tares, and perhaps others).

Even when he explained some parables to his followers, he never suggested that the parables teach on the period between his first and second comings. In fact, Jesus didn't say he would leave and come back until the night before his death. Matthew acknowledged that his sayings were hidden and mysterious, quoting Psalm 78:2, in Matthew 13:35: "This fulfilled what God had spoken through the prophet: 'I will speak to you in parables. I will explain things hidden since the creation of the world.' " Jesus could have easily told the audience, or at least his disciples, how these parables tied into the future of the church. But he didn't.

JESUS' SELF-DISCLOSURES

In other places it seems Jesus wanted his followers to understand the nature of his mission as the suffering servant:

> Taking the twelve disciples aside, Jesus said, "Listen, we're going up to Jerusalem, where all the predictions of the prophets concerning the Son of Man will come true. He will be handed over to the Romans, and will be mocked, treated shamefully, and spit upon. They will flog him with a whip and kill him, but on the third day he will rise again" (Luke 18:31–33).

This was clear enough. However, we also read in verse 34 that the disciples "didn't understand any of this. The significance of his words was hidden from them, and they failed to grasp what he was talking about."

Why didn't they understand? Was it because they couldn't break out of the eternal (undying) Messiah paradigm? Or did God himself "hide" the meaning from them? We don't know. But if we study all of the similar disclosures Jesus made, we see sixteen passages where he told his disciples what he was going to do (some are duplicates).[2] Each passage that records the disciples' reaction makes it plain they did not understand what he was saying.

While he was with them, they never did understand. Right up to the end of his ministry they were asking, "So is this the time when you will reveal your kingdom?" (Acts 1:6; cf. Luke 19:11). Even the question they asked at the Mount of Olives—"What will be the sign of Your coming?" (Matthew 24:3 NASB)—may be misleading to contemporary readers, in sounding like they knew he would leave and come back. But the term *coming* was also used of a triumphal entry, or presentation of himself, as king. They probably still thought that this "coming" could happen any day.

PARADIGMATIC THINKING

A paradigm is a model, a way of thinking. Once people have become used to seeing something one way, they have trouble seeing other ways of interpreting the same thing. The Jews of Jesus' day had a paradigm, a way of viewing the Old Testament and the predictions of Messiah. While Jesus didn't fit their view very well, they never succeeded in forming a new paradigm that included two messianic comings. They looked on in confusion, and usually Jesus gave them little or no help forming a new understanding.

Notice, for instance, the paradigmatic thinking of the crowd in John 12:34. After Jesus mentioned being "lifted up" on the cross,

> The crowd then answered Him, "We have heard out of the Law that the Christ is to remain forever; and how can You say, 'The Son of Man must be lifted up'? Who is this Son of Man?" (NASB).

Jesus didn't answer their question. Because they couldn't conceive of a dying Messiah, they tended to shift the Son of Man's identity in order to compensate. This likely was the norm throughout Jesus' life.

THE LAST NIGHT

At the Last Supper, Jesus made a series of significant statements. After dinner, he said,

> Dear children, I will be with you only a little longer. And as I told the Jewish leaders, you will search for me, but you can't come where I am going. (John 13:33)

Then we read that Peter asked, "Lord, where are you going?" (v. 36). Clearly, Peter still didn't know what was about to happen, and Thomas echoed this confusion. When Jesus said, "You know the way to where I am going," Thomas answered, "No, we don't know, Lord. . . . We have no idea where you are going, so how can we know the way?" (14:4–5). They were completely baffled.

Then, when Jesus promised that those who received the Spirit after his departure would receive a revelation of him, Judas Alpheus asked, "Lord, why are you going to reveal yourself only to us and not to the world at large?" (v. 22). They were incredulous that he wasn't going to reveal to the world his true identity as King Messiah. Remember, this conversation occurred the night before his death. Even at this late date, none of his disciples realized that he intended to die, rise, leave, and return.

In the same conversation Jesus said, "These things I have spoken to you so that you may be kept from stumbling" (16:1 NASB). Later he expanded: "Yes, I'm telling you these things now, so that when they happen, you will remember my warning. I didn't tell you earlier because I was going to be with you for a while longer" (v. 4). He was longing to open their eyes to the whole plan: "There is so much more I want to tell you, but you can't bear it now" (v. 12). He only gave hints: "In a little while you won't see me anymore. But a little while after that, you will see me again" (v. 16).

Again, dismay and confusion reigned as the disciples asked each other, "What does he mean when he says, 'You won't see me, but then you will see me,' and 'I am going to the Father'? And what does he mean by 'a little while'? We don't understand" (vv. 17–18). His only response:

I have spoken of these matters in figures of speech, but soon I will stop speaking figuratively and will tell you plainly all about the Father. (v. 25)

Why would Jesus need to wait for a later time to tell them plainly what he meant? Most commentators give no adequate explanation,[3] but the answer is readily available: The time was not right to reveal the mystery hidden for ages past. *Only after the cross could he throw back the curtain to reveal God's plan for the ages.*

As we read this exchange we should sense that Jesus was pursuing a course identical to what God earlier pursued in the Old Testament; i.e., telling them things they didn't understand but would remember after the events occurred. Following the resurrection, these statements all made perfect sense (cf. John 2:22), but beforehand Jesus himself acknowledged that people couldn't grasp what he was saying. Ask yourself: Why did Jesus say it was "necessary" to speak in parables? (John 16:25).

AFTER THE RESURRECTION

After the resurrection, Jesus met with the disciples and fully explained himself:

> Then he opened their minds to understand the Scriptures, and He said to them, "Thus it is written, that the Christ would suffer and rise again from the dead the third day; and that repentance for forgiveness of sins should be proclaimed in His name to all the nations, beginning from Jerusalem" (Luke 24:45–47 NASB).

What a Bible study this must have been! Notice what he "opened their minds" to: the Old Testament predictions of the suffering servant. Now they understood that he and King Messiah were one and the same but revealed in two separate comings.

After the cross, Jesus expected people to recognize what had happened. He said to the men on the road to Emmaus, "O foolish men and slow of heart to believe in all that the prophets have spoken! Was it not necessary for the Christ to suffer these things and to enter into his glory?" (vv. 25–26). "Then beginning with Moses and with all the prophets, He explained to them the things concerning Himself in all the Scriptures" (v. 27). These men had seen Psalm 22 and Isaiah 53 fulfilled and had already heard reports of the resurrection. Jesus apparently felt the picture was now clear.

Why did Jesus wait until after his resurrection to tell them these things? Why couldn't he have opened their minds earlier? Why did he speak in "figurative language" before but plainly now? He was intentionally veiling his mission up until a certain point in time. As with God through the Old Testament, Jesus wanted a situation where he could say "I told you so," while at the same time he didn't want people to know what he was doing until after he did it.

CONCLUSION

Once we admit that the suffering servant prophecies were deliberately obscured and that Jesus perpetuated the obscurity, the whole business cries for an explanation. Paul says it was a secret God kept to himself alone, not revealed to previous generations. Why would God feel the need to keep Jesus' mission secret? Why would Jesus continue the policy of concealment even as the hour of climax approached?

The best answer is that this was part of the cosmic war with Satan. Jesus had to keep the secret until the right time so his enemy would walk into the net prepared for him, as Paul says in 1 Corinthians 2:6–8. No other answer is suggested (we will look at some of the critical issues in appendix 4), and because of that passage's importance to the meaning of the mystery, its exegesis becomes pivotal.

Although the cross and Jesus' two separate comings (with the previously undisclosed age between) accomplish numerous other goals, according to Scripture, none of them would require secrecy. On the other hand, the disarming of Satan (Colossians 2:15) and the victory won through Christ's death probably did require surprise. Unless we believe God is orchestrating both sides of a pseudo-war where the players have no choice about what they do (e.g., that God compelled Satan to conspire to kill Jesus, even though he didn't want to), we almost have to conclude that Satan didn't understand how devastating the cross would be to himself.

Secrecy only from human players would be a waste of time. If they were confused but Satan knew what was going on, he would have no problem telling people under his influence how to respond. Also, the cosmic significance assigned to the hidden mystery in multiple passages often focuses on the angels, fallen or unfallen. Paul's insistence that "we are not fighting against flesh-and-blood enemies, but against evil rulers and authorities of the unseen world" (Ephesians 6:12), underscores that spiritual warfare, now substantially won, is at the heart of God's purpose for the church (as discussed in chapter 5). At the cross God silenced the logic of rebellion once and for all, and without coercion or force. Satan signed his own death warrant, oblivious to what he was doing. He took the logic of rebellion to its logical conclusion: self-destruction.

ASSESSING GOD'S SECRECY

In chapters 4 and 5, and appendices 2 and 3, we've considered substantial evidence that God kept Jesus' mission a secret until the last minute. I have suggested that the purpose for concealment has to do with spiritual warfare and future cosmic security based on its citizens' understanding of God.

In this appendix we'll look at a number of critical questions and possible contrary evidence to my suggestion. Questions like the ones below often come up when I lecture on the subject.

SATAN'S BLINDNESS

It is one thing to say the disciples didn't perceive or understand what Jesus was saying, even though he announced his intention to die and rise from the dead, but how could Satan miss such a clear declaration?

Never forget that, unlike God, Satan is not omniscient. He is far more intelligent than humans are, yet he is limited in knowledge and understanding. Again, we have no evidence that he can tell the future or read people's minds, and neither is he omnipresent, even through the agency of his many demons. These limitations raise at least two possibilities.

Satan may have made the same mistakes everyone else did, and for the same reasons. Whatever caused the disciples' failure to comprehend what Jesus was saying may have caused Satan to fail as well. Perhaps God was actively blocking his understanding—a distinct possibility based on the passive voice in the phrase "[it] was hidden from them" (Luke 18:34). The middle voice would simply mean they were too blind to see what he was saying.

Perhaps Satan too suffered from paradigmatic thinking that left him unable to consider an alternative mission for Jesus, one not involving a world takeover. Either way, he must not have grasped the meaning of Jesus' words.

An additional possibility is that Jesus only gave these disclosures when he discerned that Satan was not around. When talking to the disciples in the upper room about his death and departure, Jesus said, "I will not speak much more with you, for the ruler of the world is coming, and he has nothing in Me" (John 14:30 NASB). If Jesus only talked about confidential information when no demons were listening, this might help explain why he gave disclosures of the future in odd settings that sometimes seem rather out of context.

If Satan thought Jesus was here to begin his kingdom, why would he try to tempt him? Didn't he do this so he could disqualify Jesus from being a "spotless lamb" sacrifice?

This motive, which some have suggested to explain why Satan tempted Jesus, implies that Satan fully understood what Jesus was here to do, but we don't know Satan's motives on this occasion. If Jesus committed sin, it probably would have disqualified him from being king, just as it would have disqualified him from being the sacrificial lamb. The temptations raise multiple theological problems involving the Trinity, the kenosis (or "emptying") of Jesus, his ability to sin ("impeccability") and more. Therefore, I'm not going to attempt a full explanation here. Suffice to say that passages like those on the temptation of Christ would have to be reconsidered if we accept that nobody, including Satan, knew Jesus planned to die for sin.

WERE ALL PEOPLE SO BLIND, AND SHOULD THEY HAVE BEEN?

If nobody knew the meaning of the suffering servant predictions, why does Simeon cite one of Isaiah's Servant Songs when he sees Jesus as a baby? (Luke 2:25–32).

It seems that Simeon was giving a prophetic word, since he speaks in verses similar to that found in the prophets. If so, he was inspired to say what he did, but perhaps without realizing the full implications. He would have been just like the Old Testament prophets who predicted "the sufferings of Christ" without knowing to whose suffering it referred (1 Peter 1:12). Prophets don't always understand what they utter, as Daniel indicated after receiving one of his visions: "I heard what he said, but I did not understand what he meant" (Daniel 12:8). On another occasion he said, "I was greatly troubled by the vision and could not understand it" (8:27). If Simeon was speaking a prophetic word in this passage, he may never have understood the full implications. Our best evidence remains that nobody, including Simeon, understood the mystery because it was "hidden in God" (Ephesians 3:9 NASB).

If nobody knew Jesus was the suffering and atoning servant, why did John the Baptist declare, "Behold the lamb of God!"? (John 1:36).

Again, John may have been speaking under prophetic inspiration rather than from his own understanding. Jesus said John was a prophet, so the same argument (as for Simeon) would apply. We know John's understanding was not complete, because he later became so confused he had to send messengers asking whether Jesus was in fact Messiah (Matthew 11:2–3). When people asked John his own identity, he would refer to Isaiah 40:3: "a voice shouting in the wilderness, 'Clear the way for the Lord's coming!' " (John 1:23). In the context for this prediction, Isaiah was clearly referring to the coming of Messiah, but in his second coming: "Then the glory of the Lord will be revealed, and all people will see it together" (Isaiah 40:5). So John probably expected a kingdom like everyone else, which likely is why he sent the messengers to ask Jesus if he was Messiah after all: No kingdom had appeared, and Jesus wasn't acting like a king.

If the predictions of the cross were so hard to understand, why did Jesus and an angel reprove people for failing to understand them?

On two occasions, people were rebuked for failing to see Jesus' death and resurrection for what they were. In Luke 24, two angels said to the women who came to the empty tomb:

> Why are you looking among the dead for someone who is alive? He isn't here! He is risen from the dead! Remember what he told you back in Galilee, that the Son of Man must be betrayed into the hands of sinful men and be crucified, and that he would rise again on the third day. (vv. 5–7)

On another occasion, Jesus rebuked the men on the road to Emmaus:

> You foolish people! You find it so hard to believe all that the prophets wrote in the Scriptures. Wasn't it clearly predicted that the Messiah would have to suffer all these things before entering his glory? (vv. 25–26)

The important thing to see in both incidents is that they occur only *after* the resurrection. Jesus and the angels apparently felt that since the crucifixion and the resurrection had now occurred, they should have been able to connect the dots. Instead, it seems not a single person was waiting for the resurrection; people remained locked in their paradigm of Messiah as a reigning king who cannot die. The disciples were so certain that Jesus had died once and for all that he had to eat fish in front of them to convince them he wasn't a ghost (vv. 36–43). Before the cross, Jesus himself acknowledged that the disciples didn't understand and implied that they *couldn't*: "There is so much more I want to tell you, but you can't bear it now" (John 16:12). His position clearly changed after the resurrection.

Why haven't I read this in commentaries before?

I have never done a thorough survey of the history of interpretation on this issue. My fragmentary reading indicates that this interpretation of events is indeed rare. In fact, I have yet to read anyone who fully argues this case. But that may not be surprising.

From the early centuries, Christian apologists have been eager to demonstrate the clarity of Old Testament prophecy regarding Jesus' death for sin. However, as we have seen, that argument only holds water *after* the life of Jesus.

Interestingly, I was first fully introduced to the difficulties in Old Testament predictions of Messiah's first coming through discussions with Jewish scholars. As one Jewish history professor said, "Since the time of Jesus, the lion does lie down with the lamb. The problem is that only the lion gets back up!" During these discussions, I was impressed by the strength of my own paradigmatic thinking. I'd always been taught that only a fool would miss the predictions of the suffering and death of Jesus because they were so clear. But conservative Jewish scholars see suggestions like the idea that Messiah comes twice as completely unsupported by Scripture. From their perspective, Jesus simply failed to fulfill Old Testament messianic prophecies.

In the years that followed, I began looking at the question from the perspective of a first-century Jew. I had to admit that from their vantage, the prophecies were not only unclear but totally confusing. At the same time, I felt their explanations for prophecies of the first coming were tortured and inadequate in their own right.

I think a desire to have an unambiguous case for the prefiguring of Jesus has led Christian readers to exaggerate the clarity of these predictions, at least as they appeared during Jesus' day. Bible teachers today discuss how spiritually blind the disciples and others were to miss what was happening; nonetheless, we look at these events from the Christian perspective, and from our view, after the life of Jesus, they are clear. Jewish readers ask, "Of what use are predictions that can only be deciphered after the fact?"

While in seminary, I did a verse-by-verse analysis of every significant first-coming prediction, in part because I was bothered by these complaints, which I sensed were on some level correct. While pondering an honest answer to such questions, I was driven to the conclusion that God had purposely constructed the predictions this way. My suggestion that he did so to provide his enemy with an opportunity to destroy himself contains some speculation and may not be the whole answer. But I have not seen any other satisfactory answer that adequately explains the obvious ambiguity in these prophecies.

I think this is a novel teaching that goes against the Reformation teaching that "the devil is God's devil."

I don't think so. Luther's famous statement is true and in no way contradicts what I am arguing in this book. Satan is *not* at liberty to do what he wants; otherwise, we would probably all be dead. On the other hand, God has given him a surprising amount of freedom, as all human history demonstrates. Even in cases where God controls Satan's evil actions, the question remains: How does God control him? One possibility is that he does so by simple decree, as seen in Job. But it may be that in this case God got Satan to do what he wanted, not by force, but by allowing him to do exactly what his own evil heart desired.

God is fully capable of causing things to come out a certain way by suddenly withdrawing his protective hand. One example is Isaiah 7:20, where God says he will hire a "razor" from beyond the Euphrates to shave the land of Israel—the horrifying Assyrians. But we need not assume that God directly *compelled* the Assyrians to attack Israel; they were interested in that anyway. All God did was remove his protecting hand because of Israel's sin.

You refer to a "prophetic gap," which identifies this argument as being from the dispensational school of interpretation. Therefore, reformed theologians should reject this view.

Not true. Both reformed and dispensational interpreters accept a prophetic gap (skipping from Christ's first to his second coming in the same passage with no indication of any time passing). This is unavoidable, and Jesus himself indicated a prophetic gap in the way he interpreted Isaiah 61, as we saw earlier (see Luke 4:17–21).

After studying this question for years and discussing it with reformed scholars, I am convinced that the whole question has nothing to do with the reformed/dispensational debate. The question of the meaning of the mystery hidden has nothing to do, for instance, with the nature of the kingdom when Jesus returns. All agree that Jesus will rule when he returns, whether it's a theocratic kingdom or simply eternity future. Reformed theologians see the prophecies of the second coming in many of the same passages dispensationalists do. Both schools also see the first-coming predictions the same way. So this is simply not an area of disagreement between the two schools.

One reformed scholar, Grant Osborne, professor of New Testament at Trinity Evangelical Divinity School, read my paper on the subject of the mystery hidden for ages past and was in guarded agreement while feeling more study was needed. He said the paper was important and urged me to write a formal research paper and present it to the Evangelical Theological Society (of which he was the president at the time). I turned down the offer because I am a pastor with a good-sized church to lead, and I have never felt called to work in the academic world. I told him if he thought it was so important, he should write the paper and present it. Though that never happened, I bring it up to illustrate that reformed thinkers have no more problem with this position than anyone else. To be fair, when I discussed it with D. A. Carson, he was more negative. He agreed that God wrote prophecy in a way that obscured Jesus' career, including the cross. He also agreed that Satan did not understand what the cross would accomplish. However, he felt my suggestion that God had arranged things this way in order to fool Satan, "went too far." He felt events were clear enough that Satan should have understood.

In summary, I have written on this theory of the mystery and its relation to spiritual warfare in the hope that people will consider it, not on the basis of which school of theology it belongs to but on the basis of biblical exegesis. I personally am critical of both the dispensational and reformed approaches at points, and I don't feel committed to either. Neither am I affiliated with either view. It doesn't matter, because theological conclusions should be based on sound exegesis, not on affiliation.

ENDNOTES

Chapter 1

1. *www.barna.org/barna-update/article/21-transformation/252-barna-survey-examines-changes-in-worldview-among-christians-over-the-past-13-years* (accessed 16 March 2009).

2. *The New Living Translation* (NLT) of the Bible takes an interesting approach. Instead of word-for-word translation, its committee translated "thought for thought." This often is an excellent way to translate with accuracy, for the simple reason that we express thoughts today differently than biblical authors did then. The NLT is not a paraphrase, such as *The Message*, where the author gives his interpretation of what was written and said. On the other hand, *all* translation includes some interpretation, because words and expressions have a certain semantic range of meaning. We refer to certain translations as "literal," but translators *always* have to choose which of several words or expressions to use in translation. The NLT approach allows for more interpretation than most, and I have used it as the default version throughout this book. However, wherever I feel it takes too much liberty, or where the actual wording is important, I have preferred *The New American Standard Bible* (1995 edition) (NASB), one of the most literal word-for-word translations we have.

3. Many authors stress the victory Jesus won over Satan in a way that makes it sound like Satan isn't very dangerous and can't win battles against the church. I disagree. The victory won at the cross refers to the ultimate cosmic war between God, the church, and Satan. But that doesn't mean Satan can't win local victories, and substantial ones at that. He has utterly defeated entire churches and even denominations in the history of Christianity, rendering them ineffective in serving God, or even making them disappear altogether. He can also win battles in individual Christians' lives.

Otherwise, why would Peter tell us to be on the alert lest he "devour" someone? Of course we want Christians to feel secure in Christ, and we have good reason to reassure them that Jesus will get the last word, but sometimes efforts to alleviate fear can get out of control and begin to imply that there is no danger.

CHAPTER 2

1. Biblically, cherubim first appear when God stationed two of them at the garden of Eden (Genesis 3:24). The angelic figures attached to the ark of the covenant were cherubim (Exodus 25:18). God appeared enthroned above the cherubim (Psalm 80:1). There are striking and confounding descriptions of cherubim in Ezekiel 1 and 10.

2. The Old and New Testaments refer to immense numbers of angels; the term *myriads* means tens of thousands. Revelation 5:11 (NASB) refers to "myriads of myriads" of angels, and while the NLT translates this "thousands and millions of angels," more accurately it means *hundreds of millions* of angels (see also Psalm 68:17; Daniel 7:10; Deuteronomy 33:2; Nehemiah 9:6; Hebrews 12:22). It is possible that Matthew 18:10 indicates that children have guardian angels, which again would imply that angels are exceedingly numerous. Some people mistakenly believe that angels are the spirits of humans who have died; Hebrews 9:27 shows that this is false.

CHAPTER 3

1. Liberal scholars generally deny that the serpent was Satan. Rather, they say it was just a mythical creature or a talking snake. Gordon Wenham says, "Early Jewish and Christian commentators identified the snake with Satan or the devil, but since there is no other trace of a personal devil in early parts of the OT, modern writers doubt whether this is the view of our narrator" (Gordon J. Wenham, *Word Biblical Commentary Vol. 1, Genesis 1-15*, [Dallas: Word, Incorporated, 2002], 72). However, as we will see in Chapter 19, early parts of the Old Testament do refer to a personal Satan and demons. Also, one of the "early Christian commentators" who said this passage referred to Satan was John in the book of Revelations, 12:9, which states that the "dragon was thrown down, the serpent of old who is called the devil and Satan" (NASB).

2. Some interpreters suggest that Adam and Eve's knowledge was the *experiential* knowledge of evil. But this doesn't fit God's statement in verse 22:

"Behold, the man has become like one of Us, knowing good and evil" (NASB). Adam's knowledge was like God's, which was not experiential. Rather, just as God decrees what is good and evil based on himself—on the unchanging reality of his very essence—so humans began doing the same thing, that is, deciding what is good or evil *based on self.*

CHAPTER 5

1. Origen, and Gregory of Nyssa, thought Satan made this mistake because he failed to realize that Jesus was deity in human form. Gregory argued that the humanity of Jesus cloaked his deity: "The Deity was hidden under the veil of our nature, so that, as with ravenous fish, the hook of the Deity might be gulped down along with the bait of flesh" (*Great Catechism,* 24). Thus God made Satan think he could trade the enslaved human race for something more valuable—the death of Jesus (this is the so-called "ransom theory"), and, instead, Jesus used his divine power to rise from the dead. However, this is implausible. Satan would have known Messiah was divine because he would have known Isaiah 9:6. Again, one demon complained that Jesus had come before the appointed time; why would demons submit to his name if they didn't know he was divine? How would his followers, and even his enemies—but not Satan—know he claimed deity? Also, the idea that God would offer to pay Satan for humanity elevates Satan unreasonably. Jesus' references to offering himself as a ransom refer to his paying the sentence owed to God's justice.

2. Some feel this passage is not referring to Satan but to the human rulers who put Jesus to death. That's possible, although unlikely in my opinion. Paul uses the term *god of this world* (or *this age*) to refer to Satan (2 Corinthians 4:4). Also, the "mighty powers in this dark world" refers to demons (Ephesians 6:12). The term here in 1 Corinthians 2:6 is *aeon houtos,* rather than *kosmos,* though the sense is similar. In addition, if Paul was referring to Pilate, Herod, and Caiaphas, why would he use the present tense, "who are passing away," when all of them were already dead or at least no longer in power? This phraseology suggests the passing of the present age, or the *kosmos* (1 John 2:17).

   David Prior leans toward human rulers, but says, "What does Paul mean by the rulers of this age . . . ? It could be earthly rulers, such as Pilate and Caiaphas, representing Roman and Jewish wisdom, or it could refer to demonic powers" (*The Message of 1 Corinthians: Life in the Local Church,* The Bible Speaks Today, Vol. 50 [Downers Grove, Ill., InterVarsity Press, 1985]). Warren Wiersbe says, "Paul may have been referring to the spiritual and demonic rulers of this present age (Romans 8:38;

Colossians 2:15; Ephesians 6:12ff). This would make more sense in 1 Corinthians 2:6, for certainly Pilate, Herod, and the other rulers were not recognized for any special wisdom. The wisdom of this age has its origin in the rulers of this age, of which Satan is the prince (John 12:31; 14:30; 16:11). Of course, the spiritual rulers would have to work in and through the human rulers. So perhaps we must not press the distinction (John 13:2, 27)" (*The Bible Exposition Commentary* [Wheaton, IL: Victor Books, 1996, c1989]).

Whether or not Paul has the demons in view here, we can still conclude that Satan didn't know God's plan, because Paul says the mystery was hidden in God alone (Ephesians 3:9).

3. God confirms that he purposely veiled the Old Testament prophecies of the first coming in 1 Peter 1:10–12: "As to this salvation, the prophets who prophesied of the grace that would come to you made careful searches and inquiries, seeking to know what person or time the Spirit of Christ within them was indicating as He predicted the sufferings of Christ and the glories to follow. It was revealed to them that they were not serving themselves, but you, in these things which now have been announced to you through those who preached the gospel to you by the Holy Spirit sent from heaven—things into which angels long to look" (NASB). According to this passage, even the prophets who foretold the suffering servant didn't know to whom the passages referred. Notice it's the first coming of Christ ("the sufferings of Christ and the glories to follow") that confused them. Even after careful search and inquiry, God never told them who the suffering servant was. Peter says God only revealed to them that a later generation would be served by these predictions, so they didn't need to know who it was. This must be the case, again, since Paul says the mystery was a secret "hidden in God."

Interesting as well is the last phrase: "things into which angels long to look." Apparently the angels are astonished by what they see in this revealed mystery. Like the passage in Ephesians 3:10, Peter seems to imply that the entire universe is learning a lesson they will never forget from the work of the cross and its result in the church.

CHAPTER 6

1. Bill Hybels and Mark Mittelberg, *Becoming a Contagious Christian* (Grand Rapids: Zondervan, 1996), 120.

CHAPTER 7

1. Theologians debate whether this binding of Satan is a one-time event that happened during Christ's ministry or something we should do in prayer anytime we plan to plunder Satan's house. Most who believe this refers to a unique event that happened at the cross or during Jesus' ministry, also cite Revelation 20:2, about Satan being bound for a thousand years. Some believe this prophecy is referring to the church age (so Jesus bound Satan during his ministry, and he remains bound today). I don't agree. The whole reason God binds the Evil One, in this passage, is "so Satan could not deceive the nations anymore" (v. 3). This description doesn't fit the binding in Matthew 13—Satan is still deceiving the nations today. As Jesus' followers, we have power over Satan unlike any before us, and in this sense, the coming of God's kingdom in Jesus could be a binding of Satan. But I also think this could refer to something we should do in prayer whenever we go out to plunder his household. Paul stresses intercessory prayer in the context of spiritual warfare (Ephesians 6:17–18).

2. When we look at how the early church behaved, we see that "infiltration" captures the imagery of our strategy better than "invasion." Invasion suggests arrival in force and gradual domination of the enemy's land; a conventional invasion usually tries to roll the Enemy back like rolling up a carpet. But the early church didn't see itself this way—they acted like an underground partisan force. Partisans have to conceal their presence most of the time, mixing with ordinary citizens in occupied territory, waiting for the chance to strike a blow against the occupier. Consider how the wheat and the tares grow side by side and the farmer forbids any effort to separate them (Matthew 13:24–29).

   Think of the French underground during World War II. The Nazis, who had no right to occupy France, were cruel overlords. Patriotic French people formed underground nuclei of partisans to resist occupation. They met together, trained, were armed (usually by the British), and carried out orders sent in by their British controllers. Partisans must conduct themselves so as to avoid bringing down the heat of majority culture. Yet to be successful, they have to recruit others to join the movement and go out on frequent raids or intelligence-gathering forays. By day, they don't attract attention to themselves but live as normal people of the land.

   You see this kind of thinking frequently in the New Testament; God calls Christians to live as "aliens and strangers." We are aliens in the world because "We are citizens of heaven, where the Lord Jesus Christ lives" (Philippians 3:20). Paul says God has "rescued us from the kingdom of darkness and transferred us into the Kingdom of his dear Son" (Colossians

1:13; cf. John 17:14). Of course, we realize this transfer is spiritual, and that for the time being, we still live in the world system as aliens. Paul pictures himself as a partisan when he says, "I have become all things to all men, so that I may by all means save some" (1 Corinthians 9:22 NASB). As he moved from one culture to another he tried to blend in as much as possible without violating God's moral imperatives. Just as a Frenchman couldn't tell whether the man next to him on the bus was a shopkeeper or an underground fighter, people who met Paul had no way of knowing he was one of the most powerful apostles alive. He seemed like others in the society.

Peter appealed to the church, as aliens and strangers, to live excellent lives among the Gentiles in order to refute slander and avoid persecution (1 Peter 2:11–25). They should honor the king and other officials and, if they were slaves, even their masters. As a persecuted community, he wanted them to avoid any behavior that would bring unnecessary trouble. They would have enough trouble merely pursuing their mission without adding unnecessary offense.

The church has often failed to see infiltration this way and has opted for a *coup de main*, where they try to take over entire cultures by force. This was the case in medieval times, when the church enforced Christian moral views with imprisonment, torture, and even death. In place of infiltration, the church saw its role as domination, considering force to be a legitimate tool for advancing God's purposes on earth. Instead of equipping and empowering believers to spread God's Word, the church focused on protecting and controlling believers by forcing others to comply with its doctrine and morality.

Even today, some Christians look more to political solutions to evil than to winning the hearts and souls of people to God. The result is increased hostility from our culture and a distortion of the message we are called to preach. We should turn away from forceful or showy tactics and instead focus on spreading God's love, as the Bible teaches, through quiet, personal involvement with non-Christians.

3. Gerhard Kittel says, "[This] word group [*katischuo*] has the meaning 'to be able,' 'to be capable,' 'capacity,' 'power,' 'strength.' The word here means to 'be strong enough' or 'to be able' either 'to overcome' or 'to prevail' (if the reader thinks that context fits), or 'to withstand' (if we think the context fits that)." G. Kittel, G. W. Bromiley, and G. Friedrich, eds., *Theological Dictionary of the New Testament, Vol. 3*, electronic edition (Grand Rapids: Eerdmans, 1964–c1976), 397. The word literally means, "to be strong against." The question is, "strong enough to do what?" It should be obvious that city gates need to be strong enough to withstand

attack. They *never* attack others, so it would be absurd to think of a set of gates "overcoming" an army. Thus the NRSV correctly translates, "the gates of Hades will not prevail against it."

4. The vision God gives his people in the Old Testament nonetheless does give the mandate to reach out with his love to other people (see Jonah). God tells the Israelites in Deuteronomy 7:6, "You are a holy people, who belong to the Lord your God. Of all the people on earth, the Lord your God has chosen you to be his own special treasure." He proceeds to order them to dispossess the nations in Canaan rather than try to win them. "When the Lord your God hands these nations over to you and you conquer them, you must completely destroy them. Make no treaties with them and show them no mercy. Do not intermarry with them. Do not let your daughters and sons marry their sons and daughters, for they will lead your children away from me to worship other gods" (vv. 2–4). This concern about contamination, intermixing, and imitating the nations dwindles nearly to the vanishing point in the New Testament. Carving out an area and living there apart from other peoples would be unthinkable. Our commission is to go.

5. In fortress theology, Christians have concluded that we, the church, are in a fortress under attack by Satan. Their view of the church's strategy is primarily defensive—that is, we have to guard our people from the dangers of the world-system. This usually involves some form of separation from the world; a misunderstanding of the concept of holiness. To be holy means to be *distinct* or *different*, not necessarily to be separated in the sense of avoiding or leaving the world. Christians should be different because we are more loving and selfless than others, not because we are culturally detached.

Fortress theologians focus on the Old Testament instructions to avoid contamination from the surrounding countries. They think we too need to form safe havens for believers and should not go to "worldly" places like bars or rock concerts. We should break off friendships with ungodly people and should never watch ungodly shows. The whole emphasis is on defense and avoidance. Of course, most fortress theologians also say Christians should witness, but success is unlikely when Christians live in a separated, isolated mentality.

Jesus and the rest of the New Testament directly reject fortress theology. Jesus went to raw parties in the homes of tax gatherers and even had prostitutes among his followers. The Pharisees and other leaders (fortress theologians of their day) criticized him for being the friend of tax-gatherers and sinners. But he said, "Healthy people don't need a doctor—sick people do. I have come to call not those who think they are righteous, but those who know they are sinners" (Mark 2:17). Paul argued that we also should "try to find common ground with everyone, doing everything [you] can to save some" (1 Corinthians 9:22). The argument that Paul was stronger than others and therefore was only describing his own ministry rather than ours, breaks down when we read on to 11:1: "Be imitators of me, just as I also am of Christ" (NASB).

Paul didn't avoid idol temples. He told the Athenians: "I was passing through and examining the objects of your worship" (Acts 17:23 NASB). He went right in and studied polytheistic religion. He quoted heathen poets and philosophers by heart (Titus 1:12; Acts 17:28) and actually forbade withdrawal from the world-system when he cried out with horror, "[I never told you to avoid] unbelievers who indulge in sexual sin, or are greedy, or cheat people, or worship idols. You would have to leave this world to avoid people like that" (1 Corinthians 5:10).

Jesus made his position on this clear during his prayer for his followers before the crucifixion: "I'm not asking you to take them out of the world [*kosmos*], but to keep them safe from the evil one" (John 17:15). We are not to seek refuge from worldly people and situations, because then we would lose our effectiveness in the offensive war God sent us to wage. The only exception would be Christians who feel too weak to be around sinful situations; these may have to withdraw from the world until they gain enough spiritual strength to withstand potentially tempting situations.

Believers who fear the *kosmos* usually create their own subculture—including language, music, art, and even dress—that becomes a barrier for non-Christians. Fortress Christians lose their vital engagement with those who need them most: the lost mass of prisoners we are to rescue. Some fortress theologians have even persecuted non-Christians on the theory that they pose a threat to the faithful.

Perhaps the most extreme example of fortress theology was the medieval church, which literally sought to protect the faithful by exterminating unbelievers throughout *Christendom*, a term roughly synonymous with Europe. But some churches today that argue against Christian involvement in "worldly" events become quite extreme in their own right. Abundant evidence suggests that fortress theology is still popular, as it has been throughout Christian history.

6. Peter Wagner says, "Our initial research indicates that there has been *no appreciable growth* in the American evangelical population as a whole over the last ten years" (cited in William Chadwick's *Stealing Sheep: The Church's Hidden Problems with Transfer Growth* [Downers Grove: InterVarsity Press

2001], 64). According to a recent study by the Barna Group, "Simply put, each new generation has a larger share of people who are not Christians (that is, atheists, agnostics, people associated with another faith, or those who have essentially no faith orientation)" (George Barna, "A New Generation Expresses Its Skepticism and Frustration with Christianity," September 24, 2007; *www.barna.org/FlexPage.aspx?Page=Barna Update&BarnaUpdateID=280*, accessed 3/12/08). Christine Wicker marshals studies from multiple evangelical sources and concludes, "The truth behind all these numbers is that evangelicals are not converting and cannot convert non-Christian adult Americans, especially native-born white people, in significant numbers. . . . A small and declining group of people has been portrayed as tremendously powerful and growing so rapidly that they might take over the country—when in fact that number of converts among this group is down and dropping. They are rarely able to convert an adult middle-class American" (*The Fall of the Evangelical Nation: The Surprising Crisis Inside the Church* [New York: Harper One, 2008], 64, 67). Other researchers agree. For a more complete list of citations from recent studies, visit *www.xenos.org/satan*.

7. Over the past decade, Xenos leaders have led research teams to dozens of the most famous and rapidly growing churches around the country to study their methods and outcomes. These include churches from a wide array of approaches—charismatic, seeker-sensitive, cell-based, emergent, house church, health and wealth, satellite churches, churches that plant churches elsewhere in the country, etc. During our early trips, team members often commented that virtually no members or staff they interviewed had met Christ as adults, or at that church.

Curious at this anecdotal finding, we began to record interviews with those who said they met Christ at a particular church, and those who said they transferred from other evangelical churches. We have determined that large, growing churches in America are gaining nearly all their growth through transfer of believers from other evangelical churches. To make sure of these results, we randomly interview as many members as possible (at least scores, and sometimes hundreds) at services or home groups. We ask them whether they consider themselves Christians, and where and how they became believers. To our own amazement, we have found that the number claiming to have become believers at that church is invariably less than 10 percent of the sample—often less than 5 percent! In some cases, our teams include dozens of researchers, and we interview hundreds of members to reduce the sampling error. I'm not going to name the churches involved, because I don't want to cause problems for them, but readers would be shocked, like we were, if this research were ever published. So far, using this technique, we have only identified three churches where more than 10 percent of their own people report that they were converted in that church.

We continue this research today, still looking for other large groups where the majority of growth comes from conversions. If you think you know of one, let us know at Xenos.org! In discussions with church research experts, I've been told that nobody has done this kind of research before. Instead, composition calculations normally are made by comparing the number of baptisms or professions of faith with the amount of growth in the church. This is how one leader concluded that his church of seventeen thousand people is 80 percent converts; they have baptized fourteen thousand people there. But this method is flawed; apparently, some churches reach significant numbers of converts but must lose them soon afterward, and meanwhile the ones who stay must be the transfers. (We also interviewed some transfers who said they were re-baptized for various reasons.) Otherwise, why would 90 percent of the people at church claim they met Christ at a different church? D. A. Carson refers to research showing that only 2 to 4 percent of converts reached at evangelistic events in the U.S. are still involved in Christianity five years later (*A Call to Spiritual Reformation* [Grand Rapids: Baker Academic, 1992], 14). According to one denominational expert in church planting, nationwide church growth averages 3 percent growth by conversion. The rest is all transfer or biological growth (members having children).

8. George Barna says, "As the nation's culture changes in diverse ways, one of the most significant shifts is the declining reputation of Christianity, especially among young Americans. . . . In fact, in just a decade, many of the Barna measures of the Christian image have shifted substantially downward. . . . For instance, a decade ago the vast majority of Americans outside the Christian faith, including young people, felt favorably toward Christianity's role in society. Currently, however, just 16 percent of non-Christians in their late teens and twenties said they have a 'good impression' of Christianity." He also points out that Christians know this shift is happening: "Ninety-one percent of the nation's evangelicals believe that 'Americans are becoming more hostile and negative toward Christianity' " (Barna Group, *The Barna Update*, "A New Generation Expresses Its Skepticism and Frustration with Christianity," September 24, 2007, *www.barna.org/FlexPage.aspx?Page=BarnaUpdateNarrow& BarnaUpdateID=280*. Accessed 3/12/08). See also *www.xenos.org/satan*.

9. The following table is from Clinton E. Arnold, *Three Crucial Questions about Spiritual Warfare* (Grand Rapids: Baker Academic, 1997), chapter 1.

Imagery of Warfare and Struggle in the New Testament

Image	Reference
The "strong man" (Satan) is fully armed.	Luke 11:21
Someone stronger (Jesus) conquers the "strong man" and takes his armor.	Luke 11:22
Jesus came to bring the sword.	Matt. 10:34
Jesus came to proclaim liberty to captives.	Luke 4:18
The demonized man had a legion of spirits.	Mark 5:9, 15
Jesus led the evil powers in a triumphal procession.	Col. 2:13
Jesus stripped the evil powers of their weapons.	Col. 2:15
Jesus took captives.	Eph. 4:8
The Christian life is a struggle.	Col. 1:29; 2:1; 1 Tim. 4:10
The Christian life is a struggle against evil forces.	Eph. 6:12
The Christian life is a struggle against sin.	Heb. 12:4
The desires of the flesh wage war against the soul.	1 Peter 2:11
Christians are called to struggle for the faith.	Jude 3
Paul struggled for the gospel.	Phil. 1:30
Paul "fought the good fight."	2 Tim. 4:7
Christians are soldiers.	Phil. 2:25; Philem. 2; 2 Tim. 2:3–4
Christians need to wear armor.	Eph. 6:12–17

Image	Reference
Christians engage in warfare.	1 Tim. 1:18; 6:12; 2 Cor. 10:4
Christians wield weapons of warfare.	1 Tim. 1:18; 2 Cor. 10:4; Rom. 6:13; 13:12; 2 Cor. 6:7
Angelic war in heaven	Rev. 12:7
The beast and kings of the earth will make war.	Rev. 9:19
Satan gathers the nations for a final battle.	Rev. 20:7–8

CHAPTER 8

1. Satan's followers include a third of the heavenly host (Revelation 12:4); see endnote 2, chapter 2.

CHAPTER 9

1. A few examples out of many would include Jesus' fierce denunciation of the Pharisees, scribes, and teachers in Matthew 23; Paul's reference to false teachers as "false apostles" and "servants of Satan" (2 Corinthians 11:13–15); and John's labeling of false teachers as "false prophets" having the "spirit of the Antichrist" (1 John 4:2–4).

2. A basic history of the church gives ample examples, even coming from a sympathetic author. For instance, see Justo L. González, *The Story of Christianity: Volumes 1 and 2* (San Francisco: Harper One, 1984). Cult atrocities are well documented in Walter Martin, *The Kingdom of the Cults,* anniversary edition (Minneapolis: Bethany House, 2007).

3. Although growth-hungry pastors at conferences I've attended often claim that expository Bible teaching is too slow paced and bookish for today's culture, the facts say otherwise. Calvary Chapel is probably the greatest movement of God in America today. At their original location in Costa Mesa, California, they have grown to as many as twenty thousand people (mostly converts, unlike other big churches) and have planted more than thirteen hundred other churches, including quite a few mega-churches (some of which are among the largest in the U.S.). Yet they do nothing but exposit the Scriptures every week, going through whole books, and even the whole Bible. Churches we have studied that use topical

evangelistic sermons and light, entertainment-oriented services never come anywhere near this record of effectiveness. Most people in these churches are transfers. At Xenos, expository Scripture teaching has also led to a high proportion of converts and decent growth.

4. We recommend having people study Ken Sande, *The Peacemaker* (Grand Rapids: Baker, 1991, 1997).

5. Division is different from dissent. Churches should develop clear teaching materials detailing the difference between righteous dissent and unrighteous division. Our outline on this is Dennis McCallum, "Leadership and Authority in the Church: What It Is and Isn't" (*www.xenos.org/classes/leadership/leadershipandauth.html.*) Accessed 06/05/08.

6. The notorious St. Valentine's Day Massacre of French Protestants called Huguenots occurred on 23/24 August 1572. After that extermination and the religious wars that followed, Protestantism ceased to be a significant force in France. On the Waldensians, see Dennis McCallum, "The Waldensian Movement From Waldo to the Reformation," May 1986, *www.xenos.org/essays/waldo1.htm.*

CHAPTER 11

1. George Barna shows that the most committed Christians he studies ("evangelicals"), a group smaller than atheists, agnostics, or adult adherents to non-Christian faiths in America (less than 7 percent of the sample), are "least likely to say they are 'totally committed to getting ahead in life' (52 percent)." It's good to see that conservative, Bible-believing Christians are less likely than atheists to be totally committed to materialistic advancement, but sad to see *it's still the majority!* Of the group he calls "born again" (who claim they are going to heaven because they have received forgiveness through Christ, but who may not hold all the other key biblical beliefs), he says, "This segment is the most likely of all to admit to being 'totally committed to getting ahead in life' (74 percent)." That is, they are more likely than adherents to other religions or atheists or agnostics to agree to this statement (*The Barna Update,* "People's Faith Flavor Influences How They See Themselves" [August 26, 2002]). I also believe materialism is one factor behind the consistent spiritual disinterest found in American men. Barna says, "Men remain a puzzle in America. . . . They are still less committed, less active, and less orthodox than women in almost every factor we measure" (*State of the Church 2006,* 51–52).

2. Parents in America are pushing their kids toward worldly accomplishments with rapidly increasing zeal. ABC News quoted The American Academy of Pediatrics, saying that children today spend 30 percent more hours at organized activities than children fifteen years ago (Dec. 4, 2006). One author refers to the mistaken child-pushing fad gripping our country today as "hyper-parenting" (see Alvin Rosenfeld and Nicole Wise, *The Over-Scheduled Child: Avoiding the Trap of Hyper-Parenting* [London: St. Martin's Griffin, 2001]). The growing belief that kids will be happier if they get top grades, enter top universities, get top careers, and are best in multiple sports is not surprising when it comes from non-Christian materialists. The problem is that Christians apparently agree. We hear no dissenting voice and see no real difference between Christian and non-Christian practice in this telling area.

3. For ideas on how to develop a personal ministry, see our earlier book: Dennis McCallum and Jessica Lowery, *Organic Disciplemaking: Mentoring Others into Spiritual Maturity and Leadership* (Houston: Touch Publications, 2006).

Chapter 12

1. The NLT gives an inferior translation for this passage, adding words to imply that we are only opposing humans and human reasoning. But this is not a literal translation (like the NASB), and it contradicts Paul's own statement elsewhere that "we struggle not against flesh and blood but against . . . spiritual forces of wickedness in the heavenly places" (Ephesians 6:12 NASB). Of course, there were human false teachers in view as well, but Paul saw their work as being inspired by Satan; he makes this clear in 2 Corinthians 11.

2. George Barna has constructed a fairly simple set of beliefs he calls a "biblical worldview." To qualify, one must only believe seven simple statements of central Christian teaching: that absolute moral truth exists; that the source of moral truth is the Bible; that the Bible is accurate in all of the principles it teaches; that eternal spiritual salvation cannot be earned; that Jesus lived a sinless life on earth; that every person has a responsibility to share his religious beliefs with others; that Satan is a living force, not just a symbol of evil; and that God is the all-knowing, all-powerful maker of the universe who still rules his creation today. Although this is not a highly rigorous definition, he found that "currently, only 5 percent of adults [in America] have a biblical worldview. . . . Overall, 8 percent of Protestants possess that view, compared to less than one-half of one

percent of Catholics." The rest, over 90 percent, disagreed with at least one of the points. He comments, "Most born again Christians hold a confusing and inherently contradictory set of religious beliefs" (*The Barna Update*, "Most Adults Feel Accepted by God, but Lack a Biblical Worldview" [August 9, 2005]).

3. John F. Walvoord and Roy B. Zuck are typical in their claim that "the breastplate of righteousness refers not to justification, obtained at conversion (Rom. 3:24; 4:5), but to the sanctifying righteousness of Christ (1 Cor. 1:30) practiced in a believer's life. . . . Righteous living (Rom. 6:13; 14:17) guards a believer's heart against the assaults of the devil" (*The Bible Knowledge Commentary: An Exposition of the Scriptures*, Vol. 2 [Wheaton, IL: Victor Books, 1983–c1985], 643). John MacArthur agrees. After citing the whole passage from Ephesians 6, he says, "Our spiritual weapons can be summed up in one word: obedience" (*Standing Strong: How to Resist the Enemy of Your Soul* [Colorado Springs: Victor (David C. Cook), 2006], 73). In both of these and most books on the subject, the emphasis is almost completely on the believer living a righteous life and thereby defeating Satan. I believe Paul's focus is more on knowing and believing what God has done for us.

4. Chuck Smith, *Effective Prayer Life* (Costa Mesa, CA: The Word for Today, 2000), 12.

5. See endnote 1 in chapter 7.

6. J. Oswald Sanders, *Spiritual Leadership* (Chicago: Moody, 1994), 90.

CHAPTER 13

1. The word translated *temptation* here can also mean "trial" or "testing" (as in the NRSV), yet in this context (which is not about suffering but falling into sin) the NLT has correctly chosen temptation as the meaning.

2. Some kinds of judgments are legitimate. Just as *judgment* has different meanings in English, the same is true in Greek. We could say someone is judgmental, meaning he is harsh and rejecting. Or we could say someone has good judgment, meaning he has good discernment and wisdom. That's why Jesus said, "Do not judge according to appearance, but judge with righteous judgment" (John 7:24 NASB). We are not to judge in a self-righteous or condemning way, but we're expected to be able to discern the difference between good and evil, truth and falsehood. Also, we should not try to judge people's motives (1 Corinthians 4:1–6).

CHAPTER 15

1. See chapter 7, endnote 7. Thom Rainer says, "The American church is not growing. From 1990 to 2000, the U.S. population grew from 248 million to 281 million, a 13 percent increase. In that same period, worship attendance in American churches grew by slightly less than 1 percent," *Breakout Churches* (Grand Rapids: Zondervan, 2005), 73. He adds, "Fewer than 15 percent of church members indicated that they had shared with someone how to become a Christian in the past twelve months," 74.

2. Ibid., 69–90. Members of stagnant and declining churches routinely thought their churches were growing rapidly and reaching the lost in large numbers.

3. In the research work referenced earlier (endnote 7, chapter 7), we also often meet with staffers when studying other churches. We routinely ask what percentage of people in their groups they thought were converts won in their own groups. Some pastors admit the percentage is low—18 percent in one case, but usually 25 to 40 percent or more. Yet the surveys in those same churches show that only 3 to 9 percent are actually converts reached at those churches. So far, no pastor has come closer to the truth than *five times* the actual number. We don't believe the pastors are lying, but they appear to believe that they are doing five to fifteen times better than they are. See *www.xenos.org/satan* for more information on this research. On the other hand, it's interesting to note that the same staff that can break its statistics down in a dozen different ways from memory is unable to give a statistic for the convert vs. transfer composition of its people. So far, all have admitted that they don't study that question. Perhaps some leaders don't really want to know the answer to this question. See William Chadwick, *Stealing Sheep: The Church's Hidden Problems with Transfer Growth* (Downers Grove, IL: InterVarsity Press, 2001). Chadwick thinks church leaders purposely conceal the truth about transfer growth and that they also purposely seek transfer growth by launching strategies only likely to win transfers. While I cannot agree with him that accepting transfers is the moral equivalent of shoplifting, I think his argument deserves to be heard.

4. In our studies referenced above, so-called emergent churches and health-and-wealth churches were the worst in terms of how many of their people say they met Christ in that church. We saw a clear correlation between how far groups get away from expositing Scripture as the authoritative Word of God and low levels of convert growth.

5. See backing for this claim in Dennis McCallum and Jessica Lowery,

Organic Disciplemaking: Mentoring Others into Spiritual Maturity and Leadership, chapter 1.

6. George Barna, *Growing True Disciples* (Ventura, CA: Issachar Resources, 2000), chapters 6–7. Even by his extremely inclusive definition (where discipleship might mean participating in an online spiritual chat group), only a minority of American evangelicals have been discipled. By the stricter standard (that I would accept) where discipleship would entail a weekly meeting with a mentor, Barna's figures appear to show that as few as 3 percent of American evangelicals report being discipled.

7. See chapter 12, endnote 2.

8. Professor Alvin Reid found, "Of the 350,000 churches in the U.S. . . . less than 1 percent is growing by conversion growth" (Alvin Reid, *Radically Unchurched: Who Are They—How to Reach Them* [Grand Rapids: Kregel Academic, 2002], 23). Researcher David Olson writes, "In reality, the church in American is not booming. It is in crisis. . . . If trends continue, by 2050 the percentage of Americans attending church will be half the 1990 figure" (David Olson, *The American Church in Crisis: Groundbreaking Research on a National Database of Over 200,000 Churches* [Grand Rapids: Zondervan, 2008), 16. Also, Julia Duin, in *Quitting Church: Why the Faithful Are Fleeing and What to Do About It* (Baker, 2008), cites studies from evangelical and secular sources showing a large-scale exodus from churches and no growth.

CHAPTER 17

1. For a sympathetic survey of "core shamanism" see Michael Harner, *The Way of the Shaman*, 3rd ed. (New York: Harper & Row, 1990).

2. The earliest clear mention of demon possession I have found in Jewish literature is in a highly fanciful account where an angel explains how to heal in Tobit 6:7–9: "Then the young man questioned the angel and said to him, 'Brother Azariah, what medicinal value is there in the fish's heart and liver, and in the gall?' He replied, 'As for the fish's heart and liver, you must burn them to make a smoke in the presence of a man or woman afflicted by a demon or evil spirit, and every affliction will flee away and never remain with that person any longer. And as for the gall, anoint a person's eyes where white films have appeared on them; blow upon them, upon the white films, and the eyes will be healed.'" We should feel glad that such passages are absent from the canonical books of the Bible! How

remarkable it is that Scripture, coming from this same social and cultural background, is completely free from such transparent superstition.

3. Although present in a couple of early manuscripts, this addition is rated as "certain" by conservative and liberal scholars alike. Evans says, "The addition probably reflects the church's growing interest in fasting." C. A. Evans, *Word Biblical Commentary Vol. 34B, Mark 8:27–16:20* (Dallas: Word, Incorporated, 2002), 47.

4. Some authors think Christians should never address Satan or a demon; John MacArthur argues that only Jesus and the apostles had authority to address and exorcise demons (John MacArthur, *Standing Strong: How to Resist the Enemy of Your Soul* [Nashville: David C. Cook, 2006]). I don't agree. While most cases of taking authority over demons did involve Jesus or an apostle, that's to be expected, considering that most of the New Testament is about their ministries. On the other hand, we see Philip (not the apostle, but Philip "the evangelist," as he is known), in Acts 8:5–7, healing and casting out demons. Because this Philip was in Samaria, he couldn't be the apostle Philip, because Acts 8:1 indicates the apostles stayed in Jerusalem.

Chapter 19

1. Gerhard Kittel said, "It is striking how rarely the *Satan* notion is expressed in the Old Testament," adding, "The few Old Testament references initiated . . . further development in pre–New Testament Judaism, and this finally produced many combinations of the Satan concept with originally very different ideas (e.g., an identification with the evil principle or with the angel of death), and the attributing to Satan of many features which derive from such independent sources as the story of fallen angels, with no original reference to Satan. It should be stressed that the idea of Satan originally had nothing whatever to do with human impulses or with the fallen angels" (*Theological Dictionary of the New Testament* [Grand Rapids: Eerdmans, 1976], 2:74). We have seen that this is untrue.

2. G. Earnest Wright reflects the liberal consensus: "The world of Satan with his powers and principalities of darkness is a development in later Judaism. . . . So definite is the Old Testament in its exaltation of God that all things good and bad were ascribed to him. The doctrine of Satan only gradually came into being to alleviate the difficulties inherent in this view" (*The Old Testament Against Its Environment* [Chicago: H. Regnery Co., 1950], 91). In a circular fashion, liberal scholars argue that Satan

was absent in preexilic Judaism, and then used the presence of Satan in preexilic books to argue that those books or sections must be postexilic! This is a secular perspective. More correctly, the Old Testament writers ascribe bad events to God (including Satan's actions) because of God's permissive will. He has the ability to prevent such events, but did not, usually for judicial reasons. See also Kittel: "Judaism was prepared for the adoption of demonology, namely, in its realization that there is in man a will which resists the attempted fulfillment of the Law and which is thus to be ascribed to demonic influence. It is by inner necessity, therefore, that in these writings [the intertestamental, pseudepigraphal books] the demons are closely linked with Satan. . . . A broader basis was thus given to the doctrine, for now, as distinct from the Old Testament, all evil was no longer traced back to the rule of God" (Kittel, *Theological Dictionary of the New Testament*, 2:16).

3. Liberal scholars base their case on an argument from silence (the fall of Satan is not discussed until later, and they don't count Ezekiel's prophecy, denying that this refers to Satan), and from anecdotal cases, like that in Numbers 22:22 (NASB). There we read that as Balaam was going to curse Israel, "the angel of the Lord took his stand in the way as an adversary against him." The word *adversary* is the word for Satan, thus showing, they claim, that Satan was just a term for angels or people who were standing in opposition, usually on God's side against evil. In fact, the word *Satan* can be used this way, but that has no bearing on whether Israelites also believed in a fallen evil angel called Satan.

4. The Old Testament also discusses unfallen angels. Gleason Archer points out that "Genesis mentions cherubim; Joshua refers to a prince of the angels. Their function was said to be the delivery of messages to Abraham, Moses, Joshua, Gideon, and various prophets such as Isaiah, Zechariah, and Ezekiel. Thus as early as the Torah we find the angels revealing the will of God, furnishing protection for God's people, and destroying the forces of the enemy" (*A Survey of Old Testament Introduction* [Chicago: Moody, 1968], 403).

5. Wright, *The Old Testament Against Its Environment*, 78, 87, 91.

6. Ibid., 92–93. This also accounts for why we see no incantations involving God in the Old Testament. J. I. Durham says, "Yahweh had not withheld his name but had freely given it to Moses. . . . His sovereignty is such that he was not subject to the manipulation of his worshipers. . . . Not surprisingly, there are no incantation texts in the Old Testament. Yahweh could not be controlled, or even altered in his set purpose, by men"

(*Word Biblical Commentary Vol. 3, Exodus* [Dallas: Word, Incorporated, 2002], 288).

7. During the past few decades, Christians have demonstrated a willingness to fabricate mythology about demons or to believe fabricated material. The result is loss of credibility before the watching world and disgrace for the name of Jesus. Aside from this area of spiritual mapping, much more serious problems have arisen because Christians have been in the vanguard of a movement during the 1980s and 1990s to champion the notion of Satanic Ritual Abuse (SRA). This craze seized the whole country for over a decade, resulting in the imprisonment of many innocent people as well as splitting churches, families, and friends. Christian counselors nationwide reached the conclusion that tens and perhaps hundreds of thousands of children were being ritually raped in satanic cult meetings. As one who lived through this and had my church damaged profoundly in the process, I remember how people who believed this myth would excoriate and persecute anyone who expressed the slightest skepticism about these wild stories. Doubters were viewed as unbelievers and often as likely child molesters in their own right. I remember watching the staffers from one Los Angeles day care led away in chains after being charged with the most grotesque sexual games with preschool children. I shook my head in disbelief—they included elderly women. It just didn't make sense to some of us who work with people. At its height, according to a survey, 70 percent of Americans believed in these sexually abusing satanic cults (A. S. Ross, "Blame It on the Devil" in *Redbook* [June 1994]: 88).

In the end, evidence gradually accumulated so powerfully against this view that finally it was pounded into relative silence (although some still come forward with these stories). Most Christian books written about Satan during the 1980s and 1990s reflect credulity on this movement. Today, authors, speakers, and counselors who championed the SRA craze are embarrassed to have been involved.

Most proponents of SRA held to an allied doctrine at the time: that MPD (multiple personality disorder) was *prima facie* evidence of demonization and childhood sexual abuse, a notion that also has since largely been discredited. My criticism of those who foisted this foolish movement on the church is not just that they were credulous; the real problem was that neither the advocates nor other church leaders stopped to ask the most important question: "What does the Bible say?" In both these cases, the answer was "nothing." How could we come to believe that God would have failed to mention this crucial insight in his Word? For any still tempted to believe the lurid testimonials that occasionally come up, I recommend the excellent study of the aftermath by Debbie Nathan and Michael Snedeker, *Satan's Silence: Ritual Abuse and the Making of a Modern American Witch Hunt* (Lincoln, NE: Authors' Choice Press, 1995, 2001). The lesson should be clear: Don't teach doctrines that are not well-supported in Scripture.

APPENDIX 1

1. George Barna says, "Six out of ten Americans (59 percent) reject the existence of Satan, indicating that the devil, or Satan, is merely a symbol of evil. Catholics are much more likely than Protestants to hold this view—75 percent compared to 55 percent—although a majority of both groups concur that Satan is symbolic" (Barna Research, "Americans Draw Theological Beliefs From Diverse Points of View," *www.barna .org/FlexPage.aspx?Page=BarnaUpdate&BarnaUpdateID=122* [accessed 5 June 2008]). More recently, only 29 percent of Americans strongly disagreed with the statement "The devil, or Satan, is not a living being, but a symbol of evil" (Barna, *State of the Church 2006* [Ventura, CA: Barna Group, 2006], 22).

2. My own book on the existence and nature of God is *Christianity: The Faith That Makes Sense* (Wheaton IL: Tyndale, 1996). Also good for popular reading are Lee Strobel, *The Case for Faith: A Journalist Investigates the Toughest Objections to Christianity* (Grand Rapids: Zondervan, 2000) and *The Case for a Creator: A Journalist Investigates Scientific Evidence That Points Toward God* (Grand Rapids: Zondervan, 2006). A classic from the 1940s is C. S. Lewis, *Mere Christianity* (New York: HarperOne, new ed., 2001). For more academic readers, see J. P. Moreland, *Scaling the Secular City: A Defense of Christianity* (Grand Rapids: Baker Academic, 1987).

3. Liberal interpreters mistakenly claim that the serpent is not Satan. This is bound up with their view that the Jews didn't develop a belief in Satan until late in their history, a view we discussed in chapter 19. Their theory contradicts Revelation 12:9. See also chapter 3, endnote 1.

4. Protestant thinkers from Luther on have been quick to point out that "the devil is God's devil" and that he cannot do anything God doesn't allow. Some go further, saying Satan never does anything without *explicit* permission from God. For instance, Erwin Lutzer says, "He cannot act without God's express permission; he can neither tempt, coerce, demonize, nor make so much as a single plan without the consent and approval of God" (*The Serpent of Paradise* [Chicago: Moody, 1996], 102). I think some of this verbiage is misleading. What Satan does is God's will in the sense of

his permissive will, or what some theologians call God's "effectual will." That means God *could* prevent what Satan does, but he doesn't. So one must conclude that, on some grander scale, God wills that the universe be the way it is, including the existence and actions of Satan; otherwise, he would change it. However, this is different than saying Satan has explicit permission for each and every thing he does, or that God gives "approval." The language of Lutzer and others makes it sound like Satan goes to God and asks permission for each action, then God decides whether he wants that or not. This has God actively directing Satan's actions, and I think it confuses God's permissive will with causality, or intentionality.

When thinking about this, remember that Satan's actions are against God's *moral will*, which God declares in the Bible in clear terms, and therefore evil actions like Satan's are *against* the will of God. But when we speak of God's permissive will, we mean everything that happens in the universe, whether good or evil, is within his greater plan. These things are only "God's will" in the secondary sense that he has not prevented them from happening, though he could have. Here, a hierarchy of values may come in. For instance, is it better for God to allow freedom of choice or to prevent the possibility of evil? He has sovereignly chosen an answer to this question by creating freedom of choice, which resulted in the fall of Satan and others. That doesn't imply that God *caused* them to fall, or that they come and ask his permission for the other evil choices they make.

Careful thinkers will see a significant difference between the view that God's permissive or effectual will allows freedom, including evil, and the view that God gives "approval," let alone causes, each thing that happens. The latter view is total fatalism, where all choices on our part are only apparent and really pointless. This is neither the biblical view nor the view of the reformers (and I'm not suggesting that authors like Lutzer teach this, although I worry that one could reach this conclusion from misleading language). The Bible says our choices are significant because (1) we have no way to know in advance what is God's effectual will, and (2) what matters for us is God's *moral* will, because that describes what he actually wants rather than what he allows to happen. Although Calvinist and Arminian theologians debate many areas, this is not one of them; they agree we should not represent God as the direct cause of Satan's evil, even though he has willed to permit it.

The idea that Satan gets express permission for each and every action he takes on earth is based on cases like that in Job, where he was only allowed to do certain things with permission. Also, Satan "demanded permission" to sift the disciples on the night of Jesus' crucifixion (Luke 22:31; notice that *you* here is plural in Greek; it was not just Peter, but all the disciples). These and other accounts show that Satan does not have a free hand in this world but is limited by God. However, it does not follow that just because he got explicit permission in one case involving a believer, he gets express permission for everything he does. Rather, he operates under the more general concept of God's permissive will, which can and does include many things of which God disapproves. Consider that everything Adolf Hitler did was within God's permissive will; this doesn't mean he got permission from God for each act but that God permitted a world where people are free to defy his moral will. This more general view of God's permissive will accords with the warnings we read about the dangers Satan poses to believers; such would be nonsense under a fatalistic view wherein God has predetermined every action.

APPENDIX 2

1. George Ladd, *I Believe in the Resurrection of Jesus* (Grand Rapids: Eerdmans, 1975), 66. Unfortunately, Ladd also concludes that the early church imported their preferred meaning into the Servant Songs out of wishful thinking. This flies in the face of New Testament revelation, including Jesus' own statement that the Scriptures say the Son of Man must suffer and be treated with contempt (Mark 9:12). What would Jesus be referring to if not the Servant Songs? The mere fact that people didn't see the Messiah in these passages doesn't mean he isn't there; it just means they had no idea there would be two comings.

APENDIX 3

1. Many interpreters see these two parables as predicting the church being infiltrated by evil and corrupted. The birds in the mustard plant and the yeast are symbols of evil. While this is debatable, no one doubts that the mustard seed and others predict gradual growth as the pattern for the church.

2. In this list of passages, I have put an asterisk by the ones that mention a reaction from the hearers: Mark 8:31–32*; 10:45; 9:9–10*, 12*; 9:31–32*; 10:32–34; Matthew 16:21–22*; 20:17–19; 17:22–23*; Luke 9:22; 9:44–45*; 18:31–34*; John 3:14; 10:15–20*; 12:32–34*; 16:16–18*, 25. The passages either say nothing about what the hearers thought or specify that the hearers did not understand what he was saying, often adding that the meaning was "hidden" from them.

3. For example, G. R. Beasley-Murray explains, "Jesus is a riddle to those who fail to perceive his role as mediator of the kingdom of God. It is comprehensible therefore that the revelation in Jesus should be described in our passage as given *en paromias* [in parables, or metaphor]" (*Word Biblical Commentary Vol. 36, John* [Dallas: Word, Incorporated. 2002], 287). He thinks Jesus is saying that later, when the Spirit comes, things will become clearer. This makes it seem like the change was in the disciples' perception, but Jesus clearly says *it is his own clarity of speech that will change*, not the perception of others. The contrast here is not "you now see it this way but soon will see it that way"; it's "I'm speaking this way, but soon will speak that way." Most commentators take a similar line, arguing that Jesus was speaking clearly but that the people were too blind to see it.